FRAMEWORKS FOR SPORT PSYCHOLOGISTS
ENHANCING SPORT PERFORMANCE

Karen Lee Hill

WITHDRAWN

Frameworks for sport
psychologists by Hill,
Karen Lee

D1339294

Library of Congress Cataloging-in-Publication Data

Hill, Karen Lee, 1947-
    Frameworks for sport psychologists / Karen Lee Hill.
        p. cm.
    Includes bibliographical references.
        1. Sports--Psychological aspects. 2. Psychologists. I. Title.

GV706.4 .H54 2001
796'.01--dc21

00-038894

ISBN: 0-7360-0014-3

Acquisitions Editor: Michael S Bahrke, PhD; **Developmental Editor:** Jennifer Clark; **Assistant Editors:** Derek Campbell and Laurie Stokoe; **Copyeditor:** Jacqueline Eaton Blakley; **Proofreader:** Sarah Wiseman; **Indexer:** Nancy Ball; **Permission Manager:** Heather Munson; **Graphic Designer:** Nancy Rasmus; **Graphic Artist:** Denise Lowry; **Cover Designer:** Jack W. Davis; **Printer:** United Graphics

Printed in the United States of America   10 9 8 7 6 5 4 3 2 1

Human Kinetics
Web site: www.humankinetics.com

United States: Human Kinetics, P.O. Box 5076, Champaign, IL 61825-5076
800-747-4457
e-mail: humank@hkusa.com

Canada: Human Kinetics, 475 Devonshire Road Unit 100, Windsor, ON N8Y 2L5
800-465-7301 (in Canada only)
e-mail: hkcan@mnsi.com

Europe: Human Kinetics, P.O. Box IW14, Leeds LS16 6TR, United Kingdom
+44 (0) 113 278 1708
e-mail: humank@hkeurope.com

Australia: Human Kinetics, 57A Price Avenue, Lower Mitcham, South Australia 5062
08 8277 1555
e-mail: liahka@senet.com.au

New Zealand: Human Kinetics, P.O. Box 105-231, Auckland Central
09-523-3462
e-mail: hkp@ihug.co.nz

This work is dedicated to my family,
especially Bill, Jennifer, and Christin.
You have enhanced my life
in untold ways.

Ψ CONTENTS

Ψ PREFACE

"I'm going to cause you all sorts of trouble," the tall, athletic woman announced with a smile as she strolled into the office. "I'm Lisa Irons." We shook hands as she slumped down in the chair. "I don't know if you can help, but I'm desperate," she sighed. "I've tried everything else and nothing works, so I figure this can't hurt."

How do psychologists account for the thoughts, feelings, and behavior described in the preceding paragraph? Is Lisa Irons normal? How can sport psychologists understand and help her?

Sport psychologists may understand and work with Lisa in various ways depending on their theoretical perspective. This perspective, or *model*, determines which thoughts, emotions, and actions are selected as important and which are neglected as inconsequential. These models are the focus of this book.

Understanding Sport Psychology and Theory

Sport psychology is the study of individual and group human dynamics in the context of sport. As its name implies, it has its origins in both psychology, the study of the human mind and behavior, and sport studies, primarily physical education. With one foot in each discipline, sport psychology struggles to carve out its niche and establish an identity in each.

While sport psychology draws from both physical education and psychology, it differs significantly from them. For example, physical education emphasizes bodily aspects of movement, while sport psychology emphasizes the mental and emotional aspects. And unlike much of mainstream psychology, sport psychology is not oriented toward healing of mental disease and disorder. Rather, it aims at enhancing the sport experience and developing the self through sport.

Sport psychology's focus is on performance enhancement and personal growth through sport, including "deep core" change mediated by sport experiences (Oglesby 1987). Sport psychologists usually refer to those they serve as *athletes* or *clients* rather than *patients*, and a session with a client is a *consultation* rather than *therapy*. The primary purpose of sport psychology is to promote personal growth while providing athletes of all ages and skill levels with mental and emotional skills to produce their best possible performance.

All disciplines, including sport psychology, must produce theoretical models to unify data, generate hypotheses, and explain findings. Sport psychology's current models are borrowed from their parent disciplines. The behavioral model dominated physical education even before Skinner codified it in psychology. Models from psychology, such as the psychodynamic and humanistic models, have also been borrowed and adapted to sport. This book outlines prominent models from the discipline of psychology and explores how they are applied in sport psychology.

What Are Theoretical Models?

How many times have you heard a comment or thought dismissed because it's "just a theory"? Yet formulating theories is vital to our well-being and advancement. Humans have a fortunate compulsion to understand and "make sense" of themselves and their surroundings. We constantly collect data through observation of our environment and ourselves in an attempt to understand what we experience. As we make our observations, we organize them into models, or *schema*, of how the world operates, and these models guide and influence our behavior.

Theoretical models suggest questions, explanations, and predictions for the phenomena they describe. The theoretical position of the psychologist influences practice in significant ways. Each theory offers a different view of the human condition and reality. For example, consider the different approaches to and explanations for anxiety. To the psychodynamic practitioner, anxiety is the result of unresolved conflicts emanating from the unconscious mind. For the behaviorist, anxiety is a classically conditioned response to environmental stimuli. To the neuropsychologist, it is a hardwired, naturally selected fight-or-flight trait with evolutionary origins. And to the cognitive practitioner, it is the result of unrealistic, ruminating thought patterns. Each of these theoretical explanations of anxiety poses a different origin of anxiety and prescribes a different approach to treatment.

Does one "correct" model exist? What are the chances that we can create or discover one model that fits everyone's experience of mental and emotional phenomena in sporting activities? In sport psychology, which aims to understand and describe "best" performances, one must challenge the assumption that any *one* logical or reasonable model can account for peak performance. As Robert Kirshner said, ". . . the universe is under no obligation to make sense . . ." (Ferris 1997, p. 40)—and neither are its inhabitants. It is possible that as evolved organisms, humans are so complex and variable that no theoretical model reliably and realistically describes the human psyche. This does not mean that we should abandon our search for theoretical models that come closer and closer to providing a framework for our observations of reality. However, we must keep in mind that not only will the search be imperfect, but it may well be impossible. So theoretical models are necessary for the advancement of our knowledge of ourselves, and some models will move us closer to true understanding, but *the* model—a global theory that unifies and explains all human experience in sport—may not exist.

If we tentatively accept this possibility, an important follow-up question is, "Of the models that do exist, which is the 'best'?" Unfortunately, research in sport psychology that examines the relative benefits of the different models as a whole is lacking. For example, there are not any studies in which athletes are randomly assigned to work with sport psychologists who use different models and then are measured on a specific outcome variable. Such research would be valuable to the discipline, but until it is available sport psychologists must select their frameworks based on studies that exist and personal experience with models that work for clients.

Why Study Theories?

In February 1997, Slife and Williams published an article in *American Psychologist* arguing for a new subdiscipline in psychology to be called *theoretical psychology*. This article initiated an ongoing dialogue regarding the importance of theory to the discipline of psychology, including 10 pages of commentary on this topic in the January 1998 issue of *American Psychologist*.

This recent attention to theory in sport psychology's parent discipline reminds us of the importance of the role of theory in advancing the discipline of sport psychology. Sport psychology, like psychology, is in danger of drowning in a sea of isolated data points that desperately need to be grounded in theory if we are to create a global picture of sport and sport behavior. These theories generate hypotheses for research, which build the knowledge base of the discipline.

In addition to theory's importance to the discipline, understanding and commitment to theory is critical for practitioners so they can

- establish a personal counseling theory,
- dialogue with professional colleagues, and
- inform clients and the public about sport psychology.

What is your personal counseling theory? How do you account for the success of a Doug Flutie or the failure of the U.S. men's ice hockey team at the Nagano Olympics? All sport psychologists make assumptions and interpretations about the nature of human performance, values, and emotions. It is vital that you are clear about your own assumptions, for they will direct your interpretation and treatment of athletes. Awareness of one's values and intellectual predisposition is a critical first step in establishing one's personal counseling model, and understanding the strengths and weaknesses of various models is part of this process.

The adoption of a personal counseling model is not a one-time event. It is an evolving process intertwined with other aspects of professional growth, including complete training in the counseling models. The theoretical models presented in this book are valuable because they can be used to promote a common dialogue among professionals about the nature of humans; the causes of behavior, thoughts, and emotions; and the interactions of these critical human capacities.

How would you articulate your counseling goals and processes to an athlete? Understanding the theoretical orientation of the sport psychology practitioner is a basic consumer right for athletes. In fact, an article in the November 1995 issue of *Consumer Reports* advises all consumers of psychological interventions to ask about the theoretical orientation of the consultant on the first visit (Consumers Union 1995, p. 734). The study of theories will help you provide athletes with a clear explanation of interventions and provide a framework for the work that you do together.

Understanding Theories and Their Applications

You are probably using this book in conjunction with a sport psychology textbook that provides an introduction and literature review of various sport psychology topics such as personality, motivation, and goal setting. This volume will help you connect these important topics by approaching them in the context of unifying theories that interpret and explain them.

In this book, a single case study is interpreted by each theoretical perspective to demonstrate how different theories attend to different client issues and result in different treatments. Sample process plans for the case of Lisa Irons are presented for each theoretical model. In these interpretations, you will be able to witness the application of theory to practice and understand how your own theoretical orientation provides a blueprint for the treatment of athletes. The interpretations of the case study also serve to reinforce and illustrate the explanations of the theories. For example, if you have difficulty grasping the concept of a defense mechanism from the explanation of the theory, a practical example in the case study will help to clarify the concept.

After reading the explanation of a theory and examining the case process plan illustrating the use of that theory, the next step is to apply the theory to new material. This book includes additional case material at the end of each chapter that you can use to practice applying the model described in the chapter. This practice will give you an opportunity to interpret an athlete's issues and apply the model to a new situation. In my own classes, I follow these case studies with an assignment in which students have to write their own case studies demonstrating important concepts in the particular theory under study. I find this learning progression—read an explanation of the theory, examine a demonstration of the theory in a case study, apply the theory to new case material, and write your own case study illustrating the theory—provides students with a useful working knowledge about both the theory and practice of sport psychology. This book is designed to mirror that learning progression and guide you through the important process of adopting your own consulting theoretical position for application in your future practice.

Ψ ACKNOWLEDGMENTS

I wish to thank the following individuals who have given me their time, advice, and invaluable insights in the course of writing this book:

- Dr. Carole Oglesby, a longtime friend and supporter, and an incurable optimist.
- My family and friends, who encouraged me when things were going well and happily distracted me when they weren't.
- My friends and colleagues at Penn State University, especially the Penn State, Delaware County Library staff, and Deli lunch bunch.
- The staff at Human Kinetics, especially Jennifer Clark, Steve Pope, Michael Bahrke, and Lynn Hooper-Davenport.
- The reviewers, whose comments and suggestions contributed to the quality of this work.

Finally, I am grateful for the work of my fellow sport scientists, coaches, and athletes, who have increased our knowledge of sport psychology and persist in the quest for excellent performance.

Ψ INTRODUCTION

The theoretical assumptions held by the sport psychologist guide the intervention process. The theory defines the underlying causes of the athlete's problems, guides the process for solving these problems, and suggests which types of intervention techniques should be used. The impact of different theoretical orientations can best be illustrated by analyzing a single case study using different theories.

In each of the following chapters, the case of Lisa Irons will be interpreted by the theory defined in the chapter. The interpretation presented in the "Process Plan" section of each chapter will allow you to compare the different theoretical approaches and see how each theory influences the intervention process in Lisa's case. Each process plan represents only one of many ways that the ideas presented in the chapter could be used to guide Lisa's work with a sport psychologist.

Read the case study presented in this introduction to familiarize yourself with Lisa's situation. As you study the basic concepts of each theory, reflect on how they apply to Lisa's situation and think about ways the model might be applied to her case. Compare your thoughts with the ideas presented in the chapter's process plan. It is often helpful to refer back to the case study and read it again as you study the process plan.

The Case of Lisa "the Cheetah" Irons

"I'm going to cause you all sorts of trouble," the tall, athletic woman announced with a smile as she strolled into the office. "I'm Lisa Irons." We shook hands as she slumped down in the chair. "I don't know if you can help me, but I'm desperate," she sighed. "I've tried everything else and nothing works, so I figure this can't hurt."

Her initial consultation continued with Lisa reporting the following:

"I'm a 39-year-old professional golfer. I've been pretty successful on the LPGA tour for 16 years, but recently—within the past two years—I seem to be in a slump. My game is not consistent, or maybe I should say it is consistent—consistently bad! On one hole my drives will be long and straight, but who knows about the next hole? Each day it seems like I have a different problem with my game. I never know what's going to be working for me when I go out on the course.

"My confidence is in shambles along with my game, and it's really getting me down. At first I just thought this was one of the ups and downs of the tour, but it's gone on for so long now. I've gone to my teaching pro to try to get my game straightened out, but it just hasn't helped.

"Within the last year, I also started keeping a journal to see if I could figure out what's going wrong in my game and my life, but I really don't know what to do. I am tired of the tour and tired of everything, I guess. I have a lot of nervous energy, but I can't seem to focus it. I've always had high expectations for myself and a sense that I can do whatever I put my mind to, but I haven't accomplished my goals of winning major tournaments and becoming a top player. I'm worried that I might not live up to my potential. I've started thinking about retirement, but I hate to quit before seeing more success on the tour."

That is the essence of Lisa's introduction. Lisa summarized the important aspects of her life in a brief autobiography that she left with the sport psychologist:

I first started hitting golf balls when I was five. My dad, a police officer, was working the late shift. He would come home in the morning, fix breakfast for my older brother and me, drop my brother off at school, and then take me with him to the driving range. He sawed off one of his old clubs and bought me some balls to hit, mostly to keep me busy while he hit. I remember trying to hit like he did. I loved to watch the balls sail up and out into the grassy field. I started trying to mimic hitting like my dad. The more I mimicked him, the more attention he gave me. He started showing me how to swing. Since my birthday was just after the cutoff date for school, I had almost two years of going to that driving range with my dad. It was a great time. I loved it. Dad knew the pro at the range, and soon I was having informal lessons. I loved the attention.

While I remember going to the golf range just about every day, my mom and dad also encouraged my brother and me to try other things. We could experiment and try anything, from drums (one of my brother's trials) to ceramics (one of my poorer choices). The only rule was that we had to finish what we started. So when I signed up for those three months of ceramics lessons, I had to finish them, but I hated every minute. I guess I can truthfully say that I had a nearly ideal middle-class childhood.

I played in my first real golf competition, the state junior championships, at age 10. I was disappointed that I didn't win, but I did finish in the top 10. Looking back, I think my expectations were too high given my experience and practice schedule. After that tournament I recognized that if I wanted to compete at the highest level I had to be more committed. I started practicing every day, seven days a week. I put in three or four hours of practice on school days and five or six hours of playing and practice on weekends and school vacations. My life started to revolve around golf. When I increased my practice time, I expected—really felt entitled, I guess—to start playing better right away. When that didn't happen, I started "blowing up" in tournaments. I consider myself an easygoing person generally, but when I feel I've been treated unfairly or with disrespect, my anger just seethes until I explode. I remember feeling that some people in junior golf disrespected me by dismissing my early good showing as luck. I wanted to show them in the worst way, but then I would go out and bogey or double bogey and just explode.

As I started to play better, I was noticed by club professionals, people associated with junior golf and the media. While all this attention made me more self-conscious, I thrived on it to some extent. I was the runner-up in the state junior tournament my sophomore year, won it when I was a junior, and reached the final match play competition in the national junior tournament my senior year.

As I became more interested in and skilled at golf, my playing created more of a strain on our family. The high school I attended did not have a girls' golf team, so my family had to bear all of the financial and support burdens. It was a struggle. I knew my parents were making lots of sacrifices so I could play tournaments. I was often torn between my feelings—I wanted to play and compete in the worst way, but each competition seemed to require so much from my mom and dad that I felt bad about making them struggle with the costs of my golf. It was particularly bad when I wasn't playing well because I felt like I was letting them down in addition to all the other pressures of competition.

High school golf paid off, however, because I won a full athletic scholarship to a small Sun Belt college with a great tradition of fielding top women's golf teams. I don't think I've ever been as happy as I was playing college golf. We had a great team and I loved being part of it. That's where I picked up my nickname—the Cheetah—because I often came from behind with a birdie blitz that won the match. I played the national college team circuit and traveled all over the U.S. We won the AIAW national championship twice, and everyone on the team was great friends. I really never had friends who shared my enthusiasm for golf before, and I felt great about being a leading player with my team. I no longer had to worry about the financial cost of playing. It was one of the best times of my life.

After college, I decided to give the LPGA tour a try. I was a rabbit, chasing the tour from one site to another—trying to qualify—for a year or so. That was a tough time for me. I missed the camaraderie of my college team, and I was back to having financial worries again. The competition on the tour made it quite different from college golf. The skill level was much higher, and I felt like an outsider. It definitely took me a long time to get to know the other players and stop feeling so lonely. On top of all this pressure, I had to increase my practice and playing time in order to bring my game up to the professional level, and in that process I injured my lower back. Up until this time I had enjoyed a relatively injury-free sport career, and dealing with major injury was outside of my experience. I jumped back and forth between rest and just playing with the pain. It is an aggravating, recurring problem that has haunted me during my entire professional career.

I finally "found" my professional self when I won my first tournament. So far in my career I've won some smaller tournaments, but only one major. I'm starting to wonder if that major win wasn't just a lucky fluke, because I haven't been able to win a big one again. I'm disappointed that I'm not in the top tier of women on the tour at this stage of my career even though I have always had a burning desire to get to that level—until recently. In spite of my meager win record in the major tournaments, I've been fortunate in that I've played well enough to be in the money and support myself in golf. A golf equipment company sponsors me, but I'm afraid that if I don't start winning they will drop me.

Recently I've thought more about retirement. I'm not sure if it's because I'm not playing well and I'm frustrated, or because I'm turning 40 this year, or because my back and other aches and pains are finally taking their toll. I look at other pros on the tour and I see some of them playing their best golf at my age or older. I can't figure out what's wrong with me. I often feel confused about what to do, and it's getting me down. The confusion and my poor play make me nervous about my future. It has been hard for me to concentrate because my thoughts keep jumping around among concerns about my play, my health, my financial situation, retirement, and everything else.

Chapter 1

THE PSYCHODYNAMIC MODEL

The *psychodynamic model*—the "grandfather of all models"—traces its heritage from Freudian psychoanalysis and is the oldest of the modern theoretical models. Therefore, many of the concepts of contemporary models reflect aspects of the psychodynamic perspective. For instance, the *transference* concept—that individuals recreate relationships based on early significant relationships—is a thread found in modern family systems models. In addition, the basic premise that individuals seek pleasure and avoid pain is central to the behavioral model. The psychodynamic model is of more than historical significance, however. It continues to be updated by modern theorists such as Mahler and Kohut, and the focus on the dynamic nature of development is found in the most contemporary of theories— chaos and complexity theory.

Basic Concepts

Sigmund Freud, Carl Jung, Alfred Adler, Karen Horney, Heinz Kohut, Otto Kernberg, and Erik Erikson are some of psychology's Hall of Famers known for their work with psychodynamic models. Of these, Sigmund Freud is the name most often associated with the psychodynamic approach. Freud is often referred to as the "father of psychoanalysis," with psychoanalysis being one branch of the psychodynamic perspective. The psychodynamic perspective is distinguished by its concepts of inner conflict, the unconscious, defense mechanisms, and transference.

The Dynamic: Inner Conflict and Its Resolution

All psychological models must account for how thoughts, actions, and feelings are derived. What is it that determines how we act and feel as individuals in the variety of situations that we experience? In the psychodynamic model, management of inner conflict is a basic process that shapes personality, including our behavioral, cognitive, and emotional responses to life. While internal conflict is common to psychodynamic theories, the model accommodates various views on its nature.

In Freud's view, inner conflict is caused by the push and pull of three competing forces found within the self. Freud named these inner forces the *id,* the *ego,* and the *superego.* The id constantly and relentlessly seeks the pleasure associated with fulfilling biological drives and cravings of the body. Freud identified two biological urges, the *libido* (sexuality) and *aggression,* that motivate humans and contribute to intrapersonal psychic conflict.

Freud delineated the role of the libido in his theory much more completely than the role of aggression. This psychoanalytic emphasis on sexuality, which Freud considered a universal human drive even in infancy, permeated his view of human personality development. Sexuality is the Freudian master motive. In modern psychodynamic terms, sexual wishes encompass a broad spectrum of bodily pleasures, such as eating a good meal, relaxing with a massage, and hitting a home run. Sexual wishes are not just genital sensations. Likewise, expressions of aggressive wishes include feelings of anger and hate, as well as a desire to destroy, including self-destruction.

These innate biological drives act as sources of motivation, prompting the person to act to satisfy the drives and gratify the self through the pleasure enjoyed when drives are temporarily appeased. Conflict results when the unrealistic and irrational pleasures sought by the id are thwarted by the restrictions imposed by reality. Life in the "real world" is filled with restrictions that block the selfish id from its quest to satisfy biological urges "anytime, anywhere, anyhow," setting the stage for inescapable conflict and anxiety.

The ego is the mediator between the limitations of the real world and the indomitable persistence of the id for self-satisfaction. It negotiates the push and pull between individual satisfaction and pleasure and real-world limits such as scarcity and the need for social order. The ego must perform a balancing act between fulfilling the unrelenting drive for pleasure of the id and dealing with the restrictions imposed by reality, including the laws, morals, and rules of society.

The ego develops by successfully negotiating these conflicts through various defense mechanisms. It protects the self by either transforming the blatant desires of the id into acceptable thoughts, behaviors, and feelings or controlling id desires by repressing them to the unconscious, where they are locked away and "unknowable" to the self. Through these processes the ego struggles to control the anxiety caused by the clash of the id's pleasure principle with the ego's reality orientation.

Laws, ethics, and moral rules that enable humans to live together in social settings as taught to the infant and child by caregivers are internalized to form the third force of the mind—the superego. In the psychodynamic model, "others," particularly parents and significant others, have a profound influence on personality because their teachings, values, and morals are internalized by the superego. The superego provides another roadblock for pleasure satisfaction—the guilt-producing conscience—and it judges the ego's efforts in controlling the id and measuring up to the morals, values, and cultural ideals of society. When the ego is successful in turning the pleasure drives of the id into socially acceptable and valued outcomes *(sublimation)*, the superego "judges" the ego as "good." However, when the ego is unsuccessful in sublimating the biological urges of the id, the superego judges the ego harshly and fills the person with feelings of guilt, disgust, and self-loathing. Failure to resolve inner conflicts results in repression of the conflict to the unconscious and feelings of anxiety over the inability to negotiate a solution.

The complex struggles among the id, ego, and superego form the basis of Freud's explanation of the self's mental processes. Freud also theorized that there were common developmental challenges that all individuals must negotiate in the course of their lives. He organized these universal challenges into a fixed stage theory of development. Because all of the stages involve the ego mediating a sexual desire of the id with restrictions of the real world and judgment of the superego, Freud's theory is referred to as the *psychosexual stage theory of development*. The psychosexual stages are classified by the part of the body receiving sexual gratification and are called the *oral, anal, phallic, latent,* and *genital* stages. Each stage is characterized by its own challenges to the ego.

An example of one of these universal challenges is the Oedipus complex of the phallic psychosexual stage. The challenge of the Oedipal complex for a male is to resolve the conflict of his intense love for and desire to possess his mother with the fear of his father's rage should he act on this love. In this conflict, the ego must negotiate a settlement between the id's desire to possess the mother and the fear of retribution (sometimes viewed as fear of castration) from the father for attempting to steal the mother from the father. Successful negotiation of this conflict occurs when the boy's sexual feelings for his mother are repressed to the unconscious and he begins to identify with his father. If the boy does not successfully negotiate this conflict, he becomes fixated in this stage of development. According to Freud, this fixation tends to result in difficulty later in life. For example, a boy who is fixated in the phallic stage never identifies with his heterosexual father, which, according to Freud, may lead to homosexual behavior, guilt, and shame.

Freud's developmental stages are outlined in table 1.1.

Table 1.1 Freud's Psychosexual Stages of Development

Psychosexual stage	Age	Description
Oral	First year of life	Sexual energy is expressed through the mouth; fixation may result in smoking, overeating, or dependency later in life.
Anal	2-3	Sexual energy is expressed through the anus as toilet training takes place; fixation may result in excessive messiness (anal expulsive) or in excessive neatness (anal retentive).
Phallic	3-5	Sexual energy is expressed in the penis and clitoris; fixation results in a lack of identification with same-sex parent.
Latent	6-12	Sexual energy is latent or dormant as the child prepares for mature sexuality.
Genital	Puberty to adulthood	Sexual energy is transformed into mature sexual love that includes gratification of one's sexual partner.

Not all psychodynamic models are based on Freudian concepts of psychosexual conflict. Alfred Adler, a contemporary of Freud, rejected Freud's emphasis on sexuality and biological urges as the prime cause of inner conflict. Adler proposed that it is the helplessness and inferiority experienced in infancy and throughout life that fuels inner conflict. In Adler's view, humans are constantly striving for superiority, which he defined as seeking to fulfill one's potential. Other psychodynamic theorists and practitioners, such as Jung, Kohut, Mahler, and Horney, have contributed additional concepts to the psychodynamic model and have disputed various aspects of Freud's brand of the psychodynamic. While it is important to remember that the psychodynamic model has many variations, Freud's work, especially his conceptualization of inner conflict, provides the basis for these later variations.

The Unconscious

We have all had experiences in which we overreacted to an event in unexplainable and, by our own standards, uncharacteristic ways. These reactions often surprise and disturb us as we wonder, "Where did *that* come from?" The psychodynamic answer to that question focuses on the *unconscious*. The concept of an unconscious part of the mind is one of the great contributions of Freud's theorizing on the human condition. The unconscious in psychodynamic theory is a part of the mind that is unknown. Painful thoughts, emotions, and disturbing mental images are repressed or restrained in the unconscious for self-protection. The dynamic model views the mind as the place where opposing forces—thoughts like "I'd really like to punch my teasing brother" (aggressive drive of the id) and "Good children don't fight" (social internalization of the superego)—coexist and interact, producing conflict. This conflict is irritating and often painful to the person. When it cannot be resolved, the conflict is pushed down or repressed into the unconscious, where it remains "unknowable" and therefore less painful. However painful, unresolved conflicts repressed in the unconscious are not neutralized and totally contained. Repressed issues leak out, usually in disguised forms—through dreams, language metaphors, "slips of the tongue"—causing behavioral symptoms and often problems for the individual.

According to the theory, the most common sources of unresolved conflicts are events in early childhood. As infants we come into our world with tremendous physical and emotional needs and desires that seek fulfillment. Fulfillment of these desires is often blocked by the needs of others and the limits of the environment to provide satisfaction. Consequently, childhood is a time when selfish desires are in perpetual conflict with social and environmental limits. Total wish fulfillment is impossible, so the child copes with unresolved conflicts by repressing them into the unconscious. Furthermore, young children have the capacity to be astute *observers* of the world around them, but they are unsophisticated *interpreters* of their environment. This "seeing without understanding" produces confusion and conflict for the psyche. It also creates a personally constructed, subjective view of reality that may or may not correspond to a more objective interpretation of actual events.

Defense Mechanisms

In the supermarket, a toddler ignores his scolding mother by looking away from her and staring intently at a peanut butter jar; a four-year-old covers her ears with her hands and closes her eyes while her father reprimands her for disobeying him. These common childhood behaviors are examples of universal human defensive responses to conflict and discomfort. In the psychodynamic model, they are evidence that humans seek to defend themselves from emotional pain and discomfort such as shame, guilt, and anger. Throughout life individuals collect a repertoire of defense mechanisms that protect them from the pain of their conflict issues. *Defense mechanisms* are recurring patterns of thinking that serve to protect the person from overwhelming anxiety by either repressing conflict issues in the unconscious or by distorting reality to disguise the conflict in a less threatening form. As their name implies, they protect the self from the painful anxiety, shame, and guilt of knowing the conflict material by providing a process in which the conscious mind is presented with safe, alternative mental thoughts that reduce the pain by keeping the true issue masked in the unconscious. These defenses are self-protective and adaptive, at least in the short run. Therefore, removing defensive mechanisms can lead to considerable turmoil for the person and must be done with great care.

Because defense mechanisms are the ego's agents of repression for the unconscious, they are a focus for analysis in the psychodynamic approach. Enabling the client to understand and recognize defense mechanisms is a major goal of psychodynamic interventions, as this provides a key for unlocking the imprisoned conflicts of the unconscious. Because the unconscious holds unresolved conflict issues, removal of defense mechanisms is done with great care and it is expected that the client will resist dealing with the pain of these issues. While analysis of defense mechanisms is a focus of the psychodynamic model, the defenses are not seen as flaws, but are instead respected as evidence of the client's ego strength and ability to protect the self. Examples of some common defense mechanisms in sport situations are presented in table 1.2.

Transference

Emphasis on the person's past as a major component of present feelings, thoughts, and behaviors is a third focus of the psychodynamic model. This focus is reiterated in the psychodynamic explanation of important relationships in the person's life. The concept of *transference* postulates that

Table 1.2 Examples of Selected Psychodynamic Defense Mechanisms

Defense	Definition	Example
Denial	Refusal to accept reality or recognize a true source of anxiety	Pitcher's immediate response to giving up the winning home run in the ninth inning is "No, no! I don't believe it. This can't be happening."
Rationalization	Justifying an unreasonable action of feeling by manufacturing reasons for it	"I didn't play well because I forgot to wear my lucky socks."
Regression	Behaving in a manner that is characteristic of an earlier stage of development	The coach has a temper tantrum when an athlete makes an error
Displacement	Expressing unwanted feelings or thoughts by redirecting them from a more threatening, powerful person to a weaker person or object	A shortstop is angry at the coach for berating him in public after making an error, so he yells "shut up" to the batboy who is chattering to other players
Inhibition	Controlling thoughts or activities to avoid feelings of anxiety	An athlete avoids rough play or contact with opponents to inhibit her assertiveness and avoid anxiety
Reaction formation	Exaggerating a thought or feeling to help repress the opposite feeling or thoughts	An athlete is always early to practice and games to defend against wishes to be tardy and show up when he pleases
Sublimation	Diverting unwanted impulses into socially approved thoughts or behaviors	A person with strong feelings of aggression becomes a champion boxer
Repression	Actively pushing painful memories out of awareness	A football player having no memory of the "spearing" incident that led to his paralysis
Projection	Attributing one's own undesirable traits to others	A volleyball player who is angry with her coach acts pleasant toward the coach but complains to teammates that the coach is mad at her

(continued)

Table 1.2 *(continued)*		
Defense	**Definition**	**Example**
Splitting	Dividing the world into "good versus bad" dichotomous categories and operating in an "all or none" fashion	After one bad call, an athlete declares the referee incompetent and "always against our team"

people construct their relationships in the present by reproducing emotionally important aspects of their past relationships (Ursano, Sonnenberg, and Lazar 1991, p. 42). Memories of past interactions and relationships are superimposed on successive relationships because individuals tend to replay and utilize past experiences to forge new relationships in the present. This is not to say that present relationships are exactly like past relationships. However, transference infers that important present relationships are woven using both new experiences and past sets of memories from old significant relationships. The new relationship becomes a vehicle for working out issues from old relationships, but this process is unrecognized by the person. In sport this might be seen when an athlete weaves old sets of memories, attitudes, and feelings toward his father into a new, intense, interactive relationship with his coach.

For humans, the most significant early relationships are with parents, and current psychodynamic theorists accord great importance to the client's relationship with the mother, father, and other early caregivers. Of particular interest are the characteristics of the bonds of attachment formed with early caregivers and the subsequent movement toward independence from these caregivers. Because all humans are born in a state of almost complete helplessness, issues of attachment to caregivers in order to successfully deal with infantile helplessness are of consequence to individuals as they mature. Optimal attachment to the primary caregiver alleviates the person's helplessness and provides the necessary sense of security for growth toward independence. For this reason, both the nature of early attachments and subsequent movements toward separation or individuation are important areas of inquiry in psychodynamic consultations. If these processes of attachment and individuation are less than optimal for the person, they cause conflict and pain in later relationships with others. Other significant relationships, such as sibling relationships and romantic involvements, are also of interest in the psychodynamic model.

Transference phenomena have important implications for the relationship between the client and psychologist. The transference concept predicts that the client will create a relationship with the counselor that recapitulates important aspects of the client's early relationships. Additionally, past relationships of the *psychologist* may unknowingly be brought into the consulting session, a process called *countertransference*. In the psychodynamic model, it is incumbent on the psychologist to constantly guard against bringing her own material into the counseling session. The psychologist is expected to maintain a keen awareness of her feelings and thoughts, analyze them, and deal with them so that they can be controlled and kept out of the counseling relationship. This requires that the psychologist be diligent about knowing and understanding the self in addition to working toward the goal of self-understanding for the client.

Goals and Procedures

"Know thyself," the ancient Greek philosophical taunt, is a concise description of goals in the psychodynamic model. In this model, knowing and understanding both the conscious and unconscious aspects of one's inner life enhances the self. The reworking of past anxiety-causing conflicts, especially those repressed to the unconscious, promotes healing and guides the self toward a more rewarding, mature set of behaviors, resulting in greater productivity, success, and happiness.

"Working through" past anxiety-producing conflicts is accomplished through analysis of defense mechanisms, transference, and other windows of the unconscious mind, such as dreams and disguised metaphors in language. The analyses are initially done by the psychologist, who offers interpretations of the client's material to the client. These interpretations are crafted by observing patterns in the client's reports of thoughts, behaviors, and feelings across a variety of situations. The therapist seeks to explain the significance of the client's distortions of certain past events and show how the client's present worldview is related to past misinterpretations. Revelation of past unconscious material allows the client to re-evaluate automatic patterns of thoughts, feelings, and behavior from a more mature position. During this analysis it is imperative that the client understands and is willing to accept the material as it is interpreted or analyzed by the psychologist. Lack of acceptance is viewed as resistance and as a sign that the client is not prepared, or lacks the security, to examine the troubling material and emotions surrounding his conflict issues. Overcoming the client's resistance usually takes considerable time and leads to the long series of consultations that often characterizes psychodynamic approaches. As the consultations progress, the client begins to recognize his own patterns and is able to engage in self-interpretation and self-analysis. Self-analysis signifies the progress of the client in understanding himself and is a goal of the model.

Accessing the Unconscious: Free Association, Dream Analysis, and Projective Tests

Free association is a technique for accessing the unconscious in which the client is instructed to relax and say whatever comes to mind without censoring or altering the free flow of thoughts. The client is not to be concerned about the content or coherence of the thought stream and is asked to verbalize all thoughts and feelings without judging or censoring them in any way. Free association revelations may be humiliating or shameful to the client, and expressing one's view of the world leaves the client feeling vulnerable. It is important that the client senses a high degree of safety and acceptance in the free association process so that her perspective of the world can be revealed.

The practitioner actively seeks to assure the client that the office is a safe environment and that the client's needs will be given precedence. Some actions that promote this sense of security are discussing confidentiality with the client and informing the client of safeguards employed to protect personal files. Providing an office environment that is secure, soundproof, and quiet, perhaps with separate entrances and exits so clients do not encounter other people, is also helpful. Often the psychologist will deliberately sit out of direct view of the client to assure that the presence or reactions of the practitioner do not inhibit the client's free flow of thoughts, and to make the client feel more at ease.

The material that results from the client's free association is used to detect patterns of thoughts, feelings, or fantasies, which reveal the client's defense mechanisms. Through analysis of these defense mechanisms and of latent or hidden meanings in the free associations, the client's more primordial issues can be uncovered.

The importance of the client's past history in the psychodynamic model requires the therapist to assist the client in connecting present distress with past painful memories and feelings. Bringing these past conflict issues to the surface requires courage on the part of the client to be vulnerable in the reliving of these painful issues so that they can be understood and resolved. Although the client is expected to resist this reliving of painful events, with the help of the therapist, resistances can be recognized for what they are and overcome. Painful issues can be resolved because the client now, no longer a child, has more resources to understand past feelings and experiences and also has the support and resources of the therapist to assist in this challenging endeavor.

Dream analysis, like free association, is a technique that provides clues to the client's unconscious issues, as dreams are seen to contain hidden material. In fact, dreams can be viewed as the sleeping version of free association. Dream material is often considered less guarded than free association material, but it also contains its own resistances and defenses. Dream material is related to the client's past history and analyzed for its patterns and latent meanings through interpretations of disguised metaphorical and analogous images.

Another technique used to bring out the hidden material of the unconscious is *projective testing.* In projective tests, such as the Thematic Apperception Test and Rorschach inkblot test, the client is asked to view amorphous stimuli (such as an inkblot) and describe what she sees in the stimuli. Because these stimuli are amorphous, the client projects hidden material from her own psyche into her interpretation. This material is then analyzed and interpreted to reveal the client's unconscious thoughts and feelings. Changes in projective tests, free associations, transference, and dream material over time can be used as assessment tools. The changes in these materials are seen as reflections of personality changes and identify progress in self-understanding.

Analysis of Transference

The transference concept posits a re-creation of both troublesome and positive attachments and individuation issues through subsequent relationships with other important individuals during the life span. If the processes of early attachment and individuation are incomplete for the person, they cause conflict and pain in later relationships with others. Because unresolved relationship issues are painful, they are often relegated to the unconscious. In the psychodynamic model, the technique for uncovering these conflict issues of relationships is through the analysis of transference. In consultations, the psychologist deliberately presents herself as a blank wall so that issues from the client's past relationships can be cast onto the relationship between the client and the psychologist. Then, by analyzing this transference relationship between the client and the psychologist, the unknown and painful conflicts of the past can come into view and be understood and resolved.

Because the psychologist deliberately puts little of herself into the relationship, the client's relationship with the psychologist is "created" by the client's own psychological material, which is then analyzed in the session. For example, if during a consultation the client notes that he feels that the psychologist is "laughing" at material from his free associations, the psychologist might choose to ignore the content of the free association and explore why the client feels that the psychologist is laughing at or mocking him. If the client is open to examining his reaction to the therapist, then together they might explore other times the client felt that important people in his life laughed at or mocked him. The goal is to identify past instances, usually from childhood, in which an important person in the client's life shamed or mocked him; bring the unresolved pain from that relationship to the surface; then seek to understand it, and thereby resolve it. Understanding of these unresolved relationship issues promotes healing and alleviates the need for problematic feelings and behaviors in the client.

The Psychodynamic Model in Sport Psychology

Although some of the early works in sport psychology (Ogilvie 1966) had a psychodynamic flavor, employment of the psychodynamic model has been limited, especially in the United States. Critics of this model cite its origins in clinical psychopathology and its rather long time frame of treatment as aspects of the model that dispose against its use in athletic settings.

Additionally, in the area of research, the critical role of unconscious processes in the psychodynamic approach makes it difficult to establish cause-and-effect relationships through empirical studies. Silva states that "the inability to predict behavior under certain psychic events has led some psychologists to maintain that deterministic (psychodynamic) models can explain all but predict nothing" (1984, p. 63). Gill agrees, stating that the psychodynamic model is based on "after-the-fact explanations . . . and offers few testable predictions, especially about healthy personalities," which makes it unsuitable for both applied work with healthy athletes and research (1986, p. 26). Apitzsch defends the psychodynamic approach and offers a different reason for its unpopularity, stating that "researchers from North America are, by and large, ignorant of the existence of scientific studies on psychodynamic theory reported in languages other than English and, therefore, too hastily jump to conclusions concerning the usefulness of this theory" (1995, p. 113).

One argument supporting the use of the psychodynamic model with athletes is that contemporary efficacy studies indicate that the psychodynamic model requires a client who is introspective, has a fairly healthy ego, is motivated to change, and is capable of facing the self honestly (Corsini 1994). These characteristics do apply to some athletes, so the model may be appropriate for athletes who desire insight as well as relief from symptoms. Though some claim that because the psychodynamic model has its origin in psychopathology it is therefore not appropriate for healthy athletes, all theoretical models in psychology must relate to and outline the genesis of both "normal" and "pathological" feelings, thoughts, and behaviors. Consequently, this model should not be dismissed solely for its original relationship to psychopathology.

Because psychodynamic theories rely on self-knowledge in order to promote growth, these models share the self-development mission of sport. Psychodynamic consultations aim at reconstructing aspects of the individual's basic personality and are not limited to resolving specific issues. Goals of self-understanding and deep personality change require a commitment of considerable time and make the psychodynamic model unpalatable to athletes who are oriented toward solving a specific performance problem rather than self-development. However, "when the client wants understanding as well as symptom relief or when the 'secondary gain' of the symptom leads to either failure of the direct approach or the substitution of a new symptom for the old one," then a psychodynamic approach may be indicated (Corey 1996, p. 43).

In the few instances in which the psychodynamic model is included in the sport literature, the topic most often associated with it is the athletic personality, especially the "injury-prone" sport personality (Begel 1992, Gill 1986, Hunt 1996, Nideffer 1989, Silva 1984). Sanderson discussed defenses such as escape and avoidance as underlying dynamic issues that may explain the phenomenon of injury-prone athletes (1977). Hunt has published several works examining the psychodynamics of risk and injury with attention to the role of unconscious conflict in risk-taking and management of injury (1995, 1996). In "Psychological Aspects of Scuba Diving Injuries," Hunt's methods included conducting clinically oriented research interviews to "illuminate ways in which short-term psychological treatment can facilitate insight into dangerous and/or 'injury prone' behavior, the psychodynamics of injury denial and depressive reactions to injury" (1996, p. 254).

Apitzsch and his colleagues conducted research focusing on a different psychodynamic angle (1993, 1995). They used a projective test, the Defense Mechanism Test, to examine athletes' defense mechanisms, reasoning that the stress and anxiety related to important athletic performances engages athletes' intrapsychic defensive processes so that anxiety can be reduced. In their research on soccer players, Apitzsch and Berggren (1993) focused on the adaptive and maladaptive nature of defense mechanisms, hypothesizing that adaptive uses of defenses enhanced performance while maladaptive uses of defenses decreased performance. For example, the defense mechanism of denial may be adaptive if it encourages a player to persist in a losing match where chances of winning are slim. Ignoring the threat of losing the match causes the athlete to play with vigor and hope, preventing her from giving up. However, denial may be maladaptive if it causes an athlete to ignore the reality of the strength of an opponent in a match, resulting in a reduction of effort by the athlete and underestimation of the opponent (Apitzsch 1995). Their study presents cases that illustrate how analysis of an athlete's defense mechanisms, and determination regarding situations in which these individual defenses are adaptive or maladaptive, can be used to predict athletic performance.

Another sport topic that has garnered psychodynamic interest is running. Berger and Mackenzie investigated the thoughts, behavior, and emotions of a female jogger over a four-month period, using a clinical case study methodology (1980). *Case studies* are in-depth analyses of a client's situation and interpretation of his issues using psychodynamic concepts. They describe the client's presenting problems, the content of dreams, free association material, the psychologist's analysis of defenses, the client's reactions to interpretations, and the outcome of treatment in exacting detail. Case studies are the traditional form of descriptive research in the psychodynamic model. Some of the most famous case studies were written by Freud, who advanced this type of descriptive research to an art form. In this particular study, the data were three interviews with a trained clinician supplemented by the client's personal journal entries. Free association, fantasizing, and stream-of-consciousness writing after jogging sessions provided the material that was interpreted to support four hypotheses or propositions. The supported propositions were

1. "Participation in sports involves the experiencing of a wide spectrum of emotions ranging from agony to ecstasy." Among the emotions reported by the client were aliveness, anger, competency, control, fear of death, guilt, and power (p. 364).

2. "Sports such as jogging are conducive to introspection as well as to thinking in general." The client reported a range of cognitive activities including daydreaming, self-talk, reviewing past conversations with others, self-hypnotic experiences, and meditations (p. 365).

3. "Engagement in sport satisfies inner psychodynamic needs." In this case, evidence of obsessive-compulsiveness and use of defense mechanisms such as repression surfaced while jogging. A relationship between jogging and family dynamics was also interpreted (pp. 366-369).

4. "Awareness of private, phenomenological experiences associated with sport can be useful for gaining self-understanding." This proposition was supported by the insights the jogger felt she obtained from her athletic endeavors. These insights "expanded her self-awareness and self-understanding" (pp. 370-371).

This case study epitomizes the form of inquiry, methodology, and quality of knowledge that can be gained from use of aspects of the psychodynamic model.

The use of the psychodynamic model to investigate the "meaning" of sport is exemplified in a scholarly essay in Sachs's *A Psychoanalytic Perspective on Running* (1984). In this essay, Sachs outlines various psychoanalytic meanings runners attach to their running activity by exploring the workings of the dynamic consciousness, childhood fantasies, and multiple determination (multiple meanings) in running. He illustrates a psychoanalytic approach to understanding the antidepressant effects of running using a case study of a male runner. Among the psychoanalytic interpretations attached to the running case study, Sachs suggests that

> running might act as an antidepressant on a simple level by discharging the repressed aggression in physical activity. Similarly, the physical pain suffered during long runs or races might replace the superego punishment for causing the loss. The feeling of being inadequate or unable to survive without the lost object might be countered as the runner demonstrates self-sufficiency and gains a realistic increase in self-esteem. Another way psychodynamic theory might explain why running relieves depression is that it invokes a total denial of the loss. The independence and self-sufficiency fostered by the running might on an unconscious level be equated with the statement, "I am so self-sufficient that I don't need anyone and therefore have not suffered a loss." In this dynamic the running does not relieve the depression by aiding the process of grieving but defends against it by denying the loss through an illusory self-sufficiency. (p. 103)

Throughout this work, Sachs analyzes case studies of runners to demonstrate how running can promote expression of conscious and unconscious internal conflicts from all phases of psychosexual development. His application of psychoanalytic concepts to running provides a good example of how sport behavior can be interpreted as a latent expression of the person's dynamic unconscious through the psychodynamic perspective. Furthermore, he suggests that running activity can be used as an adjunct tool in psychotherapy.

It should be noted that the rather scarce reference to psychodynamic concepts in sport psychology research might not reflect its relative importance and use to the practitioner. It is difficult to ascertain how many sport psychologists working in the applied domain use psychodynamic theory and techniques, either exclusively or in concert with other models, when working with athletes. Additionally, while Freudian psychoanalysis is the prototypical psychodynamic theory, it is important to remember that other branches of the psychodynamic tree may be more applicable to sport and self-understanding of athletes. Of particular note are the theoretical twists in the Adlerian psychodynamic model that emphasize the importance of social context. Adler's emphasis on how people interact with each other and the individual's struggle to find a place of significance in social groups are topics of interest in the world of sport, especially team sports, as well as in the world at large.

Misuse of Psychodynamic Interpretations: A Football Is Not Always a Fetus

Imagine you are an athlete reading about sport psychology and you come across the following narrative:

> The hiking of the football between the legs of the center into the quarterback's hands becomes a ritual denoting male birth envy. According to the rules (created by males), all players must await the "birth" in stillness. Action (life) cannot take place until after the birth of the ball. Prior to the snap, there is no action, save for occasional fetal kicks of a blitzing linebacker (based on ideas from Dervin 1991).

How would you react? In "Sports, Athletes, and Games in a Psychoanalytic Perspective," Dervin provides interpretations of sport and athlete behavior, showing how analogies, symbolic meanings, and latent meanings can be culled from athletics (1991). These interpretations are intended to help sport psychologists view sport from a psychodynamic perspective. The interpretations are generalized and are not connected to the material of a specific client. Dervin did not intend that his interpretations should be applied to all football players, but misrepresentation and misapplication of psychodynamic interpretations by some critics have prompted many to dismiss this perspective because it is often taken out of context. Taken out of context, psychodynamic interpretations seem bizarre. Freud's severest critics argue that he simply discovered that everything in the world is only separated by two degrees of freedom. Add the existence of an unconscious with a hidden agenda and the power of interpretation by analogy, and all human behavior can be interpreted in multiple ways—all fictional accounts created by "shrinks" who never played the game.

The problem with applying these "generalized interpretations" to all athletics is that they violate the psychodynamic model by distancing the interpretation from the client. Because this model centers on the client's personal material, interpretations apply only to the client. The farther away the interpretations stray from the specific client, the less validity they possess. Psychodynamic interpretations need to be culled from repetitive patterns in the client's own material. They need to be anchored in the free associations, history, defenses, and transference material of the client and presented to the client for examination. Interpretations must resonate with the client's experiences, thoughts, and feelings because the psychodynamic approach is a person-centered rather than problem-centered approach to performance behavior.

It is not surprising that when athletes read interpretations from other athletes' material or generalized interpretations that are not connected to a specific athlete's situation, they often reject them outright. While this rejection can be interpreted as athlete defensiveness, it is the misuse of psychodynamic methods, specifically the generalization of interpretations, that is the crux of the problem. While generalized interpretations that do not stem from individual material should never be imposed on athletes, they are useful for training practitioners in the psychodynamic model by suggesting options for interpretations. They can be used to "summon the psychoanalytic spirit not to nail in hard facts but to probe, to suggest analogies, to tease out latent dimensions" as Dervin suggests (p. 164).

Summary

The psychodynamic model is based on Freud's conceptualization of the role of the unconscious and the dynamics of the person's psychosexual development. Major concepts of this model include the following:

1. Personality and motivation are based on dynamic interactions among aspects of the self—the id, ego, and superego.

2. Much of this dynamic internal interaction takes place in the unconscious and is not recognized by the individual. Defense mechanisms are often employed to handle internal conflicts and can be enhancing or debilitating.

3. While individual treatments vary, there are common elements of the psychodynamic model that are relatively stable:

   a. an interest in the client's past history

   b. active participation of the psychologist in providing interpretations and guidance

   c. concern with keeping the practitioner's issues out of the treatment and concentrating solely on the client's material

   d. a "working through" of the client's inner conflicts and unconscious issues so that the unknown is revealed and can be handled with maturity

Because this model centers on the individual client's personal material, interpretations apply only to the client. The farther away the interpretations stray from the specific client, the less validity they possess.

Process Plan for Lisa Irons's Case:
Psychodynamic Perspective

Before working with Lisa, it is necessary to assess her case to determine whether she is a suitable candidate for psychodynamic techniques. Part of this assessment would include educating Lisa about the psychodynamic approach. Because understanding is a goal of the psychodynamic model, Lisa must understand the assumptions and process of the psychodynamic model as a first step in understanding herself and creating a working alliance with me. If Lisa agrees that this approach might be beneficial for her, I would also discuss issues such as time commitment and financial obligations, so that she has a clear understanding of her commitments to the work. Lisa seems to have sufficient ego strength, intelligence, and motivation to benefit from the psychodynamic approach. Her journal-keeping and autobiography indicate that Lisa is looking for the understanding provided by an analytic-oriented approach and not just symptom relief from her slump. Although we will certainly address issues associated with her slump, I will work with Lisa so she understands that unconscious issues may be the source of her slump and that resolution of these issues will lead to relief. If she agrees to commit to this work, she seems a likely candidate for a successful psychodynamic intervention.

As part of the assessment process, I would ask Lisa's permission to talk with her pro. I am not seeking the professional's opinions of Lisa or her problems—that information must come directly from Lisa through our work together—but I want to confirm that Lisa's problems are not solely caused by basic biomechanical errors that require a biomechanical solution.

I would start with some projective testing with Lisa, looking for basic personality patterns that influence her approach to life. Techniques such as free association, dreams, symptoms, humor, and language slips will be used in our sessions to identify unconscious issues. Free association can be applied to elements in Lisa's current life or past events of importance. Changes in Lisa's free association material and dream analysis material can be used as assessment tools, as they reflect personality changes and progress in her self-understanding.

In applying the psychodynamic model to Lisa's case, I would be extremely interested in exploring more about her sporting history, especially as it relates to her early sporting experiences in her family. Lisa's sense of confusion may emanate from a split—a conflict between her old patterns of thinking and behavior, which have served her well in the past, and a need to change and adopt new strategies in order to cope with her present-day realities. This type of conflict spawns generalized anxiety, irritability, and distractibility that could certainly influence motor performances.

It is evident from the information presented that Lisa has a strong superego that dictates what she "should" be doing. For example, she has internalized her parents' rule of not being a quitter. Superego judgments against quitting a project, whether it is ceramics as a child or quitting the tour before accomplishing major tournament victories, is contributing to Lisa's conflict regarding retirement from the tour. This pattern of pursuing a goal regardless of circumstances may have contributed to Lisa's past successes but may be unrealistic in her present, different circumstances. I also would use free association to have Lisa expand on her autobiography comments about getting recognition as a child. For example, her reference to imitating her father at the driving range might be related to her current strivings for recognition as a professional golfer. I will not impose my interpretations on Lisa, but if I detect a pattern in her striving for recognition, I will suggest that this is an unresolved issue for her.

I noticed a marked discrepancy between Lisa's facial expression (smiling) upon entering my office and her words ("I'm going to cause you all sorts of trouble") and her body language when slumping down in the chair. This discrepancy could reflect the strength of her superego, so I would explore the unconscious superego "rules" that might cause this sort of break between facial expression and verbal/body language. I would want to explore whether Lisa believes that she must "always be pleasant," for instance.

Of equal importance will be an exploration of the strength of Lisa's ego in relation to her athleticism and her ideal self. Her accomplishments indicate that she has mastered a great deal in relation to the game of golf. This mastery should be mirrored in her view of herself (ego) as an athlete, and that view should be solid and strong. Lisa's confidence springs from the strength provided by her mastery and accomplishments in the game as an elite athlete. When this ego strength breaks down or develops weaknesses, and it fails to match her superego view of her ideal self, then Lisa is subject to "leaky self-confidence" and questions herself as an athlete. This can lead to distrust of her ego-centered "athletic self," which will negatively influence her golf performance. Her competitive performances must be anchored in her athletic self, and it is this self that she must trust so she is free to perform without interference from internal and external distractions.

Central to Lisa's ego strength as an athlete are her defense mechanisms. These can serve to both enhance and detract from peak performance, so much of our work will be devoted to analyzing them. I will work with Lisa so she recognizes and understands her defenses. I will make interpretations from her comments to identify those defenses she uses in relation to her athletic performances. As she begins to understand her own defenses, Lisa will reinforce those defenses that contribute positively to her performances. Sublimating her anger at losing because of a muffed bunker shot, for example, into energy and desire to fuel deliberate practice on mastering that shot, is a defense that Lisa might value and strengthen. At the same time, I will help her to understand how some of her defenses actually do her harm and need to be worked through or replaced with more effective defenses.

Defenses are latent in Lisa's free association, dreams, jokes, and other manifestations of mood, thoughts, and behavior. Denial is a defense in which the client ignores painful realities and acts as if they do not exist. Because Lisa never makes reference to any intimate personal relationships in her adult life, I would want to explore whether that defense serves to separate her personal life from her professional life in a positive way—that is, in a manner that promotes her best athletic performances—or whether it is a source of guilt and anxiety that her career has left her isolated and alone.

With time, Lisa can be expected to form a transference relationship with me that will mimic other important relationships in her life. As with defense mechanisms, these transferences will eventually be analyzed for content. When defense mechanisms and transference relationships are first identified by me and revealed to Lisa, she may respond by resisting the interpretations. Dealing with these expected resistances will also constitute part of our work together. We will work to identify, and have Lisa accept, her resistance before attempting to interpret any content or the meaning of the resistance. Because my interpretations are only hypotheses that I present to Lisa for consideration, it may be difficult to discern her resistances from what she might view as faulty interpretations. However, all of my interpretations will be based directly on Lisa's material and I will not make any interpretations based on one or two incidences in that material. In our sessions, my role is to listen and to identify Lisa's patterns, and I do not offer any interpretations that I cannot connect directly to her material in multiple situations. It is the repetitive nature of Lisa's responses that I will bring to her attention first. As she begins to self-identify her patterns, we can explore their meaning and underlying causes, but this deeper exploration is only possible after Lisa accepts the existence of the patterns and lowers her resistance.

Early in our work, Lisa may resent that I adopt an abstinent approach and seem to be "just listening" without bringing any "contributions" to the sessions. We will have to discuss her response to my blank screen approach, and that discussion may lead to information about what kind of response Lisa desires from me. Her reply is likely to unveil unmet desires from past relationships, which we can explore.

During our work, I will be alert for countertransference distortions—my propensity to let my material and my own psychic patterns interfere and distort my view of Lisa. For example, I would monitor my own parenting inclinations to "save" Lisa from disappointment by guiding her toward retirement and an "easier" lifestyle.

The primary goal of the psychodynamic approach is to provide Lisa with an understanding of the nature and unconscious origin of her patterns, especially her emotional patterns, of responding to the challenges of life. This understanding and awareness will allow her to consciously alter her problem-solving approaches and vary her repertoire of responses to life's challenges. The psychodynamic goal is to promote fundamental change in Lisa that will lead to global changes in all aspects of her life, including her performance as a golf professional. My goal is to foster Lisa's self-development, not to provide isolated symptom relief from her slump.

Additional Case for Discussion

The following case study focuses on an issue of increasing concern in sports, eating disorders. Examine this case from the psychodynamic perspective and create a process plan for Meghan Dane. After reading later chapters, you might want to return to this case and interpret it from the perspective of other models.

It is important to consider the qualifications of the sport psychologist in treating this athlete. What type of training and licensing should the sport psychologist possess? If the athlete selected a sport psychologist without the proper credentials, what options are available to the sport psychologist for ensuring proper and ethical treatment of the athlete?

Meghan Dane was born big, weighing 13 pounds and 4 ounces and measuring 24 inches in length. She always knew she was big for her age. Baby pictures showed a healthy, round little face with chubby cheeks. Her parents' stories confirmed it, too. Meghan remembers that her mother always called her "chunky monkey" when she was a toddler and that "Mother was proud that I was over the top of my age group for size during all my pediatric checkups. It was like a contest, and Mother was happy when I was at the top of the charts."

"Not that I minded," Meghan continued. "I apparently loved to eat and was seldom content to be without something in my mouth. My baby pictures all show me either eating or furiously chewing on a pacifier, which I refused to give up." When she was four years old, Meghan entered a preschool program and her father insisted that the pacifier stay at home. Meghan compensated by sucking her thumb, a habit she continued well into grade school, especially when she was afraid or anxious.

At age six, Meghan started elementary school at her Catholic parish school. She recounts, "I weighed 80 pounds and was over 4 feet tall in first grade. I was by far the biggest child in the class, which meant I was always last in line because we always lined up by size for processions and special events like First Communion. About this time I started to see my size as a bad thing rather than a good thing. My mother didn't seem so proud of me now." Worried about their daughter's weight, Meghan's parents first encouraged and then demanded that she cut down on her food intake. At school some boys started calling her "Great Dane," a teasing nickname that spread around the school. Meghan remembers, "I was so ashamed. They thought I was a dog, and soon I started to feel like one." As Meghan's unhappiness about herself increased, so did her eating. She started to withdraw and found pleasure and solace in food.

The Danes' family doctor recommended that she get more exercise, so her parents signed her up for a girls CYO soccer team. Meghan remembers, "My size was a big advantage in soccer, as I could pretty much plow through the other girls and score at will. Fortunately I was pretty coordinated and not too slow, given my size. Soccer gave me a chance to put my size to use. Other girls liked having me on the team because we won games and championships. I began to see some advantages to my size and thought my good play depended on my being bigger, so I kept on eating."

Meghan really enjoyed soccer and was becoming a skilled player. When she was 10 she was invited to play on a traveling team. She started to slim down a little, but was still much bigger than other girls her age. In fact, she was bigger than most of the 12-year-olds on the team. Because of her size, others often forgot that she was only 10 years old and expected her to act and play with the maturity of the older girls on the team.

At age 13, Meghan moved into a more competitive soccer league. She recalled, "All of a sudden, I was struggling to score, and for the first time in my life I started to sit the bench as a second-string player. My new coach felt that my weight was slowing me down, and I could see that the more skillful and agile players were making me look bad. I started feeling like my teammates deliberately did not pass the ball to me because I was too fat. I didn't trust them, and I just knew everybody was thinking about how fat and slow I was."

After a particularly bad soccer tournament in which she made some critical errors that caused her to be benched and eventually resulted in her team's losing in the early rounds of the tournament, Meghan decided everything was wrong because of her weight. She reported, "I decided to lose weight no matter how hard it was. I took control and simply stopped eating. At first the hunger pangs were painful and I felt horrible. However, I felt I deserved the pain for all my years of 'being a pig.' After only three months of starving myself, I lost 50 pounds and was down to 130 pounds on my 5-foot 11-inch frame. I looked better and I started playing better. But

I still wasn't content; 50 pounds was not good enough. I was still fat, so I continued to diet. I lost 20 pounds more and was still fat. However, starving myself made me feel dizzy and disoriented, especially during soccer practice, so I started eating before practice. As soon as I put on one pound, I knew I would have to do something about eating before soccer, so I started eating and throwing up to keep my weight down. I managed to play well enough to get a college scholarship, and next year I will start playing NCAA Division I soccer. I'm afraid the increased competition and level of play will be too much for me. I'm still controlling my weight by eating and throwing up, and I've added laxatives and diet pills to my weight control scheme, but I'm afraid it's not enough. I really want to succeed in college soccer, but I'm afraid and anxious about failing. I don't understand why I'm so anxious all the time. I need to understand so I can change this. What should I do?"

Suggested Readings

Brenner, C. 1973. *An elementary textbook of psychoanalysis.* New York: International Universities Press.

Cramer, P. 1991. *The development of defense mechanisms.* New York: Springer-Verlag.

Freud, A. 1946. *The ego and the mechanism of defence.* London: Hogart Press.

Horner, A. 1991. *Psychoanalytic object relations therapy.* New York: Jason Aronson.

Malcolm, J. 1982. *Psychoanalysis: The impossible profession.* New York: Vintage.

Sachs, M. 1984. A psychoanalytic perspective on running. In *Running as therapy: An integrated approach,* edited by M. Sachs and G. Buffone. Lincoln, NE: University of Nebraska Press.

Chapter 2

THE BEHAVIORAL MODEL

In contrast to the psychodynamic emphasis on understanding the hidden inner life, behavioral theory focuses on conditioning, or learning, from the environment as the force that shapes the person. Behaviorists disregard the insight of psychodynamic interpretations in favor of behavioral extinction and re-education techniques that can be empirically measured and verified. The fathers of behaviorism—Watson, Pavlov, Thorndike, and Skinner—were convinced that learning from the environment, not the unconscious inner life, determines people's actions. The study of learning and behavior first centered on classical and operant conditioned behaviors. Pavlov outlined the processes of classical conditioning in his 1927 work *Conditioned Reflexes*. Experimental evidence for operant conditioning was first published by Thorndike (1898) and then popularized by the many works of B.F. Skinner, beginning with *The Behavior of Organisms*, published in 1938. Recently, the effects of social and observational learning on behavior have also interested psychologists.

Just as psychodynamic theory encompasses multiple variations, behaviorism has developed into a variety of subtheories. Initially, behavioral theory centered only on observable behaviors and environmental factors that accompanied these behaviors. Thoughts, feelings, attitudes, and the "mind" of the individual were viewed as a "black box" not subject to objective, empirical study. These "private events" were basically discounted, which led to criticism of behaviorism because it could not account for fundamental covert psychological concepts such as personality. Subsequent refinements of behaviorism included private events by viewing them as learned events that can be unlearned and modified through conditioning techniques. Additionally, the role of one's social environment and the impact of others on personal behavior through vicarious learning was injected into behavioral theory by Mischel (1973) and Bandura (1986) with their work on cognitive social-learning theory and social cognitive theory, respectively. Today the umbrella of behavioral theory includes consideration of the interactions among cognitions, emotions, actions, and social and physical environments.

Basic Concepts

Behavioral theory conceptualizes humans as learning organisms with the capacity to learn accounting for personality, thoughts, emotions, behaviors, and most aspects of the self. *Learning* is defined as a relatively permanent change in behavior that occurs as a result of experience. Behaviorists assume that learning in the form of classical, operant, and sociocultural conditioning shapes people. Both normal and abnormal behaviors are learned and can be unlearned. Therefore, the focus of consulting sessions is on the client's learned experiences as reflected in his present behaviors and learning processes.

Classical Conditioning

Ivan Pavlov, a Russian physiologist, discovered classical conditioning when he was conducting research on digestion with dogs. As part of his digestion studies, Pavlov measured saliva production as the dogs were presented with food. During the course of his experiments, he noticed that at first, the dogs only salivated when food was presented to them. This was an expected involuntary response to the stimulus (the food). But as the dogs acquired experience with the research protocol and presentation of the food, they began to salivate before the food was presented. This annoying phenomenon in his digestion experiments eventually became Pavlov's life work.

What Pavlov discovered was that environmental events in his research protocol, like sounds made by his lab assistant in preparing the food, became associated with the presentation of the food, and the dogs began to salivate at these earlier cues, or *stimuli*. He began to deliberately present environmental events, like ringing a bell, to see whether these events could elicit salivation in the dogs. He found that a once neutral environmental event, like the ringing of a bell, could produce a new behavior—in this case salivation—when paired simultaneously with a natural (unconditioned) stimulus such as food.

Conditioning involves making associations between environmental events and organism responses. In classical, or Pavlovian, conditioning, a neutral stimulus is repeatedly associated with an unconditioned stimulus so that the neutral stimulus creates a new response from the person. In classical conditioning terminology, the starting point is that an unconditioned stimulus (UCS—the presentation of food) creates an unconditioned, or unlearned, response (UCR—salivation). A neutral stimulus is then paired with the unconditioned stimulus. As conditioning or learning proceeds, the originally neutral stimulus becomes a conditioned stimulus (CS—the bell) as it becomes associated with the unconditioned stimulus (food) to produce a newly learned response, or conditioned response (CR—salivation). In classical conditioning, the conditioned response and the unconditioned response are often the same behavior (in this case salivation), but now the behavior occurs in a new situation, one in which it never occurred before (with the ringing of the bell). This process is summarized in figure 2.1.

Pavlov and his followers found that almost any involuntary or reflexive action of an organism could be classically conditioned. For example, we

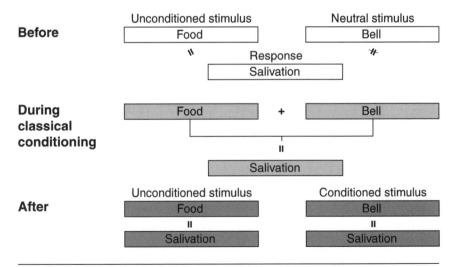

Figure 2.1 Model of classical conditioning.

reflexively withdraw from hot surfaces. If you live in a home where flushing the toilet causes the shower water to become very hot, you will soon be conditioned to jump away from the water when you hear the toilet flush. In this example, the sound of the flushing toilet is the conditioned stimulus. Before that sound was associated with a burst of hot water, it did not produce the behavior of jumping away from the shower water. As you learned that the flushing of the toilet will be followed by hot water, you acquired the adaptive behavior of jumping away before the water turns hot, a new behavior in this situation.

Behaviorists believe that classical conditioning can account for some of our involuntary emotional responses to situations. John Watson and his colleague, Rosalie Rayner, performed some classic experiments in which they conditioned fear in a young boy, Little Albert. Like most toddlers, Albert reacted with a startle reflex to loud noises. Watson and Rayner gave Albert a white rat to play with. Albert's initial response was one of intrigue and curiosity when playing with the rat. The researchers subsequently started following the appearance of the friendly rat with a loud noise that startled Albert and made him cry. Soon Albert started to cry and exhibit fearful actions, a new behavior, as soon as the white rat appeared. In this way the once delightful playmate became a feared and avoided object. For behaviorists, similar conditioning processes can account for some of our emotional responses as environmental stimuli become associated with fearful experiences and then produce feelings of fear just by themselves.

Stimulus generalization and discrimination are important assumptions of classical conditioning. *Stimulus generalization* refers to the process in which stimuli similar in nature to a conditioned stimulus produce the conditioned response. In Little Albert's case, the researchers reported that Albert eventually exhibited symptoms of fear whenever anything white and fluffy was introduced to his environment. Albert generalized the qualities of whiteness and furriness from the rat to other objects and consequently became fearful of an entire range of white, fluffy objects. *Stimulus discrimination* occurs when stimuli similar to the conditioned stimulus do not produce conditioned responses. For example, Pavlov's dogs learned the difference between the tones of different bells and would salivate to one tone but not the other.

Generalization and discrimination of stimuli add complexity to the classical conditioning process and are necessary for this type of learning to be adaptive. If humans never generalized stimuli, multiple experiences would be necessary to learn not to touch hot objects; one would have to learn not to touch the stove, matches, boiling water, and hot radiators in separate learning experiences. Conversely, if stimuli discrimination were not possible, one might go through life being equally fearful of tigers and kittens. Stimulus generalization provides an explanation for the acquisition of problematic behaviors, emotions, and thoughts. Anxiety, for example, may be learned in one situation and then generalized to similar situations where it is inappropriate. Stimulus discrimination provides an explanation for the process of abandoning the inappropriate anxiety generalization and effecting a cure.

The process of classical conditioning includes an acquisition period in which the initial learning takes place. During this process, the conditioned stimulus and the unconditioned stimulus must be paired consistently and almost simultaneously, always with the conditioned stimulus appearing before the unconditioned stimulus. Classically conditioned behaviors can be extinguished by repeatedly exposing the learner to the conditioned stimulus without the unconditioned stimulus. After extinction has taken place, there are often instances of recurrence of the conditioned response, referred to as *spontaneous recovery*.

Classically conditioned behaviors are also mediated by thoughts and beliefs. An example of classical conditioning that often fails because of prior learning in the form of thoughts and beliefs is a treatment for alcoholism in which the alcoholic drink is laced with a nauseating drug. Theoretically, in a perfect classically conditioned response, this should cause the alcoholic to avoid alcohol. However, this procedure often fails because of the alcoholic's prior learning about the treatment. If the alcoholic thinks it is the drug, not the alcoholic drink, producing the nausea, the classical conditioning process is derailed.

Operant Conditioning

In classical conditioning, the learner associates two stimuli to produce a conditioned response that is usually involuntary. In the 1950s, B.F. Skinner began to work on the conditioning of voluntary behaviors. His work led to the codification of the process of operant conditioning. In *operant conditioning*, the learner associates behaviors with consequences. Behaviors are learned through coincidental reinforcement or punishment following a specific behavior (athlete's lucky charm is associated with winning); through *shaping*, in which successive approximations toward the target behavior are rewarded or punished; or through planned situations in which you "catch" someone doing something right or wrong and reinforce or punish it, respectively. It does not matter whether the consequences are planned or serendipitous; behaviors that are reinforced increase, and those associated with punishment decrease. The learner automatically associates a behavior with the positive or negative effects it produces for the self. If the effect of the behavior has consistent positive consequences, the learner will repeat the behavior. If the consequences of the behavior are consistently negative, the learner will decrease or abandon the behavior.

These assumptions dismiss the forces of the learner's inner life by postulating that behavior is shaped and maintained by its consequences, not by free will or personal agency. Although the inner life of the individual is not a focus of the behavioral viewpoint, when it is recognized, it is viewed as an early stage of behavior. Thoughts, attitudes, emotions, and other personal events are acquired by the same process as behavior—that is, through shaping due to positive and negative consequences.

In operant conditioning terminology, a behavior's positive consequences are called *reinforcement*. There are two types of reinforcement, positive and negative, with both strengthening the probability that a behavior will be repeated. *Positive reinforcement* results in rewarding the person with a desired pleasure—for example, giving someone a piece of candy for finishing a job. *Negative reinforcement* involves the removal of an unpleasant event and is satisfying because the unpleasantness is relieved. Taking an aspirin and the consequent relief from headache pain is an example of negative reinforcement. The behavior of taking an aspirin is reinforced and likely to recur the next time one has a headache.

The timing and consistency of reinforcement affect the acquisition and strength of a behavior. In general, continuous, immediate reinforcement (in which the person receives the reinforcement each time the behavior occurs) accelerates the acquisition of a behavior. With continuous reinforcement, however, there is a possibility of *satiation,* which occurs when a person has had enough of the reinforcement and no longer desires more. With satiation or a drop-off in the continuity of reinforcement, the frequency of the behavior acquired by continuous reinforcement usually declines. Partial reinforcement, in which the reinforcement intermittently follows the behavior, extends the time required for acquisition of a behavior, but tends to make the behavior more consistent and persistent. Different schedules of reinforcement affect the characteristics of a behavior pattern. The various schedules of reinforcement and their properties are summarized in table 2.1.

A negative or unsatisfying consequence of a behavior is called *punishment*. Punishment always decreases the probability of a behavior recurring and is therefore useful for altering or eliminating unwanted behaviors. As with reinforcement, punishment is most effective in altering behavior when it immediately follows the behavior and is consistently applied.

Both punishment and reinforcement have disadvantages. The disadvantages of reinforcement are as follows:

- It can create a feeling of being manipulated.
- Reinforcers are often extrinsic rewards, which can undermine the intrinsic joy of an accomplishment.
- Reinforcers can raise the rate of responding above a person's optimal

Table 2.1 Schedules of Reinforcement in Operant Conditioning

Type	Definition	Example	Characteristics
Fixed ratio	Reinforcement occurs after every "x" number of responses	Football tackle gets a helmet sticker after every fourth sack	Produces high rates of responding; however, performance drops off immediately after the reinforcement because motivation sags after the reward
Variable ratio	Reinforcement occurs after every "x" average number of responses, but the specific number varies from reinforcement to reinforcement	In fishing, casting the line into the water is reinforced by a "catch" after an average of 15 casts	Produces very high, steady rates of responding and is resistant to extinction
Fixed interval	Reinforcement occurs after a fixed amount of time has passed	Young athlete gets a "star" on Friday after perfect attendance at practice for a week	Response is diminished after reinforcement is delivered because the athlete knows that time must pass; in the example, the young athlete will not be motivated for Monday's practice by the reinforcement
Variable interval	Reinforcement occurs after an average of "x" units of time have passed since the last reinforcement	Coach has athletes running sprints in which they sprint various amounts of time (2 minutes, 3 minutes, or 4 minutes, but an average of 3 minutes) until the coach blows the whistle; athletes are then rewarded with a rest	Produces low but steady rate of responding

level, resulting in making work of the once playful activity (for some, playing sport for a paycheck makes it a job rather than a spontaneous, voluntary activity).

The following are some disadvantages of punishment:

- It tells the person what *not* to do rather than what to do.
- An authority may administer inappropriate punishment (if the coach makes athletes run laps for punishment, the running becomes a negative activity, which is not always desirable, especially in a sport that requires aerobic training).
- It may engender negative emotions, which may be associated with the punisher or the activity.
- The punished person may react with a fight-or-flight response, either lashing out or disengaging from the coach or sport.
- Its effects depend on the presence of the punisher, and the punished individual learns not to "get caught."
- The unwanted behavior may increase if the person views the punishment as reinforcing because it brings attention.

As with classical conditioning, operant conditioned behaviors can be extinguished and are subject to spontaneous recovery. Consequently, behaviors that oppress an individual can be deconditioned or unlearned by manipulating the environment. Behavioral treatment also requires addressing the issue of relapses. Clients must be taught specific techniques to deal with relapse so that spontaneous recovery of the unwanted behavior does not derail the person's progress.

Sociocultural Conditioning—Modeling

A third type of learning is *vicarious conditioning* or *observational learning*. Humans have a fortunate and wonderful capacity to learn by observing others. If we note that another person experiences positive consequences as the result of a behavior, we are likely to model that behavior ourselves at a later time. If we observe negative consequences resulting from behavior, then we vicariously learn not to copy that behavior or pattern.

Observational learning is influenced by the qualities of the model, with those held in high regard more likely to influence the observer-learner. Children often model parents and heroes such as professional athletes because they respect and admire them. Likewise, models that are perceived as outstandingly successful and similar to oneself are more likely to be imitated than models who are ordinary and different from oneself.

Bandura (1986) and other social behaviorists refer to our capacity to imitate others as *social learning* because of the importance of other people to the learning process. The importance of private mental events, such as expectations and attitudes, in interpreting and therefore mediating the conditioning process is also a strong theme in social learning theory. Social behavioral theories focus more attention than other behavior theories on the contributions of a person's cognitive events to learning. Social behaviorists have combined behavioral theory with aspects of cognitive theory, which will be covered in the next chapter.

Goals and Procedures

The objective of behavioral interventions is to provide corrective learning experiences for the client in order to substitute self-enhancing behaviors for previously learned maladaptive action patterns. Self-understanding is not a necessary objective, but self-regulation—learning to modify and control one's behavior—is. The role of the psychologist in the behavioral model is that of teacher. The practitioner sets up opportunities for the client to learn new behaviors and abandon inappropriate actions. Behavioral consultations focus on the actions of the client rather than the "meaning" of those actions. The client's long-term history is of little interest, and immediate history is of interest only insofar as it informs the client and psychologist about how a behavior was initially learned and what environmental conditions serve to support the behavior's repetition through reinforcement.

In the student–teacher relationship between the psychologist and the client, the client takes an active, participatory role in the direction of the consultations. Unlike the psychodynamic approach, the client's presenting problems are accepted as the focus of the consulting plan and are not viewed as "acceptable" problems that hide the "real" hidden problems. The client determines the "what" of the consulting sessions, and the psychologist determines the "how," but the historical "why" is of little interest in the behavioral model.

Because the behavioral treatment plan deals with only one or two problem areas at a time, the client's role in identifying her most disturbing problems is important. In discussions with the psychologist, the problems are broken down into subcomponents and a thorough delineation of the problem behavior is created. This delineation provides the basis for setting short- and long-term goals to solve the problem. It is desirable that the client views herself as an instrumental agent in this and other aspects of the treatment.

Assessment

Once the problem areas have been identified, specific, systematic assessment procedures are initiated. Behaviorists believe that "you start from where you are," and they take great pains to determine exactly where that is. The client plays a major role in the assessment process. Few psychometric tests are employed other than behavior inventories (to clearly describe the behavior) and self-reports. The client may be asked to keep detailed records of the target behavior, including its initial occurrence, severity, frequency, and environmental conditions that affect the behavior. The initial assessment is used to appraise the stimuli and rewards that might either maintain a maladaptive behavior or promote a constructive behavior. These detailed records also provide a baseline that can be used to measure progress during treatment.

Assessment is also used to construct a precise understanding or definition of behavior. For example, anxiety and its associated behaviors can be both adaptive and maladaptive to an athlete. Only a thorough examination of the anxiety-producing situation enables the athlete and counselor to determine whether an anxiety-related behavior is maladaptive or adaptive. During the initial assessment, the history of a behavior is explored only to identify stimuli and rewards that were instrumental in establishing the behavior and to identify coping mechanisms that the client has employed effectively or ineffectively in the past. Conditions that are currently maintaining the behavior are considered more important than past history, which is only useful insofar as it sheds light on the current situation.

Accurate, detailed assessment provides the data necessary for establishing specific, measurable goals. Assessment continues throughout treatment and provides the measuring tool for goal attainment. Continuous assessment documented by the client's accurate recordkeeping is a central component of treatment.

Goal Setting

Systematic assessment provides the information needed to establish the client's long- and short-term goals. Assessment and goal setting are complementary components in the behavioral model. Examination of behavioral assessments determines not only what behaviors will be modified, but how the environment can be modified to promote success and how "success" will be defined in goal setting.

The qualities of effective goals have been the subject of many investigations, yet issues regarding the requisite characteristics of goals continue to be debated. Are goals more effective if they are general or specific? difficult or moderate? closed or open ended? process or outcome oriented? The best evidence for the effectiveness of goals in sport psychology is a meta-analysis done by Kyllo and Landers (1995). *Meta-analysis* is a statistical method of measuring the effectiveness of an intervention over multiple studies. Kyllo's and Landers's meta-analysis indicates that setting goals can improve performance by 0.34 of a standard deviation. This meta-analysis, which will be discussed in detail later in this chapter, also indicates that moderate, absolute, and combined short- and long-term goals have the greatest effect.

A common formula for designing effective goals is the SMART system (Bull, Albinson, and Shambrook 1996), which recommends goals that are *s*pecific, *m*easurable, *a*ction oriented, *r*ealistic, and *t*imed.

- **Specific.** Specificity refers to a detailed description of the precise target behavior. The characteristic of specificity often includes the exact requirements for the environment as well as the behavior.

- **Measurable.** Effective goals are measurable, and the measuring method is included in the goal statement. Self-reports and accurate recordkeeping provide a baseline to judge the progress of the client and promote self-monitoring of behavior.

- **Action oriented.** Behavioral goals are action oriented rather than conceptual. Strict behaviorists interpret actions as behaviors that are observable by others, but some behaviorists include self-observed behaviors, such as thoughts and feelings, as suitable behaviors for goal setting. It is important that the client have as much control over the desired action as possible, which suggests that the goal should be based on individual performance (for example, "I will only eat 1,500 calories per day") rather than on outcome ("I will lose 5 pounds this week").

- **Realistic.** Establishing the degree of compliance or achievement is part of the realistic nature of effective goals. Goals must be attainable for the client given his current level of achievement, but challenging enough that their achievement will be an acknowledged accomplishment. Goal setting often requires frequent adjustment of specific goals to attain this Goldilocks precision of "not too hard, not too soft" goal levels.

- **Timed.** The final characteristic of effective goals is that they are timed. They have a "due date" recorded in the goal statement, a date in the future when the goal should be accomplished. This timed component of goals contributes to client motivation.

Some goal-setting systems recommend two additional characteristics to the SMART acronym, *e*lastic and *r*epeatable, resulting in SMARTER goal setting. *Elasticity* refers to setting goal standards with a window target rather than a one-point target—for example, setting a golf score target of between 88 and 92 rather than one of 90, or a track time between 3:58:30 and 4:00:00 rather than 3:59:30. These window targets are thought to be preferable because they are more flexible and more likely to be viewed as achievable by the athlete. They are also less likely to result in a self-limiting mind-set if the athlete is having an exceptional performance. The range target mitigates against the self-fulfilling prophecy phenomenon that might accompany a single-point target.

Repeatability requires that the athlete be able to meet the goal more than once before it is considered mastered. It is the first step toward consistency of the new standard of performance. Being able to meet a goal more than once before moving on to higher aspirations is also a morale booster and tends to build confidence in the athlete's new level of achievement. The athlete is less likely to attribute goal attainment to luck and more likely to see it as a growth of talent.

Techniques

Identification of problem behaviors and assessment recordkeeping are responsibilities usually assigned to clients with the assistance of the psychologist. However, strategies for addressing problems are usually designed by the psychologist. The psychologist, as teacher, designs the lessons, creates a systematic plan, and guides the client through the educational process. A vast array of behavioral techniques is available to the psychologist. It is the psychologist's responsibility to select the specific techniques, incorporate them into an efficient and effective program, and individualize them to meet the client's needs. Most techniques fall into one of three categories—reinforcement, exposure, or behavioral coaching techniques.

Reinforcement Techniques

Reinforcement techniques use classical or, more often, operant conditioning principles to extinguish, shape, or reinforce specific behaviors. Often referred to as *behavior modification,* these programs attempt to create specialized environments that control or manipulate reinforcers. If the goal is to extinguish a behavior, then an environment that does not provide reinforcers is created. If a new behavior is to be added to the client's repertoire, then an environment with appropriate reinforcement for compliance and/or punishment for noncompliance is designed.

Exhaustive and continuous assessment is crucial to behavior modification techniques because the techniques are based on identification and manipulation of environmental reinforcers. Sometimes it is difficult to ascertain exactly what conditions are reinforcing a client's behavior. Objective recordkeeping and input from the client are often the only way to identify reinforcers. Once the reinforcers have been identified, the psychologist designs a program that manipulates them. This can be quite challenging, especially if the reinforcer is something that cannot be eliminated from the client's routine. Eating, for example, is a reinforcer that cannot be eliminated and is supported by variable interval reinforcement schedules, which make it difficult to change. This partially explains the poor success rate in weight reduction programs from a behavioral perspective.

Behavior modification programs depend on the use of rewards to encourage target behaviors. Behaviorists make a distinction between reinforcers and rewards. As stated earlier, a reinforcer is any factor that is associated with and increases the frequency of a behavior. A reward, however, can be something that is not directly connected to the behavior. Rewards are assumed by the psychologist and client to be positive events, but they have not necessarily been shown to strengthen the target behavior. Going back to the weight reduction program as an example, the program might be designed so that reinforcers such as high-calorie foods are reduced in the client's home environment. Good-tasting foods are associated with eating behavior and are reinforcers. The program design might also include a reward, such as getting a massage or buying new clothes after a week of successful dieting. The rewards—new clothes or a massage—originate from the external environment rather than from the client's internal self. They have not been shown to affect the client's eating behavior in the past, and technically they are not reinforcers, although they may become reinforcers in time.

The practice of using extrinsic rewards in behavior modification programs is controversial because there is evidence that they may undermine the client's intrinsic motivations to continue the target behavior. When the extrinsic reward is withdrawn, the desired behavior may decrease. Research on the effect of extrinsic rewards on intrinsic motivations is contradictory. Cameron and Pierce's meta-analysis of 96 experimental studies on the effect of reward on intrinsic motivation shows that "verbal praise enhances intrinsic motivation and that other rewards and reinforcement leave intrinsic motivation largely unaffected. A small negative effect occurs when tangible rewards are promised without regard to a standard of performance" (1994, p. 398). They concluded that use of extrinsic rewards seems to be a viable technique for altering behavior as long as the rewards are attached to specified levels of performance.

The ultimate aim of behavior modification programs is to teach clients techniques that they can use to set up self-management programs. Encouraging the client to control his own life and organize his environment to promote personal success is the meta-target behavior of behavior modification. Behavior modification strives to assist clients by teaching them how their learning and environment affects their behaviors. It encourages clients to be in control of their own lives by engaging in new learning experiences and controlling their environments.

Exposure Techniques

Avoidance of specific situations or environments can be extremely debilitating to a person and can negatively influence personal achievement. People avoid situations for a variety of reasons, most of which are related to fear or anxiety associated with the situation. When avoidance of an anxiety-producing situation is impossible, people are forced to perform in an over-aroused state and performance is often impaired. *Exposure techniques* use experience, sometimes accompanied by relaxation methods, to acclimate people so that they can participate fully in personally stressful environments.

The basic format of exposure treatments involves the client going into the anxiety-provoking situation, often with the supporting presence of the psychologist, and experiencing the situation for longer and longer periods of time. It is important that the client stay in the anxiety-provoking situation long enough to feel some degree of comfort or at least a reduction of stress from the beginning to the end of the session. With repeated experiences and declining stress levels in the anxiety-producing situation, the client's experiences counteract her expectation of harm. She "learns" not to respond in an anxious fashion to the formerly stressful environment. Acclimation, which is reinforced by decreasing stress levels, is eventually achieved.

A variation on the basic exposure technique is *systematic desensitization* (Wolpe 1958), in which the client is educated about the physiology of anxiety and gradually exposed to anxiety-producing situations. Symptoms of nausea, dry mouth, and muscle tension, for example, are explained in terms of fight-or-flight behavior. Together, the client and psychologist construct a hierarchical list of anxiety-producing stimuli for a particular behavioral situation. The list is graded from mild to extremely stressful. The client is then taught some form of relaxation strategy—such as progressive relaxation, in which various muscle groups are tensed and relaxed to teach the client what relaxation feels like. Operating under the assumption that simultaneous anxiety and relaxation are incompatible, the client is told to imagine the mildest stressor on his list while employing the relaxation strategy. Increasingly, the client is able to relax in the imagined stressful situation. When he can imagine himself in the mildest stressful situation without any anxiety symptoms, the client proceeds to the next stressor on the list and continues up the hierarchical list of stressors, learning to relax at each new level. Eventually, the client advances from imagining the stressors to actually experiencing them, again in hierarchical order from mildest to severest.

Learning relaxation skills is a critical component of exposure techniques. Behavioral theory views anxiety as a learned response to environmental conditions. The learned anxious responses can be unlearned by teaching a new response, relaxation. Body awareness, breathing exercises, progressive relaxation, meditation, visualization, hypnosis, autogenics, and biofeedback are some of the stress management methods that are used to teach the client relaxation. Table 2.2 describes various relaxation strategies that can be taught to clients. It is advantageous to devote time and effort to relaxation training because this behavioral skill is transferable and can be applied to a variety of problem situations.

Table 2.2   Relaxation Strategies

Method	Purpose	Comments
Body awareness	To develop conscious recognition of how one's body reacts to stressors; to develop internal awareness	Some exercises used to teach body awareness are stress awareness diaries, body scanning and inventory, and periodic recording of general body tension during the day
Breathing	To replace thoracic breathing patterns with abdominal or diaphragmtic breathing	Deep breathing, breath counting, and various controlled breathing patterns are used to replace the shallow, rapid breathing associated with stress
Progressive relaxation	To teach the individual how neuromuscular relaxation feels	Client is instructed to tense and then relax specific muscle groups while attending to the difference between the feel of muscular contraction and relaxation
Meditation	To teach uncritical focusing of attention on one thing at a time while staying anchored in the present time	Mantra meditation, breath-counting meditation, and gazing meditations are three widely used meditation practices

(continued)

Table 2.2 (continued)		
Method	**Purpose**	**Comments**
Visualization	To induce relaxation by use of imagination and positive thinking	Clients are instructed to imagine themselves in a safe, beautiful setting; sometimes affirmations are used to cue relaxation, and imagery can be guided by the psychologist
Hypnosis	To induce relaxation by means of a trancelike state	Trance scripts induce a narrowing of attention, passivity, and suggestions of muscular relaxation
Autogenics	To teach body and mind to respond to verbal suggestions to relax and let go	Autosuggestions of "warm" and "heavy" body parts are consciously practiced for a number of weeks; eventually the body responds to the autosuggestions without resistance
Biofeedback	To provide feedback and cue voluntary relaxation by use of instruments that objectively measure unnoticed physiological components of anxiety	Biofeedback instruments provide a mirror of one physiological aspect of tension, such as tension in the jaw, which can then be brought under voluntary control; eventually the client develops awareness without the feedback

Behavioral Coaching Techniques

Behavioral coaching techniques rely on modeling and practice in a safe environment to teach clients the personal skills they need to achieve. Assertiveness training, in which the client is taught how to express personal needs in an appropriate manner, is a common example of a skill set that is often taught through coaching. In the athletic environment, for example, assertiveness training might be employed to teach an athlete how to stand up for herself in competition.

In behavioral coaching, the psychologist plays a direct didactic role by providing clear descriptions of the desired behaviors and modeling those behaviors for the client. Once the client understands and has observed the new behavior, the psychologist sets up practice schedules so that the client can practice the new behaviors in a safe environment. Practice may take the form of mental practice (often called *covert conditioning* because the "behavior" is observable only by the client), role-playing in situations that mimic the actual environmental conditions of the target behavior, and repetitive practice in relatively "safe" situations that promote success (accompanied by positive or negative reinforcement). Drill and repetition are the hallmarks of behavioral coaching approaches. As the client develops some proficiency in the behavior, the psychologist will assign homework in which the client independently attempts the behavior in a real-world situation and reports on the results. Successful behavioral coaching is mediated by the client's motivational set, ability to mimic the model, and ability to attend to critical aspects of the skill being taught. Therefore, the coaching plan is constructed with these factors in mind.

The Behavioral Model in Sport Psychology

The number of sport psychology studies investigating techniques from the behavioral model or cognitive-behavioral model exceeds investigations of all other models by far. From its roots in physical education and motor learning, sport psychology inherited a strong tradition employing behavioral theory. Consequently, just as the behavioral model, with its emphasis on learning, dominates physical education, it also dominates sport psychology. Performance enhancement packages and research traditions in sport psychology reflect the strong influence of the behavioral model.

Performance enhancement packages, such as Suinn's visuo-motor behavior rehearsal and Meichenbaum's stress inoculation training, combine behavioral and cognitive techniques to improve athletic performance. Combining behavioral and cognitive techniques in one package is a popular strategy in the field of applied sport psychology. Professionals working directly with athletes find multicomponent packages effective in helping their clients. From a research perspective, however, it is difficult to ascertain the effectiveness of any one component in a multicomponent program. The behavioral model is historically associated with the empirical research tradition. Empirical research methods depend on isolating variables so that independent variables can be manipulated and nuisance variables can be controlled. Multicomponent performance packages are designed to have interacting variables, which complicates the empirical paradigm by making it difficult to isolate variables and tease out the effectiveness of individual components. Statistical advances in multivariate analysis and path analysis have improved the effectiveness of empirical paradigms in investigating these multicomponent packages.

Research into the theoretical constructs of some behavioral and cognitive techniques is also compromised in the research of multicomponent packages. Techniques such as visualization and self-talk are used in both behavioral and cognitive interventions. Although both the cognitive and behavioral models seek to intervene and alter self-talk and visualization, the nature of these concepts is fundamentally different in each model. For the behaviorist, self-talk and visualization are forms of silent behavior that are determined or caused by aspects in the environment that trigger these conditioned behaviors. The goal in the behavioral model is to condition new self-talk or visualization behaviors that are more adaptive. The cognitive practitioner, on the other hand, seeks to change the self-talk and visualizations *in order to change* other behaviors. Empirical research studies rarely discuss the different theoretical underpinnings of the variables they are investigating, making it difficult to classify studies on self-talk, visualization, and imagery into behavioral or cognitive techniques. In this work, I have chosen to discuss visualization, imagery, and self-talk as cognitive techniques. This chapter on behavioral techniques will include a review of studies on goal setting, arousal management through relaxation training, behavior modification, operant conditioning, self-monitoring and self-assessment techniques, and modeling.

The number of research studies on some behavioral techniques, such as goal setting and relaxation interventions, is sufficient to allow for literature reviews and meta-analysis. *Meta-analysis* is a statistical method of measuring the effectiveness of an intervention over multiple studies. Behavioral theory and cognitive theory are the only theoretical orientations that have generated sufficient numbers of research studies in sport psychology to allow this advancement to meta-analytic reviews.

In addition to the multitude of empirical studies investigating behavioral interventions, a majority of the case studies in sport psychology also employ interventions from the behavioral or cognitive-behavioral model. While these case studies do not have the power to demonstrate a cause-and-effect relationship between the treatment intervention and enhanced performance, they do provide information describing actual counseling plans that can be used to implement behavioral interventions with athletes.

Goal Setting

Two major reviews of the goal-setting literature in sport and exercise using meta-analysis have been published. The 1995 review by Kyllo and Landers, which was limited to goal-setting literature and examined 36 studies, is the more powerful of the two. The second review, by Meyers, Whelan, and Murphy, analyzed several cognitive behavioral interventions, including goal setting (1996). This review is more subjective, and while it contains meta-analytic procedures, it uses only three studies in its analysis.

Both reviews report that the goal-setting literature is equivocal, reflecting both affirmative and negative outcomes. Meta-analytic procedures can shed some light on these conflicting results by examining effect size to determine whether the literature as a whole supports the efficacy of goal setting interventions.

The meta-analysis by Kyllo and Landers (1995) analyzed 36 studies. The authors reported a 0.34 of a standard deviation increase in performance with the use of goal setting. Their investigation concluded, "This is evidence that goal setting is a successful technique for motivating sport and exercise performance" (p. 126).

Several additional findings from this meta-analysis regarding the nature and conditions of goal setting are of interest. Earlier investigations by Locke, Shaw, Saari, and Latham on goal setting in industrial and organizational settings suggested a linear relationship between goal difficulty and increases in performance (1981). This suggests that difficult goals increase performance to a greater extent than less-difficult goals. The Kyllo and Landers meta-analysis did not support this hypothesis, suggesting that in the domain of sport and exercise, moderate goals are superior to difficult goals in enhancing performance (p. 127). The authors concluded that further studies on the efficacy of difficult goals employing a standardized operational definition of "difficult goals" are needed.

A second hypothesis, that specific goals are more effective than vague, general, or no goals, was only partially supported in the Kyllo and Landers meta-analysis. Furthermore, the authors suggested that recommendations to employ performance goals (based on a person's performance, such as getting in 70 percent of first serves in tennis) rather than outcome goals (such as winning the match) may not be supported by research. They concluded that until further research on the outcome-versus-performance issue is completed, it is unclear under which conditions outcome and performance goals are most effective.

Regarding the issue of the efficacy of short-term and long-term goals, the Kyllo and Landers meta-analysis showed that combined short- and long-term goals seem to be superior to long-term goals alone. Furthermore, some of the studies they examined indicated that public goals are superior to private goals.

Meyers, Whelan, and Murphy in 1996 published both a qualitative review and quantitative meta-analysis of the literature on cognitive (imagery, cognitive self-regulation), behavioral (goal setting, anxiety management), and multicomponent (visuo-motor behavior rehearsal [VMBR] and stress inoculation training [SIT]) strategies. Their review included treatment evaluation studies published between 1970 and 1989. In the qualitative review of goal-setting studies, they state, "The hypothesis that specific, difficult, and realistic goals compared with nonspecific ("do your best") goals, lenient goals, or no goals, leads to improved task performance . . . has received a good deal of research attention," but evaluations of this proposition have been equivocal (p. 141). They did not address the efficacy of performance versus outcome goals, but they noted that performance goals correlate with increased participation and persistence in sport, which often results in higher skill levels. Unlike the Kyllo and Landers meta-analysis, Meyers, Whelan, and Murphy state that "the predicted impact of goal setting on physical performance has not been verified. Nevertheless, evidence does suggest that under certain conditions goal setting may enhance the motivations for involvement and promote more positive self-evaluation of training and competitive performance. Such changes may facilitate task persistence and therefore indirectly lead to performance improvements" (p. 142).

The Meyers, Whelan, and Murphy quantitative review (meta-analysis) on goal setting included only three studies but showed a moderate effect size (ES = 0.54). The authors report that "this finding suggests that goal setting interventions produce a statistically significant moderate effect over the no treatment experiences" (p. 150).

Emotional Regulation

The Meyers, Whelan, and Murphy review of the arousal management literature notes that the sport psychology literature reflects the clinical literature in that more research addresses problems associated with overarousal (anxiety) than with underarousal, in spite of the notion that athletes need to "psych up" for competition. Relaxation training using biofeedback, progressive relaxation, autogenic training, and other relaxation interventions have been shown to lower athletes' arousal levels and diminish anxiety. However, the connection between lower arousal levels and improved athletic performance is more complicated. Athletic performance is mitigated by a host of variables, including the nature of the task, athlete skill level, and attentional focus, which interact with arousal level to affect performance. Meyers, Whelan, and Murphy's meta-analysis examined 25 studies that used relaxation training to decrease arousal and 5 studies that used psyching-up strategies to increase arousal. Both interventions were found to increase performance when compared to control groups. The performance tasks improved by psyching up included strength tasks and tasks that required a burst of energy, such as sprinting and hurdling. Athletic tasks involving balance, precision, or complex skill sets seem to respond positively to interventions that increase relaxation, resulting in decreased arousal. Research on relaxation interventions, arousal levels, and performance is equivocal, and more investigations are needed to sort out the complexities of arousal management in sport.

Gould and Udry's review of research on arousal regulation strategies for enhancing athletic performance draws similar conclusions regarding biofeedback and relaxation strategies of the behavioral model (1994). Regarding behavioral relaxation strategies designed to invoke responses from the parasympathetic nervous system to counteract fight-or-flight responses, they state: "Taken as a whole, the results suggest that performance enhancement resulting from relaxation-based training is possible. However, caution is warranted in interpreting these results because of the failure to establish causal relationships between relaxation training and improved performance in much of the research" (p. 482). Additionally, Gould and Udry make a strong case for the necessity of conceptualizing arousal as a multidimensional concept. They use the term "arousal-related states" to capture the complexity and multidimensionality of arousal. Conceptualizing arousal as a multidimensional construct has important implications for behavioral relaxation strategies that are primarily oriented toward calming the athlete physiologically. Gould and Udry state that "simply instructing athletes to relax or lower physiological arousal without any consideration to the amount and mixture of arousal-related cognition needed for best performance is inappropriate" (p. 480).

Reviews on biofeedback and sport/exercise performance also reflect the mixed findings common in the arousal management literature. A review of EMG biofeedback and performance by Landers (1988) concluded that EMG biofeedback designed to reduce overall muscular tension in the body had little effect on performance. Another review of this literature by Zaichkowsky and Fuchs (1988) concluded that "the majority of the studies . . . showed reduction in EMG followed by improved performance" (p. 388).

De Witt reported on a pilot study and subsequent empirical study investigating the impact of biofeedback with cognitive and progressive relaxation interventions (1980). These studies of football and basketball players found significant differences in performance ratings as a result of the intervention. Like many interventions in the literature, this study employed a multicomponent intervention, so it is difficult to discern exactly what produced the performance ratings increases. Was it the biofeedback, cognitive self-statements, or progressive relaxation? Answers to these questions are not available.

Prapavessis, Grove, McNair, and Cable (1992) employed biofeedback with training in relaxation, thought stopping, refocusing, and coping statements with a small-bore rifle shooter in a single-subject study. Results of this study showed decreases in cognitive anxiety, somatic anxiety, gun vibration, and urinary catecholamines, as well as increases in measures of self-confidence and performance. In addition to measuring increases in performance from baseline, the authors measured state anxiety during competition using multiple dimensional measures of this dependent variable. Investigating multiple dimensions of complex concepts such as state anxiety reflects an increased sophistication of design in some sport psychology research. Recognition that individual athletes may manifest changes in anxiety in different modes—some by changes in heart rate, some by changes in galvanic skin measurements, or altered breathing patterns, or any other number of psychophysical measures—is reflected in more sophisticated research designs employing multiple measures of dependent variables. Unfortunately, these research designs are also expensive to implement, which has resulted in reliance on single-subject designs or studies with very few subjects.

In a review of studies using physiological interventions with athletes in competitive situations, as opposed to laboratory or contrived dependent variables, Greenspan and Feltz found that relaxation-based interventions are, in general, effective (1989). They state that "positive intervention results were reported in only two of the four relaxation-based interventions in which we could infer causality; however, positive results were also reported in all five of the relaxation-based interventions for which inferring causality was questionable" (p. 233). Consequently, while positive results for relaxation-based interventions seem to show promise of effectiveness, the research literature as of 1989 revealed few well-controlled empirical studies from which causality could be inferred. The inherent problems of conducting well-controlled empirical studies using competitive performance as a dependent variable continues to plague the sport psychology research literature today. Weinberg and Comar (1994) reviewed psychological interventions and reported findings similar to Greenspan and Feltz. They found that "38 of the 45 studies examined had found positive performance effects, although causality could only be inferred in 20 of these studies" (p. 406).

In addition to analyzing relaxation-based interventions, Greenspan and Feltz attempted to analyze two other classifications of interventions: behavioral interventions and cognitive restructuring interventions. However, they were able to locate only three studies of behavioral interventions that met their criteria of using competitive performance as the dependent variable. Therefore, they were unable to draw any conclusions regarding behavioral interventions in general. Vealey reported a similar situation, noting that the effectiveness of sport psychology interventions in general is supported in the literature but significant improvements in research methodology are needed to determine causality (1994). Vealey found that only two studies of behavioral interventions were designed to infer causality. In both studies, the behavioral interventions enhanced athletic performance.

Assessment Techniques

Kirschenbaum (1987) reported on the efficacy of cognitive and behavioral self-regulatory techniques, including self-monitoring. Work by Kirschenbaum and his colleagues suggests that positive self-monitoring (monitoring good performances), as opposed to negative self-monitoring, improves performance on new, poorly mastered, or difficult tasks. When tasks are easy or well mastered, monitoring instances of ineffective performances may be more effective. Kirschenbaum also agreed with the conclusion of Donahue, Gillis, and King (1980) that behavioral coaching, including providing operational definitions of skill components and using specific feedback, helps athletes self-monitor and subsequently improve their performances.

A 1993 case study by Jones demonstrates the importance of accurate, continual assessment in the behavioral model. Jones used performance profiling as part of an intervention with an international-level racket sport athlete. Performance profiling instructs the athlete to identify constructs, such as concentration, confidence, fitness, and discipline, that are essential qualities of elite performance. With the assistance of the psychologist, the athlete creates a prioritized list of these fundamental constructs. After these important constructs have been identified, the athlete completes a self-rating that assesses her current level of performance in each construct. The athlete is then asked to rate her performance on each construct during one of her best performances. This performance-profiling procedure involves the athlete in determining the constructs that are to be the focus of her intervention, provides a baseline assessment of the constructs to be improved, and provides guidance for goal setting by establishing the athlete's "best performance" standard as a goal.

In this case study, Jones also used relaxation training in the form of "a meditation-based relaxation technique similar to Benson's (1975) relaxation response" (p. 166). The relaxation training procedure was taught in stages that began in a safe environment with guidance and proceeded toward independent use of relaxation on the court during a stressful point in the competition. This progression mimicked the technique of systematic desensitization. Jones reported that as a result of these interventions, the athlete felt more relaxed, composed, and in control during matches. Pre- and post-test scores and an increase in major tournament wins supported the success of the interventions.

Behavior Modification

A review of behavior modification in sport and physical education by Donahue, Gillis, and King (1980) focused on the use of "operant technology" in three sport areas:

1. Coaching/teaching behavior
2. Physical education and sport environments
3. Skill development

This review was limited to empirical studies in which operant conditioning programs were used to develop specific skill or sport behavior. Although many of the studies in this review used single-subject designs and designs that lacked control groups, the authors concluded the following:

- Operant conditioning techniques can be used to train coaches to add specific, discretely observable coaching behaviors to their coaching practices (p. 314).
- Behavior modification is successful in reducing disruptive behaviors, increasing attentive behaviors, controlling classroom behavior, increasing practice attendance, increasing peer encouragement, and shaping appropriate gymnasium behavior (p. 319).
- Operant strategies, such as self-monitoring and positive reinforcement, are effective and efficient techniques for developing and maintaining sport skills (p. 323).

These conclusions reflect a flurry of research studies examining behavioral interventions in the 1970s. Rushall and Siedentop's publication of *The Development and Control of Behavior in Sport and Physical Education* in 1972 launched interest in this research of operant conditioning in sport. Behavioral techniques such as self-regulation using public self-reporting and reward systems were shown to increase desired sport behaviors in competitive swimming (Rushall and Pettinger 1969; McKenzie and Rushall 1974), basketball (Birdsong and McCune 1977; Jones 1977) and bowling (Heward 1978), as well as other sports.

More recently Scott, Scott, and Goldwater (1997) published the results of a case study in which operant conditioning was used to successfully improve the technique, and resulting performance, of an international-level pole vaulter. The athlete's technical vaulting skill was faulty in that he tended to not fully extend his arms during the critical planting of the pole before takeoff. This flaw had a direct negative impact on the height of his jump. The operant conditioning included prompting (as he ran down the runway, he was verbally prompted with the cue "reach"), shaping (using successive approximations to the desired complete extension of arms), and a conditioned positive reinforcer (correct arm extension broke a laser beam, which produced a beep, noting a successful trial). The results of this case study were an increase in the height of arm extension and a corresponding increase in the maximum height jumped that persisted after the study.

Behavioral contracting in an operant conditioning skill development program was the focus of a study published by Simek, O'Brien, and Figlerski (1994). This study appears to have been designed as an experimental study, but events outside the control of the researchers resulted in a case study rather than a controlled empirical study indicating cause and effect. The researchers used behavioral contracting, "the negotiation of contracts involving the reciprocal exchange of rewards" (Tooley and Pratt 1967, p. 212, as cited in Simek, O'Brien, and Figlerski) to improve golfers' adherence to a skill development package, the *Total Golf* chaining mastery program of Simek and O'Brien. This skill development package consisted of a 23-step mastery training program divided into three weeks. Steps 1 through 10 were taught and practiced during the first week, steps 11 through 19 during the second week, and steps 20 through 23 during the third week. The measured outcome variable was the average of three rounds of golf played before instructional training for baseline performance, three rounds played after the first week of training, and three rounds after the second and third weeks of training. The golfers were rewarded during the first two weeks of the program, and their average strokes per round dropped (improved) and mastery of skills in the training program was high. Promised rewards were withdrawn during the third week, and mastery of skills in the training program decreased, with fewer golfers completing the training steps. Stroke average per round after the third week also increased (performance decreased). The authors concluded, "The present results indicate that contracting can be an effective technique for helping college golfers to adhere to a structured training program to improve golf skills. Through the first two weeks of the training program, the 14 collegiate golfers mastered 93% of the skills required. However, when the expected rewards were not delivered following the second week of treatment, adherence to the training program decreased dramatically as would be expected. Only 32% of the required skills were mastered during the third week" (p. 1103). While the case study methodology does not show that the rewards caused the gains in performance and adherence to the training program in this study, it offers an interesting example of how rewards and behavior contracting might be employed in sport.

Inherent problems with providing external rewards to athletes are issues of dependence and satiation. Athletes can come to expect external rewards for performing and then quit or put forth less effort if the rewards are withdrawn, as seems to have happened in the Simek et al. study. The athlete's level of performance may become dependent on external reward structures. Satiation occurs when the athlete becomes bored or unimpressed with the external rewards and needs an increase in the rewards to motivate his best efforts. For these reasons, it is important that any external reward program provide for a gradual change from external to internal rewards for the athlete.

Exposure Techniques

Strong emotion, risk-taking behavior, and physical trauma often characterize the competitive sporting experience. These factors sometimes result in traumatic experiences for athletes, leading to fear and avoidance reactions to the traumatic episode and environmental stimuli associated with the stressful event. Exposing and habituating athletes to these stressful stimuli may help them adapt and perform better. While the sport psychology literature on flooding, systematic desensitization, and other exposure interventions is sparse, it may underrepresent the frequency with which these techniques are used in actual clinical practice with athletes.

Lee described a progressive or graded hierarchy process as an intervention for a gymnast who had an avoidance reaction to an injury (1988). The avoidance behavior consisted of refusal to perform the movement associated with the injury. The behavioral intervention in this case consisted of providing a "safe environment"—physical guidance, spotting, and use of a foam pit landing area—during performance of a hierarchical series of simple to complex movements leading up to the avoided target maneuver. Toward the end of the intervention, relapse inoculation in the form of alerting the coach to the possibility of spontaneous recovery was included in the treatment. The gymnast's performance, confidence, and motivation improved to the point that three months after the intervention, the gymnast's coach reported that she was no longer having problems with the movement. However, at a 10-month follow-up, the coach reported that the problem was recurring even though relapse inoculation had been included in the original treatment.

Exposure techniques may offer a viable method for overcoming fearful and risky aspects of sport performance; however, little research is available concerning their efficacy. More research is needed to determine efficient and effective uses of these techniques. The major disadvantages of exposure are that it may take many exposures over a long period of time to produce the desired effect, and that relapse may occur after the intervention.

Modeling

Modeling, or *observational learning,* has received attention in the motor learning literature and has been applied primarily to skill acquisition. An interesting 1979 study by Feltz, Landers, and Raeder investigated participant, live, and videotape modeling on a high-avoidance skill—a back dive. The participant modeling treatment included live modeling, followed by guided participation in which the model physically guided the learners through the target motions, and incorporation of a graded hierarchy of success experiences to increase self-efficacy. The results showed that the participant modeling treatment resulted in more successful dives and increased self-efficacy in the fearful task. There was no difference in performance or self-efficacy between the live model group and the videotaped model group. This study demonstrated how modeling contributes to inhibition and disinhibition of previously learned fearful responses. As the learners observed models engaging in threatening activities without adverse consequences, they became less threatened by the fearful task.

Summary

While a variety of treatments fall under the umbrella of the behavioral model, the following concepts are central to this approach.

1. The behavioral model seeks to understand human life in terms of observable behaviors and observable environmental events that encourage or extinguish those behaviors.
2. Emphasis in this model is on learning, especially learning via classical, operant, and observational conditioning. The solution for abnormal or maladaptive behaviors is to unlearn them and learn more adaptive behaviors.
3. The psychologist acts as the teacher by designing new learning experiences with the client. The client plays an active role in identifying the problem issues and implementing the new learning program.
4. Intervention is aimed at observable, measurable behaviors. In situations where "internal events" are the object of change, the internal behavior may only be observable by the person but it is still measured through self-reports.
5. Continuous assessment, often through detailed recordkeeping, provides a basis for measuring progress toward goals and provides a method for identifying conditioning elements such as stimuli and reinforcers.

Process Plan for Lisa Irons's Case: Behavioral Perspective

Lisa presents several issues in her autobiography that are amenable to behavioral approaches. I divide Lisa's process plan into four phases. The initial phase focuses on four tasks:

1. Building a working relationship characterized by open, honest communication

2. Narrowing the list of issues to one or two that are of highest concern to Lisa

3. Convincing Lisa that behavior change is possible and that she is responsible for her behaviors

4. Securing a commitment from Lisa to make the necessary changes in her daily life

Relationship building is a crucial first step in the behavioral process. I want Lisa to see me as a credible professional who can be trusted. I will be supportive and hope she will see me as someone who is "on her side" even when her plans are not going well. Rapport and open communication are crucial, and even though I support her efforts, I will be honest in addressing shortcomings in Lisa's behaviors when they occur. While it is not necessary that she considers me a "friend," we must view each other as likable and competent.

Lisa must provide the lead in determining what issues will be addressed, and I will provide direction on how we might address the issues. Identifying one or two issues of greatest concern to Lisa may seem simple at first. However, identification of issues also includes creating a clear, concise description of the behavioral aspects of the issue. This task of describing the issues will demand that we define and delineate issues in as much detail as possible. We will flesh out the specifics of the issue, set up some boundaries of the issue, and agree on what will constitute "success" in solving the problem. This attention to detail in defining the salient issues will give direction to our goal-setting activity. I can approach the identification of issues with Lisa in a direct manner as follows:

> Consultant 1: Lisa, I have read your autobiography, and we talked briefly when you first came. It seems that you have identified several issues of concern to you. Which of your issues do you see as being the most important to you?
>
> Lisa 2: Well, definitely the slump I'm in now. I think about my poor performances all the time. I'm really anxious about my scores. It scares me to think that I might never play any better. Sometimes it makes me want to just give up because it all seems so hopeless. I suppose that my "giving up" might be the reason I'm thinking about retirement. I know that I will have to retire sometime and I wonder what I am going to do when that day comes.
>
> Consultant 3: So it seems that your golf slump and concerns about retirement may be the most important issues facing you right now?

Lisa 4: Yes, but the other problems need to be solved, too. I'm concerned about my back becoming a more chronic problem. The pain makes me irritable and tense. My financial problems are worrisome. Sometimes I feel depressed about what's ahead and anxious about life in general. I'm very lonely.

Consultant 5: We need to limit our work to one or two issues at first. This doesn't mean that we will ignore your other concerns, but concentrating on the most important issues and solving them first will allow you to experience some success and give you the relief you need to work with the other issues at a later time. Let's make a list of your concerns and try to weigh them from most pressing to least concerning.

Using the "list and prioritize" technique, Lisa identified her performance slump and anxiety about retirement as her most immediate concerns. Other methods, such as scales and behavior inventories, could also be employed to identify Lisa's most important issues. The goal-setting process will require that we delineate these issues and break them into behavioral components that can be addressed in a step-by-step approach. Asking Lisa, "What are you doing about these issues now?" and focusing on her actions surrounding the issues will help identify both ineffective and helpful approaches to her problem. Centering the discussion on Lisa's behaviors emphasizes her role in controlling and being responsible for her current situation. I want Lisa to recognize that she can determine how she acts in a given situation and that she is responsible for her actions. I will emphasize that self-control and responsibility are the cornerstones for self-confidence—a necessary ingredient of peak performance. I will commend Lisa for acting on her own behalf in seeking help from me and her teaching pro. These actions reflect her commitment to change. I will openly discuss her level of commitment to this effort, even though I think it is sufficient, because I want Lisa to make her commitment aloud. This personal statement will reinforce her efforts and give me the opportunity to assure her of my support in this endeavor.

The second phase of the behavioral plan focuses on assessment of the behaviors involved in the two issues to be addressed—her slump and retirement. Lisa's performance slump was her presenting problem and will be addressed first. Often multiple issues presented by an athlete are interrelated in complex threads, and while I want to assure Lisa that we will not ignore her other concerns, addressing one major issue at a time will focus our efforts, attention, and resources, which will increase our chances of success. Additionally, resolving a major problem will clear some space and resources that can then be brought to bear on other issues. Resolving a major issue often results in partial alleviation of other identified problems.

For example, moving Lisa out of her performance slump will have a positive impact on her financial concerns and may provide temporary relief from pressing aspects of her retirement decision. It is not that I don't want Lisa to address her retirement decisions, but it would be more advantageous for her to deal with these decisions from a stronger personal position and while she is playing well. The retirement issues are also more future oriented, and I initially want us to focus on Lisa's present behaviors rather than the past or future.

A slump is defined as "an unexplained decline in performance from a previously determined baseline level of a particular athlete that extends longer than would be expected from normal cyclic variations in performance in a given sport" (Taylor 1988). Confirmation that Lisa's perceptions of her current performance status meet the requirements of a slump will be the first task in the assessment phase. This will require an objective review of Lisa's results from past performances to establish her baseline level of performance. Comparing this baseline level of performance with performance results from the past two years will show whether there has been an actual decline, the degree of decline, and an idea of the level of performance that will indicate that she has emerged from the slump (providing a measurable behavioral goal). Part of this review of past performances will be an identification of Lisa's normal performance cycles. Golf and other sports are up-and-down games in which cyclical performance is rather common. By measuring the cycles of Lisa's early career, we can ascertain that the current performance decrement is not simply a result of her average cyclical performance curve. This is an important point to confirm because sometimes athletes are in a normal performance cycle that they perceive as abnormal, usually due to environmental and personal pressures that happen to coincide with their normal cyclical downturn in performance. The added pressures may make the normal downturn seem more drastic than it actually is.

Determining the causes of a performance slump is one of the most difficult tasks in sport psychology. By definition, the causes of the slump are "unexplained," and often the athlete and coach have already conducted an unsuccessful search for the performance problem before consulting with a sport psychologist. Identifying causation is part art and intuition and part science and logic. The art/intuition aspect depends on the consultant's knowledge of the particular sport involved and is aided by drawing on the experiential knowledge of the athlete and, if possible, her coach. I would expend considerable effort in examining what actions Lisa and her coach have already tried. I want to know—What causal factors did they perceive? What actions did they take to attempt to alleviate the causes of the slump? What were the results? Were there any partial successes or actions that seemed to work at first but then deteriorated?

Taylor identifies four areas to examine when trying to determine the origin of slumping performance (1988). The four categories are physical, technical, technological, and psychological. The physical category includes factors related to the athlete's biological condition, such as overtraining, fatigue, changes in visual acuity, injury, and nutritional depletion. Technical causes of slumps are related to motor control issues, including timing, muscular tension, and proprioceptive problems. The technological category relates primarily to sporting equipment and implements used by the athlete, but can also include clothing and footwear alterations that may influence her "feel" while executing motor patterns. In the psychological category, causes such as anxiety, burnout (lack of motivation), self-doubt, and accumulated small stresses may contribute to extended declines in performance. These are all areas of inquiry that can be examined for causation. Referral to experts in these areas—physicians, nutritionists, teaching pros, biomechanical consultants, and equipment manufacturing experts—may be warranted.

The science/logical part of examining slump causes involves the use of reasoning procedures and models of causation. There are three models of inquiry that I use to guide my examination of the origin of extended poor performance.

1. The first model of inquiry is based on correlation as a starting point for inquiry. *Correlations* are positive or negative linear relationships between two factors. With reference to slumps, one factor will be performance level and the other will be a construct that either rises or falls with performance. It is important to note that correlations never prove causation and correlation is not a causal model. Nevertheless, it provides a reasonable starting point for inquiry into extended periods of poor performance. Performance profiling (Jones 1993) is an assessment technique based on correlation. Using performance profiling, I would have Lisa identify factors that she considers to be fundamental to elite performance. This draws on Lisa's experiences during periods of good performance to identify the personal and environmental factors that contributed to her previous personal best performances. After identifying the correlates of elite performance, Lisa will grade her present status in each factor. A contractual behavioral plan can then be implemented to move Lisa closer to her ideal state on each factor. During this assessment, I will be thinking about "third-party" factors that may be correlated to the identified primary correlates. These "hidden" factors that correlate with peak performance constructs may have a latent impact on performance. For example, if Lisa identifies "fitness" as a primary correlate of her peak performances, she might be mindful of only strength and aerobic power as components of fitness. I would suggest some related components—nutrition, balance, timing, and flexibility—as additional correlates to be examined.

2. The second model of inquiry I use involves investigation of nonlinear causal models. Positive and negative feedback loops are a particularly important aspect of causation to consider. Feedback loops involve bidirectional causation so that instead of viewing factor A (for example, lack of energy) as causing factor B (poor showing in competitions), we can examine how factor A influences factor B *and* how factor B causes a change in factor A. Bidirectional causation results in downward spirals and vicious cycles. Recognizing the feedback cycle enables us to design a behavioral plan that intervenes at multiple points in the cycle.

3. A third model to consider when thinking about causation is that behavior is often the result of several causes. It is rare that a decrease in performance that persists over a long period of time and is resistant to remediation efforts of the athlete and coach will have just one cause. It is more likely that a combination of factors is responsible for such a drastic decline, and the more factors that are identified, the more efficient we can be in creating the treatment plan. A corollary to the multiple causation model is that while multiple factors may cause the decline in performance, it is not likely that the factors will contribute equally to the performance problem. Determining the degree to which each factor is responsible for producing the decline will increase the efficiency of the treatment plan.

The third phase of Lisa's intervention plan is to create and implement a program to change the behaviors contributing to her slump. The program will include practicing specific actions, controlling pertinent stimuli in Lisa's environment, planned reinforcement, and some form of objective, continuous evaluation. The program will be designed around the constructs identified by Lisa as needing improvement through the performance profiling exercise. It will be based on Lisa's answers to the questions: "What do you want to do?" and "What can you do to get what you want or need?"

Lisa's complaints of erratic rather than stable performance and her acknowledged frustration and lack of composure during competitions suggest two interventions—establishing a performance routine and relaxation training. I expect to find that Lisa already has precompetition and preshot routines. Her years of experience on the tour and high level of skill suggest that she may have such routines. If she does not have routines, we will work together to create them. If she has routines, we will review them and perhaps alter them. Before changing her routines, however, I will make certain that she is conscientiously following her routine, giving each element of the routine the attention and time required. Athletes who have viable performance routines often unknowingly alter their routines by either hurrying through them, which affects their tempo, or by allowing elements that are not in the routine to slip in. Lisa and I will work together on the routine to assure that it incorporates actions that she sees as helpful.

In reworking her routine, we will consider Lisa's individual preferences, such as her sensory learning style, level of optimum activation, and timing issues. It may be advantageous to compare her current preshot routines with those she used when she was playing well. Identifying the changes made over the years may suggest some beneficial alterations in her current routine. However, it is unlikely that we would revert back to her old routine entirely. Our discussion of a revamped routine needs to recognize Lisa's personal and environmental needs as they exist today. The routine will be as simple as we can make it, and it will focus Lisa's attention on important performance cues. For example, her putting routine might be to walk onto the green noticing its slopes, read the green from two points, aim her putter, align her body, take a look at her exact target, bring her eyes back to the ball, and stroke with a "one, two" tempo.

Once we have a routine that Lisa feels will be effective, we will set up a practice schedule to acclimate her to it. At first the practice of the routine will be conducted in a low-stress environment, perhaps at a practice range. I will provide a check-off list containing the behaviors in the routine in the order to be performed that she consults after her stroke. She will give herself a Lickert scale grade on how well she focused on each action in her routine. She can also grade her performance, noting whether she forgot parts of the routine, did them halfheartedly, let additional behaviors intrude into the routine, and made smooth transitions from one action to the next.

An improvement in her shots would be the ideal reinforcer, but if the improvement is not perceived by Lisa, we will add a reward contingent on a specified level of practice performance. Lisa will help identify specific rewards to ensure that the rewards are meaningful and of value to her. While I will look for ways to insure that Lisa is reinforced for practicing her new routines, I will not include a punishment factor if she fails to do so. Being in a slump is a negative experience physically, emotionally, and mentally. I do not see any value in increasing the negative aspects of Lisa's situation at this point.

Lisa will log and evaluate all of her practice sessions. This encourages her to be responsible to herself and gives her confidence that she can regulate her own behavior. At our weekly sessions, we can review her progress and adjust the program to make it more responsive to her needs. Eventually Lisa will take the routine from her practice sessions out onto the course and into minor, then major, competitive environments.

Another aspect of the intervention will be relaxation training. Ideally, implementation of a relaxation-training program will begin during the off-season or during a timeout from competition. Often, however, there are time pressures on the athlete to get back on tour or ready for an imminent major competition in a short amount of time. When time is a constraint, relaxation techniques such as progressive relaxation and breath control are preferable to techniques such as autogenic training and yoga, which take longer to master.

Training will consist of my guiding Lisa through the relaxation procedures during a session. I will also provide her with an audiotape guiding her through relaxation procedures that she will use to practice relaxation in two 15- to 30-minute daily sessions. Once she masters the rudimentary relaxation skills and is reporting that she can relax at home, we will start conditioning her to relax using specific cues associated with her sport, like looking at the grooves on her club face. We will work toward enabling Lisa to relax quickly and effectively using cues that she can manipulate during competition. As Lisa becomes more proficient at inducing a relaxation response on cue, we will have her practice the relaxation procedure in environments with increasing pressure and distractions. This is an important part of the training, because while Lisa may be proficient in entering a relaxed state in her home, her relaxation skills may not hold up in competitive environments unless they are conditioned and practiced in those environments. Relaxation skills need to be tempered by the heat of competition.

The fourth phase of Lisa's behavioral intervention is designed to sustain her new behaviors and avoid relapses. A spontaneous return to old, comfortable behavior patterns is a common problem, and I want to prepare Lisa for this situation. First, I will explain the spontaneous recovery phenomena to Lisa so she understands and is aware of the issue. Increasing her vigilance about slipping back into old patterns will help her maintain her behaviors and encourage continued self-assessment. We will then create and practice a relapse prevention program that outlines exactly what actions Lisa should take as soon as she recognizes that she is slipping out of her new behaviors and back into her old patterns. Lisa's relapse prevention program will include a detailed description of the behaviors she wants to retain. For each new behavioral skill, she will designate how often she intends to practice the behavior and figure out how she will know when a slip in the behavior has occurred. Early recognition of slips is important to the process of establishing new behaviors. Lisa will then identify strategies to prevent and deal with relapses. This will be accomplished by her completing a relapse prevention worksheet. I use a worksheet presented by Ivey (1994, pp. 366-367) that addresses the following questions.

1. What is your understanding of the relapse process?
2. What are the differences between learning the behavioral skill or thought and using it in a difficult situation?

3. Who is on your side? Name the people you can depend on as your support network.
4. What environmental events—people, places, and situations— will be particularly difficult for you?
5. How will you respond emotionally to a relapse?
6. How can you act more effectively in a tempting situation or after a relapse?
7. What additional support skills do you need to retain the skill?
8. What are the probable outcomes of succeeding with your new behavior?
9. How will you reward yourself for persisting in your new behavior?

I might have Lisa practice the recovery plan by having her deliberately return to her old behavior, recognize the slippage, and practice how to implement the recovery plan. Having Lisa act out a deliberate relapse forces her to predict the details of her first lapse and increases her awareness of the relapse problem. One aspect of her relapse recovery plan will be to call for an appointment with me or another designated helper (coach). During the play rehearsal of her relapse, Lisa and I would talk through how she would set up the appointment and what might prevent her from carrying out such an action—such as embarrassment or not enough time in her schedule. For each impediment we would devise a way for her to get through the issue and take the necessary actions to get back on course.

I want Lisa to understand that her new behaviors will require a sustained effort from her for several months. During this time, she needs to be obsessive about practicing her new behaviors. At the same time, I do not want her to be totally discouraged if she does slip back into old patterns. Having a recovery plan in place is often reassuring to the athlete because she will know exactly what to do and what to expect with spontaneous recovery. Armed with a knowledge of spontaneous recovery phenomena, she is also more likely to see it as a human behavioral phenomenon rather than a personal failure or lack of personal character.

Additional Case for Discussion

The following case study describes a successful professional athlete who is having difficulty with one aspect of her game. How would a sport psychologist operating in the behavioral tradition work with this athlete?

Tenysha O'Neill took the pass, broke toward the basket, and shot. As she was going up, she felt the sharp elbow connect hard with her arm. The whistle blew and she knew she was headed for the foul line.

"Oh, crap!" she whispered to herself as she slumped toward the foul line. Panting, she moved mechanically, almost stiffly, through her routine. "Deep breath, bounce the ball twice, look at the rim, flick your wrist," she thought to herself as she put up her first attempt. The ball sailed up but failed to hit anything but the floor. It missed the rim, the net, the backboard—everything. "Airball, airball"—the chants haunted her, but she just laughed and shook her head. At least she could laugh at herself. The second shot wasn't much better. At least it hit the backboard, but it bounced like a brick, careened off the rim, and luckily jumped into Tenysha's teammate's hands for an easy lay-up. "Oh well, it could have been worse," she said to herself as play resumed.

Tenysha's fourth year in the WNBA was going well except for her ongoing foul shooting difficulties. She was a top scorer for her team, averaging 28 points and 13 rebounds per game. She was a definite starter and was valued by her teammates for her play at both ends of the court. But her free throw shooting was a public joke—49 percent this year, only a slight improvement over the 43 percent she posted last year. No matter how well she played during the game, the morning papers always reported on her foul shooting attempts—sometimes in great, humiliating detail.

"It's not like I haven't tried to improve," she protested. "Even though I hate to practice free throws, I threw up 100 foul shots—one right after another—every day, even on Sundays, during the off-season. The practice doesn't help, and it's boring."

"I really think this must be a genetic thing," she said. Tenysha's father was a standout Big Ten college player who went on to have an illustrious career in the NBA. Tenysha felt she was following in his footsteps because he was also known for his poor free throw shooting.

In addition to forcing herself to practice, Tenysha was advised by her coaches to create a preshot routine. She used her preshot routine during games, but it made little difference in her success rate. As she headed to the line during games, she always looked toward the bench, where her coaches and teammates would be signaling her to "slow down and be careful" with looks of concern on their faces. She tried, she always tried very hard—to be careful, to get everything right, to make the perfect free throw. But it never worked. Lately she just started to laugh her free throw mishaps off. "I can make shots that are ten times more difficult from the floor with two players hanging on me. I just can't understand why I have this thing about free throws. They should be a sure thing—easy.

"In spite of my joking about it, I don't like knowing that when the game is close and we're trying to protect a slim lead in the last minute, I'm the one the other team is looking to foul. I'm less effective as a player during the last two minutes of the game than at any other time, and so many games come down to those last two minutes. Sometimes the coach just takes me out. I want to contribute and make things happen. I want to be a clutch player when it comes down to the wire, but my free throw shooting makes that a problem. It's starting to make me tense just to think about it."

Suggested Readings

Bandura, A. and R. Walters. 1963. *Social learning and personality development.* New York: Holt, Rinehart and Winston.

Jacobson. E. 1938. *Progressive relaxation.* Chicago: University of Chicago Press.

Skinner, B. 1938. *The behavior of organisms.* New York: Appleton-Century-Croft.

Spiegler, M. and D. Guevremont. 1993. *Contemporary behavior therapy.* Pacific Grove, CA: Brooks/Cole.

Wolpe, J. 1958. *Psychotherapy by reciprocal inhibition.* Stanford, CA: Stanford University Press.

Chapter 3

THE COGNITIVE MODEL

Descartes's famous dictum "I think, therefore I am" might be modified by a cognitive psychologist to "I think, therefore that is how I am." *Cognitive theory* maintains that thought patterns and mental habits are primary forces in determining one's behavior and feelings. While the psychodynamic perspective views unconscious energy dynamics as central to feelings and behavior, and behaviorists view environmental influences on observable actions as the primary force, the cognitive perspective places its spotlight on mental processes, such as attention, attributions, cognitive patterns, perceptions, and memory. The cognitive model views the individual as an active participant in creating reality through information processing.

Historically, the cognitive perspective was formed in opposition to the behavioral notion that the individual was a "black box," simply responding to external environmental stimuli. Cognitive practitioners argue that the cognitive agent's internal interpretation of external stimuli is a more powerful force than the external stimulus itself. Although cognitive theory began in opposition to behavioral theory, in practice the two theories are compatible and are often employed together in treatment.

Basic Concepts

Human information processing, both its operations and products, forms the foundation of the cognitive model. From the time we are born, and perhaps even before birth, we use our senses to gather data from the world around us. We do not just record data with our bodies, however—we process it and give it meaning. We combine it with other information we have stored in our memories, reorganize it, and create our own unique perceptions about the data. We form internal representations of the external world by sorting, prioritizing, and assigning importance to the incoming data.

We engage in what information processing professionals label *bottom-up* and *top-down* information processing. Bottom-up processing refers to information coming from the environment by way of the peripheral nervous system (the senses) to the central nervous system (the spinal cord and brain). Not all environmental data is processed. Within bottom-up processing there is a loss of data because the senses are able to record only a partial spectrum of the available signals (the eyes cannot detect ultraviolet rays, for example) and attentional processes act as gatekeepers by ignoring some data and attending to other data. Top-down processing refers to the process that our brains use to organize and relate different bits of data to "create" knowledge for and about ourselves. The human brain, with its millions of synapses and complex neural networks, acts to interpret incoming sensory signals, giving them "meaning" and creating our individual realities. As we engage in this continuous up-and-down processing of data, we build on our previous information and we develop patterns of processing.

Most of the time these processing patterns serve to make our thinking efficient. Sometimes, however, they are a hindrance to the accurate and reliable creation of information.

Processing Handicaps—Dysfunctional Heuristics and Systematic Biases

Cognitive processing can be characterized on a continuum from creative, out-of-the-box processing to stringently patterned processing. The patterns of processing are referred to as *heuristics*. Heuristics are automatic, often shortcut, repetitive, patterned methods for processing information. They act like blueprints for processing data. The more we repetitively use these processing patterns, the more automatic they become. When heuristics become ingrained and reflexive, they bias our information processing by selectively assigning value to some data and ignoring other data. Heuristics enable us to process information more rapidly and with less effort as we grow and mature, but they also make our thinking processes subject to error and distortion if they are employed in inappropriate circumstances. They can lure us into a mental set or rigidity that blinds us to the need for different thinking processes. They often result in cognitive processing biases that can affect one's emotional and behavioral life. Cognitive practitioners have identified faulty thinking processes that trigger specific, often troubling, feelings. These faulty thinking processes produce cognitive distortions or faulty interpretations of reality that result in systematic, predictable errors in reasoning. For example, systematic selection of only the negative aspects of one's life often leads to an unnecessarily bleak outlook on life that is accompanied by sadness or depression. If an individual continually biases or filters thoughts to give importance to only the distressing events of each day, it tends to cast everything in a pessimistic shadow. Other examples of faulty processing patterns are listed in table 3.1.

Table 3.1 Faulty Thinking Patterns

Thinking pattern	Description
All-or-nothing thinking	Dichotomous thinking in which events are either black or white. If a situation is less than perfect, it is considered a total failure (for example, saying "My putting stinks!" after one 3 putt).
Overgeneralization	The tendency to view a single, temporary quality or event as a general, permanent state of affairs. Often the client will use the words "always" or "never" to describe a situation ("I never get a break with the refs").
Jumping to conclusions	Arbitrarily interpreting situations without data to support one's conclusions. It includes "mind-reading" ("I don't think she likes me at all") and "fortune-telling" (I know I'm going to mess this up").
Magnification	Exaggerating the importance of one's problems and shortcomings ("If I don't make this play, my teammates will hate me!").
Minimization	Minimizing one's desirable qualities ("I'm not really that good—it was a lucky shot"). Also, minimizing risks and losses to combat fear and personal disturbances ("I didn't want to beat her anyway—this is just a local tournament").

(continued)

Table 3.1 *(continued)*

Thinking pattern	Description
Emotional reasoning	To assume that the way you feel is the way things really are ("I feel inferior; I must be a second-rate athlete").
Labeling	Using irrational name-calling against yourself or others (such as saying "I'm a loser!" after making one error).
Personalization	Viewing events only in terms of yourself and holding yourself responsible for events that are not totally under your control ("The coach didn't say 'hello' when he walked by—I must have offended him").
Confirmation bias	Accepting only data that supports your current beliefs. Rejecting or finding fault with any data that does not support your current beliefs.

Content Handicaps—Dysfunctional Schemas, Assumptions, and Irrational Beliefs

In addition to automatic processing patterns, our minds also develop packets of habitual content. Beck and Weishaar (1995) organized the content of cognitive material into three categories—voluntary thoughts, automatic thoughts, and schemas. *Voluntary thoughts* are relatively current and conscious and are the easiest to change. They are also the most accessible in that most clients can verbalize and convey their voluntary thoughts to the practitioner. *Automatic thoughts* are at a deeper level. They are more spontaneous and more difficult to access. Because they are well-established, they are also more difficult to change. *Schemas* are our deepest core beliefs. They are the most stable of our thoughts and the least accessible to change.

A schema is a scaffolding or frame of reference for recording and organizing new incoming data. Schemas provide a cognitive framework that is relatively stable but has some capacity to grow and differentiate with experience. Schemas incorporate our most basic assumptions about our world and our lives. One of the most important schemas that we develop is our schema of the self. We each have a schema that incorporates a personal view of who we are and our particular place in the world.

Automatic thoughts are an outgrowth of our schemas. They are thoughts that have been repeated so often in our thinking patterns that they seem to operate spontaneously. They become our cherished and unquestioned beliefs, rules for living, and our "truths." For example, an automatic thought that could be connected to the schema of self for a young athlete is that of being a "choker"—unable to perform when the stakes are high. Each time the young athlete encounters a situation of importance, a sense of dread and lack of confidence occur as a result of his automatic thoughts about choking in challenging situations. The first thoughts that automatically pop into his head are about failure and what could go wrong.

Cognitive content—voluntary thoughts, automatic thoughts, and schemas—exists in many forms. Content can be in the form of images—visual, auditory, taste, smell, and kinesthetic images. It can also be in the form of language—verbalizations and self-talk—as well as in the form of concepts or symbolic representations of the external world.

Schemas and automatic thoughts are not simple cognitive structures. They are extremely complex. They are deep-seated cognitive structures that are relatively fixed and seldom updated. They are also not always mutually exclusive or consistent, and individuals can hold as truth two automatic thoughts that contradict each other. For example, one can believe both that "birds of a feather flock together" and that "opposites attract."

Because they occur as a result of our personal experiences in the world, our schemas and automatic thoughts are not only our models of the world but are often enmeshed with triggers that activate feelings. These cognitive structures have affective components that contribute to our moods and emotional condition. In the process of thinking, the individual manipulates and acts in accord with these internal representations of the world. For the most part, we engage in voluntary, mindful thinking that manipulates these internal representations and enables us to care for ourselves, solve problems, and get through the day as best we can. But we also tend to spontaneously rely on our schemas and automatic thoughts, especially in times of stress.

Because cognitive structures like schemas and automatic thoughts are personally created models of reality, they can be deceiving, inaccurate, outdated, and incomplete. According to the cognitive model, when our basic schemas and automatic thoughts are faulty, problematic behavior and emotions follow. For example, if the self-schema of a woman athlete includes a strong nurturing identity and she sees herself as a caretaker of others, she may be reluctant to engage in competitive situations that require her to be task oriented rather than person oriented. Furthermore, if she thinks of winning as "hurting" her opponent, she might be conflicted about winning contests.

Irrational Beliefs

Albert Ellis identified irrational beliefs—a form of automatic thoughts—as the primary cause of dysfunctional feelings and activity. Irrational beliefs are absolute "should" and "must" statements that form the core of distorted thinking in Ellis's view. He reduced these irrational beliefs to three statements that represent the core of rigid "should" and "must" thinking (1993, p. 7). These are the three core irrational beliefs:

- *I* [ego] absolutely *must* perform well and win significant others' approval or else I am an *inadequate, worthless person.*
- *You* [other people] *must* under all conditions and at all times be nice and fair to me or else *you* are a *rotten, horrible person!*
- *Conditions* under which I live absolutely *must* be comfortable, safe, and advantageous or else the world is a rotten *place, I can't stand it,* and life is hardly worth living.

According to Ellis, changing these irrational beliefs to reflect reality tends to improve functioning and contributes to a more positive outlook. Ellis believed in forcefully attacking irrational beliefs and sought to instill an attitude of "Don't 'should' on me" in his clients.

Rational Thought

A basic premise of cognitive theory is the concept of *cognitive plasticity,* which refers to the belief that thinking processes and established cognitive content can be altered with effort and persistence. Alteration of established cognitions depends first on recognition and identification of one's systematic thought biases, automatic thoughts, and basic schemas. Once these cognitive structures have been recognized, they can be challenged and changed. Consequently, while the cognitive model attributes maladaptive feelings and behaviors to faulty thinking patterns that result from faulty information processing, it also recognizes information processing skills as the solution to these faulty thinking problems. The cognitive approach teaches people to use rational thought, logic, and empiricism to recognize and reform maladaptive assumptions and distorted schemas. Both faulty cognitive processing and cognitive content can be reformed, resulting in a more adaptive and self-enhancing cognitive environment. Because thinking determines feelings and behavior in the cognitive model, this reformation of cognitive life results in positive change for the person.

Cognitive practitioners use both direct and indirect methods to challenge and produce change in the client's cognitive processes and material. Some methods are confrontational in that the therapist will emphatically tell the client that her thinking is faulty and needs to be remedied. Other methods are more indirect in that the therapist works with the client to view cognitive materials as hypotheses that are subject to reality testing. The therapist and client then set up a "test" of the client's cognitive hypotheses to determine whether they are realistic. In both the direct and indirect approach, the client and therapist work together not only to challenge dysfunctional thinking but also to identify how it contributes to problematic feelings and behavior and how it might be altered to the advantage of the client. Regardless of the method employed, the solution to dysfunctional feelings and behaviors is to change the thinking processes and the patterns that direct them.

Goals and Procedures

The goal of cognitive interventions is to identify and modify thoughts, assumptions, and schemas that foster undesirable actions and feelings. In addition to modifying dysfunctional thoughts, assumptions, and schemas, cognitive interventions are designed to reshape information processing to promote realistic thinking. While the initial short-term goal is relief from symptoms, the larger, overriding goal is to change core systematic biases in processing and deep-seated dysfunctional schemas.

Cognitive theory does not seek to replace dysfunctional thoughts and assumptions with "wishful" thinking. Thinking must be grounded in reality, even if that reality is not pleasant. Unpleasant experiences are not sugarcoated or ignored, but rather they are framed in real terms as being temporary, amenable to problem-solving, and open to alternative interpretations. There is no attempt to ignore actual events. Instead, clients are encouraged to examine actual events from a variety of perspectives using logic and reason. A basic tenet of cognitive theory is that systematic biases in thought and information processing dominate and effectively eliminate alternative ideas and processing paths to the detriment of the client. The client becomes "locked" into interpretations of reality that do not serve him well in coping and adjusting to the challenges of living a full, satisfying life. The solution is to open and expand the client's information processing skills, which increases the client's cognitive flexibility.

Therapeutic Alliance and Process Plan

The therapeutic relationship in the cognitive model is active and collaborative. The client and practitioner form a team with the aim of initially reducing the client's presenting symptoms and subsequently providing the client with the skills necessary to control cognitive processes independent of the practitioner. Interventions are viewed as learning experiences and treatment is fundamentally an educational process. There is no attempt to restructure personality.

The initial sessions are designed to establish the collaborative foundations of the helping relationship. In addition to collecting essential information from the client and explaining the cognitive model, the first session is designed to provide the client with some symptom relief. This initial success at symptom relief is considered extremely important for providing the client with motivation to continue with confidence in the treatment. Other issues to be addressed in the beginning sessions are misperceptions about the cognitive model, and an understanding of the client's current condition and expectations. Focus is on the client's present situation rather than the past or future. Detailed information regarding the presenting problem(s) also unfolds in the early work sessions. The client's descriptions of problems are probed so that the problem is described with detail and clarity. Significance is placed on the language and images that the client chooses to describe problems. Details such as frequency of the problem, situations that trigger the problem, and intensity and duration of the disturbance are recorded. Other issues to be explored include the client's personal view of the problem, the thoughts and feelings occurring with the problem, the extent to which the client feels "in control," and the client's prognosis regarding the outcome of the problem.

As treatment continues, there is a gradual shift from emphasis on specific symptoms to patterns of thinking and to themes of automatic thoughts and schemas. Challenges and tests of problematic thinking biases and schemas are planned, carried out, and debriefed. The client is taught to be her own "therapist" and becomes more self-sufficient in controlling information processing. The role of the therapist in sessions gradually declines as the client's skills and confidence increase. Termination occurs when the client and practitioner determine that the client has established more beneficial information processing patterns and can control personal feelings and behavior through his enhanced cognitive capabilities. Follow-up sessions are often scheduled at one and two months following termination, to assure lasting improvement.

Collaborative Empiricism

One procedure used to challenge problematic thinking is *collaborative empiricism*. In this procedure, the practitioner and client work together using inductive logic to "reality test" the client's thinking processes. The client's thoughts are delineated and treated as hypotheses that can be tested. Evidence is collected to both support and negate the "thought hypothesis" under study. For example, if the client claims that he is "not good at anything and doesn't enjoy much in life," evidence can be gathered using *activity scheduling,* a technique that the client uses to rate the degree of mastery and pleasure experienced during each activity of the day. The client and therapist then weigh the evidence and discuss its significance in terms of how it affects the client's worldview, personal actions, and feelings.

The client is also encouraged to engage in *metathinking*—thinking about how one thinks. Through this process, dysfunctional thoughts and systematic biases in interpreting reality are investigated and then either abandoned or modified. During this process, the practitioner does not directly challenge the client's cognitive structures but merely puts them in the spotlight for systematic investigation. The final decision to maintain, modify, or eliminate the problematic cognition in light of the evidence is made by the client. Because this process also illuminates both the positive and negative benefits of a problematic cognition, it identifies how the client's problematic cognition fulfills some of the client's needs. When attempts are made to modify or replace the problematic cognition, the alternative cognition can be examined to assure that it too will fulfill the client's needs.

Questioning is an important aspect of this collaborative investigation. The practitioner can pose questions in an attempt to encourage the client to consider multiple perspectives and incorporate additional facts into the decision-making process. The questioning is used to broaden the client's viewpoint and sometimes to guide the client to consider alternative explanations of phenomena, but it is not used to force the client's acceptance of the practitioner's views.

Aaron Beck was influential in establishing empirical investigations as a cognitive procedure. He developed his approach primarily as a treatment for depression, but it is used with many other disorders. A focus of Beck's work is identification of specific "cognitive profiles" for particular disorders. An example is the distinct negativity bias that often accompanies depression. These cognitive profiles are not used to categorize clients but rather to illuminate their thought biases to them by helping them become aware of how frequently they employ these biases. With this awareness, the client can begin to "catch" herself in the act of using the biased thoughts and increase self-monitoring of her own cognitive processes.

In addition to hypothesis testing and questioning, specific cognitive techniques can be employed to restructure the client's cognitive operations. Beck and Weishaar (1995) listed the following techniques for identifying and modifying automatic cognitions.

1. **Decatastrophizing.** *Catastrophizing* is a systematic bias toward seeing potential disaster and calamity in one's daily events. Often the calamity involves personal humiliation and anticipation of being personally diminished, if not destroyed. *Decatastrophizing* counteracts this bias by preparing the client to cope with the feared consequence. The practitioner

and client work together to establish a plan of response to deal with the catastrophe if it happens. As part of the decatastrophizing, the practitioner often asks the client to look at the catastrophic event from a long-term perspective. The expanded time frame itself tends to diminish the power of the catastrophic happening.

2. **Reattribution.** *Attribution* is a cognitive process in which the person determines the cause of an event. Dysfunctional attributions, like seeing oneself as the sole cause of a disastrous happening, produce feelings of guilt and blame that cause unnecessary discomfort. Through *reattribution*, the practitioner encourages the client to expand his attributions by considering "what else" may have contributed to the unpleasant event. The client is encouraged to consider the possibility of multiple causation and sharing of responsibility for an event.

3. **Redefining.** A person's definition of a problem often affects its possible solution. Redefining a problem in more specific and concrete terms suggests new solutions. For example, an athlete who defines a problem as "My coach doesn't like me" might redefine the situation as "I need to work harder to earn the respect of my coach."

4. **Decentering.** We are all born with an egocentric bias in which we place ourselves at the center of the universe. This is normal and healthy in infancy because it ensures that we do everything possible to make our needs known, thus assuring our survival. If this bias is not modified, however, it can lead to self-consciousness and anxiety. In *decentering*, the practitioner and client design experiences to test whether the client is the focus of everyone's undivided attention, as she believes. As the client becomes convinced that she is not always the center of attention and all eyes are not on her, anxiety lessens.

Direct Challenge

While collaborative empiricism uses investigative techniques to empirically test the client's cognitive processing and content, an alternative approach is to use direct and forceful challenges to counteract the power of systematic biases and irrational beliefs. In this approach, the therapist aggressively attacks the cognitive material of the client, exposing flaws and distorted logic in his thinking process. Confronted with the arguments of the practitioner, the client is forced to examine his cognitions and either replace or modify them. An essential aspect of this confrontational approach is that the client eventually learns to imitate the practitioner in vigorously confronting his own irrational beliefs. The power to define oneself should be under the control of the client and not any outside personalities, including the practitioner. In cases where the client seeks and accepts only approval from others, the goal is to free the client from defining the self through other people and redirect the client to be his own person.

Ellis identified specific techniques that directly challenge the client's cognitive content (1993). These techniques include the following:

1. **Shame attacking** vigorously attacks the client's fear of being shamed in public by directly facing the fear. The client and practitioner plan an exercise in which the client deliberately does something foolish in public. As the client is performing this exercise, she works on feeling only appropriately sorry or silly and not ashamed or disgusted with herself. These exercises also provide practice in coping with others' disapproval and recognizing that the result of doing something foolish is not global self-degradation.

2. **Forceful coping statements** are realistic and philosophic rational statements that the client repeats to himself. The client is taught to emotionally arouse himself and repeat these statements in order to forcefully and convincingly drive them into his cognitive self-schemas.

3. **Imagery** is recognized as a powerful cognitive mediator and can be used to change cognitive content. One technique that can be used is to have the client imagine her worst fears, experiencing her feelings of terror and horror in the safe environment of her mind until the feelings start to dissipate. The person can then be encouraged to replace her inappropriate emotional response with more appropriate feelings.

4. **Forceful self-dialogues** are exercises in which the client makes a videotape describing and disputing his irrational beliefs. The client then asks other people to view the tape to determine whether it is convincing. This exercise requires the client to not only create arguments against his irrational beliefs, but also to forcefully argue aloud and act out the disputations of his own harmful views. Having others view the tape forces the client to "go public" with arguments against his former beliefs, which often makes him more committed to disputing them. If the client's first attempt at disputing his harmful beliefs is not strong and convincing, then he must redo the tape to make it stronger. In this process the client tends to convince himself that his beliefs are questionable.

5. **Humor** is used to refute irrational beliefs by exaggerating them to the point of absurdity. Humorous songs about irrational beliefs, jokes, prayers for "perfect" people, and such can be used not only to refute irrational beliefs but also to promote laughter and combat the overly serious tendencies of some clients.

6. **Group processes and exercises** are useful for helping clients understand that others also hold irrational beliefs (they are not alone) and that

others' irrational beliefs cause them emotional and behavioral distress. Sometimes it is easier to see the connections between others' irrational assumptions and their consequent emotional disturbance than it is to see them in oneself. Group members can also be useful in helping each other dispute their irrational beliefs. Group members consequently become more skillful at recognizing and disputing irrational beliefs for both themselves and others.

7. **Role-playing** can be used to help clients identify their problematic irrational assumptions. In this technique, clients role-play a scene until they become angry, aggressive, or otherwise emotionally disturbed. They are then debriefed to identify what thoughts were going through their minds to create their emotional disturbance.

8. **Reverse role-playing** has the practitioner or another group member play the client's role and hold on to the client's irrational beliefs while the client tries to argue the practitioner out of them. This provides practice in disputing the client's irrational beliefs and often forces the client to recognize the rigidity of her beliefs.

9. **Thought stopping** is a technique that the client is taught to replace ruminating destructive thoughts with the image of a bold red STOP sign or some other forceful STOP image. It is designed to dramatically occupy the mind with messages to just stop thinking about the destructive thoughts. Meditation techniques in which the person practices maintaining an "empty" or "quiet" mind are a useful adjunct to thought-stopping techniques.

Special problems occur with these cognitive model interventions in clients who experience emotional reactions before or without conscious thoughts and clients who believe that they cannot control how they feel. In these situations the practitioner must design both educational and experiential lessons for the client to help him connect his information processing with his affective experiences. Techniques such as writing down thoughts that occur with specific moods often reveal patterns of cognitive activity and mood to the client over time. Additionally, exploration of the client's belief regarding the origin of emotional feelings is often necessary. Some clients view emotions as uncontrollable and unpredictable psychological events. As long as the client perceives that feelings are outside the scope of personal control, progress will be stalled. The practitioner must help the client investigate associations between environmental events, cognitions, and feelings in order to bring feelings into the realm of personal influence for the client.

In addition to these techniques, cognitive practitioners often employ behavioral techniques, such as relaxation training, desensitization, reward and punishment, and skill rehearsal. These behavioral techniques complement the cognitive techniques and reinforce the changes in thought processes. A useful combination of cognitive and behavioral techniques for intervening in situations of performance anxiety, for example, is thought stopping combined with breathing relaxation exercises. Anxiety is a multidimensional state in that it has affective, cognitive, and physical components. Interventions that alter more than one component are more likely to be successful than single-component interventions. Diaphragm breathing exercises tend to produce physical relaxation and calm the physical attributes of anxiety. Thought stopping dampens the cognitive contributions to anxiety, and breathing exercises and thought stopping together can break the anxiety spiral by interrupting the athletes' internal events that are feeding the anxiety.

Assessment

A central feature of cognitive interventions is the delineation of cognitive distortions and the ability of the client to not only recognize the distortions, but to understand the connections between the distortions and subsequent emotional and behavioral problems. Therefore, clients need to grasp reality and demonstrate average cognitive functioning without deficits in basic intelligence, memory, and attention processes in order to profit from these methods. Although the long-term goal in the cognitive model is a shift in personal philosophical beliefs and modification of distortions in thinking, initial goals are aimed at symptom relief for immediate problems. Assessment involves demonstrating to both the client and the practitioner that, first, immediate symptoms are declining, and then that deeper, more profound changes in information processing are occurring. These complex changes are best monitored through a combination of assessment techniques.

In addition to interviewing, assessment in the cognitive model makes use of self-report tests, journaling, debriefing of homework assignments, and skill improvement to assess the client's starting point and subsequent progress. Self-report tests, such as Beck's Depression Inventory, the Dysfunctional Attitudes Scale, and the Profile of Moods Survey can be used to show progress and recovery. Journal entries, daily recordings of dysfunctional thoughts, and formats such as the REBT Self-Help Form by Dryden and Walker (1992) guide the client in identifying and monitoring dysfunctional thoughts on a daily basis. (See figure 3.1.)

Written and experiential homework is always debriefed in subsequent sessions to assure that the client understands the purpose and outcome of the homework. These debriefings give clients the opportunity to display their skills in recognizing and challenging dysfunctional thoughts and replacing them with more realistic thinking patterns.

REBT Self-Help Form

A (Activating event)

- Briefly summarize the situation you are disturbed about (what would a camera see?)
- An A can be *internal* or *external, real* or *imagined.*

C (Consequences)

Major unhealthy negative **emotions:**

Unhealthy negative emotions include:
- Anxiety
- Depression
- Hurt
- Jealousy
- Shame/Embarrassment
- Rage
- Low frustration tolerance

IB's (Irrational beliefs)

To identify IB's, look for:
- Dogmatic demands (musts, absolutes, shoulds)
- Awfulizing (it's awful, terrible, horrible)
- Low frustration tolerance (I can't stand it)
- Self/Other rating (I'm/he/she is bad, worthless)

D (Disputing IB's)

To dispute, ask yourself:
- Where is holding this belief getting me? Is it *helpful* or *self-defeating?*
- Where is the evidence to support the existence of my irrational belief? Is it *consistent with reality?*
- Is my belief *logical?* Does it follow from my preferences?
- Is it really *awful (as bad as it could be)?*
- Can I really not *stand it?*

RB's (Rational beliefs)

To think more rationally strive for:
- Non-dogmatic preferences (wishes, wants, desires)
- Evaluating badness (it's bad, unfortunate)
- High frustration tolerance (I don't like it, but I can stand it)
- Not globally rating self or others (I—and others—are fallible human beings).

E (New effect)

New healthy **negative emotions:**

New constructive **behaviors:**

Healthy negative emotions include:
- Disappointment
- Concern
- Annoyance
- Sadness
- Regret
- Frustration

Figure 3.1 REBT Self-Help Form.
(Reprinted by permission from Albert Ellis Institute from Dryden, W. and J. Walker. 1996. REBT Self-Help Form copyright 1992.)

The Cognitive Model in Sport Psychology

Basic characteristics of the cognitive model—its brevity, focus on the present, and educational nature—make it appealing to both athletes and coaches. In combination with behavioral techniques, this model is one of the most popular in the field of sport and exercise psychology. This popularity has resulted in significant research relating elements of the cognitive model to sport. Because the cognitive model is often combined with the behavioral model in the actual practice of sport psychology, it is sometimes difficult to tease out research that tests the cognitive model alone. For purposes of organization in this book, emotion, attention, imagery, and mental practice are categorized as components of cognitive theory even though some behavioral practitioners consider them to be "covert behaviors" and components of the behavioral model.

While the behavioral model attributes performance variables to learned responses to environmental stimuli, the cognitive model suggests that the critical component for determining performance is not the environmental stimuli, but rather the athlete's interpretations of the environmental stimuli. Within the cognitive model, there are many theories regarding which cognitive processes are most important in contributing to the athlete's interpretation of the environmental stimuli and exactly how cognitive processes affect performance.

Cognitive Approaches to Arousal, Emotions, and Performance

Emotional arousal has both qualitative and quantitative components. The qualitative component referred to as *affect* or *emotion* describes the nature of the feeling. While emotions are difficult to define, humans readily distinguish among the qualities of emotions such as fear, anger, sadness, and joy because they "feel" different to us. In the cognitive model, the qualitative component of arousal is determined by decisions, thoughts, and judgments that are associated with different arousal states. For example, a perceived mismatch between the challenges facing an athlete and the resources available to her is a common cognitive aspect of anxiety. A fundamental tenet of the cognitive model regarding emotional control and performance is that thoughts related to the performance—before, during, and after—have a direct impact on emotional content, or which emotions are experienced, and level of arousal, or strength of the emotional response.

Arousal Qualities

While considerable research has been completed on the strength (quantity) of emotional response, little formal research has been done regarding the qualities or varieties of emotion experienced during sport performance. Explorations of the varieties of human emotion in non-sport settings have used cross-cultural studies of facial expression to identify seven basic emotions—happiness, surprise, interest, fear, anger, sadness, and disgust (Vallerand 1984). All other emotions can be defined as composites of two or more of the basic emotions. Questions regarding the prevalence of specific emotions or nature of the emotional medley experienced in sport remain largely unanswered, even though scholars and practitioners have acknowledged the importance of these questions (Vallerand 1984). In general, research has related positive emotions to motivation and persistence in sport, while negative emotions have been associated with termination of sport participation, decreased performance, and low personal performance expectancies (Crocker and Graham 1995).

Level of Arousal and Performance

The simplest conceptualization of arousal level places it on a continuum with low-arousal, sleeplike states on one end and high-arousal, anxiety states on the other (see figure 3.2). On this continuum, arousal is viewed as incremental vigilance, awareness, or sensitivity to one's surroundings. This view combines quality and quantity of emotion by portraying emotional quality as an aspect of level of arousal.

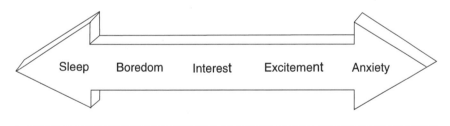

Figure 3.2   Arousal continuum.

The *inverted-U* (Yerkes and Dodson 1908) or *optimal arousal* model employs this type of continuum in modeling the relationship between arousal and sport performance. This model postulates that performance increases with arousal up to a point at which arousal interferes with performance. When performance is graphed against arousal level, the resulting graph resembles an upside-down U. Levels of activation below (boredom) and above (high anxiety) the optimum or ideal state (the top of the inverted U) produce less-than-ideal performances. The point at which performance begins to decline varies with the type of activity and personal characteristics of the performer. For example, in strength tasks, such as powerlifting, the "ideal" level of activation seems to be much higher than for a delicate task, such as the golf putt.

Criticism of the inverted-U hypothesis has resulted in alternative explanations of the activation–performance relationship. Several of these explanations specifically recognize cognitive factors as a key component of arousal. Martens, Vealey, and Burton compartmentalized arousal into two related but different forms—trait and state arousal (1990). *Trait arousal* is related to individual temperament and reflects the person's "baseline" level of arousal. Trait arousal accounts for differences in energy levels, emotionality, and general reactivity to social and environmental situations. It is reflected in one's personality, and there is some evidence that it has a genetic component. *State arousal* refers to one's level of arousal in a specific situation or context, such as a championship game. It is a level of arousal specific to an environment or social context. Both trait and state arousal are viewed as multidimensional in that they have physiological, affective, and cognitive components.

Another arousal model offered by Hardy and Parfitt (1990) employs catastrophe theory to model the relationship between arousal and performance. In this model, performance is mapped on a three-dimensional grid with physiological arousal and cognitive anxiety forming the other two axes. The model conceptualizes performance increasing with physiological arousal, much in the same manner as in the inverted-U curve. However, in this model the performance–physiological arousal interaction is influenced by the third factor, cognitive anxiety, so that the rise in performance collapses rapidly when cognitive anxiety reaches a critical magnitude. The catastrophe model predicts that high cognitive anxiety results in different outcomes, depending on whether physiological arousal is rising or declining. The interaction between physiological arousal and high cognitive anxiety accounts for both choking and the sudden record-breaking peak performances often seen in sports.

Other theories regarding the role of cognitive events, such as personal judgments, in regulating emotional arousal and performance have also been proposed. Crocker and Graham outlined two subtheories regarding the importance of goals in determining emotional responses to physical activity (1995). One subtheory regarding the relationship between emotions and goals comes from the work of Locke and Latham, who proposed that emotions are generated from subconscious judgments about how goal attainment or failure affects well-being as measured by the standard of one's personal values (1990). Positive affect follows from personal appraisal of the successful attainment of a goal, and negative affect from appraised failure in goal attainment. The strength of the affect depends on the value placed on the goal in one's value hierarchy. Attainment of a goal that corre- lates with a priority value produces more intense positive emotion than attainment of a lower-valued goal.

A second subtheory espoused by Carver and Scheier suggests that ath- letes use a negative feedback control system to reduce discrepancies be- tween actual behavior and intended behavior (1990). The size of the dis- crepancy between the athlete's goal and actual performance does not produce the emotional response—it is the rate of change in the discrep- ancy that is the key. The athlete makes an internal judgment comparing rate of change in the discrepancy in relation to the athlete's internal refer- ence regarding the expected rate of change. Emotions are generated as a response to the rate of change in the discrepancy between the athlete's in- ternal reference value regarding the acceptable rate of discrepancy reduc- tion. If the rate of change is faster than the athlete's internal reference, then affect is positive. If it is slower, negative affect results.

Vallerand proposed that reflective and subjective appraisals of perfor- mance also mediate affective states in athletic performance (1987). Vallerand's appraisal theory states that one's intuitive appraisal of a per- formance determines both general and self-related affects, and subjective appraisal of performance is a stronger predictor of emotional state than objective outcome of the performance (Crocker and Graham 1995). The athlete's performance appraisal both during and after the performance contributes to positive and negative affect about the performance, which influences subsequent performances and training.

Regardless of the model employed, arousal level and its cognitive com- ponents are viewed as a central issue in sport psychology, have received much attention in the sport literature, and have resulted in many interven- tions designed to help the athlete psych up and psych down. The literature suggests that generalizations about the arousal–performance relationship are difficult to defend because the relationship is complex and is known to be moderated by person, situation, and task variables.

Cognitive Treatments for Arousal Control

Cognitive interventions for arousal control center on cognitive restructur- ing through thought control, self-talk, and imagery. Because these tech- niques are not mutually exclusive, they are often used together and are interlaced with self-monitoring techniques. For example, a gymnast may be asked to keep a personal journal of stressful events and his thoughts that accompany these events. This information may show that his reaction to a poor practice is to say to himself, "I'll never get this move before the championship meet. Coach didn't even say anything when I missed the catch—he knows I'm going to mess up. I can't get this bad move out of my mind. My whole routine is ruined. I have disappointed everyone." Accompanying this self-condemnation is the continual replaying of the missed move in his mind through imagery.

Restructuring his cognitions would include investigating alternative perspectives, such as "I'll stay focused and take it one step at a time, making steady progress in mastering this move. I won't jump to conclusions about the coach's lack of comment. Maybe he's just trying to figure out what I'm doing wrong. I'll wait for some feedback from him. Even if my routine is not perfect, I can do my best and put in a good, competitive overall performance. I won't let one mistake get me down." The gymnast might also be encouraged to engage in mental practice in which he imagines himself successfully completing the move, and in thought stopping— forcefully directing himself to stop obsessing on a thought or image—in this case, the missed move.

In addition to restructuring the mental imagery surrounding his gymnastic performances, the gymnast might also engage in imagery that promotes peacefulness and relaxation. For example, he might imagine himself peacefully floating in a warm pool, feeling the warmth of the sun on his face, to reduce his arousal level. These types of cognitive restructuring have been shown to be effective in reducing arousal, especially in conjunction with behavioral relaxation techniques that decrease the physiological components of anxiety (Greenspan and Feltz 1989).

Some common psyching-up and psyching-down techniques employed in the cognitive model are self-talk and mental imagery. *Self-talk* is the process of verbalizing, usually silently, instructions or statements to one's self. For example, an athlete may give herself instructions to "be smooth through the turn," or encourage herself by mentally repeating, "I'm prepared and ready to succeed." Most self-talk statements relate to performance cues or self-efficacy and confidence statements, but self-talk can also be used to control emotional arousal. Self-talk statements are usually carefully constructed by the athlete in conjunction with the sport psychologist and are individualized to the athlete's needs. Choice of vocabulary is important in that the athlete must be able to personally relate to the specific words used in the statements. Some athletes respond better to words that are high impact and suggestive of the desired action. Words such as "smooooth," which has the quality and rhythm of the type of movement desired, or a staccato "go, go, go" rather than "faster, faster, faster," work better for them.

Mental imagery or visualization has also been found to be an effective technique for both psyching up and psyching down. The literature on psyching-up strategies suggests that cognitive performance preparations that arouse the athlete are advantageous for athletes engaged in tasks requiring strength or all-out physical exertion. Biddle (1985) raised several important issues regarding the mental preparation–strength performance relationship, including the question of whether different forms of psyching-up strategies, such as imagery, attention, or self-efficacy, increase the tension–placidity or energy–sleep aspects of arousal. Further research is needed on these issues.

Imagery can also be used to induce relaxation or psych down. For example, an athlete might imagine herself at a favorite beach, lying in the warm sand, listening to the sounds of the waves, in order to induce a relaxed state. Imagery and relaxation seem to have a reciprocal relationship in that imagery can induce a relaxed state and relaxation can enhance imagery (Jones and Stuth 1997). As with self-talk, the imagery must be personalized for the athlete and should be well practiced to produce the desired effect in a timely manner.

While imagery has been shown to be an effective way for athletes to psych up or psych down, the issue of whether imagery that results in psyching up or psyching down subsequently improves performance in sport is less clear (Gould and Udry 1994). As Whelan, Mahoney, and Meyers (1991) suggest, "while arousal, and perhaps anxiety itself, appears necessary, the athlete's perception of that anxiety and ability to manage it may be the variables most highly related to performance gains" (p. 313). A meta-analysis of research on the relationship between anxiety and sport performance by Kleine (1990) indicates that anxiety and sport performance are generally negatively correlated, suggesting that psyching-down strategies are more important for most athletes than psyching-up strategies.

Cognitive Model: Mental Practice and Mental Rehearsal

Imagery is a basic cognitive process, and while we often "think" using language, we can also "think" and generate cognitive content using still and moving images. There is a large body of sport psychology research relating to various aspects of mental imagery. In addition to using imagery for arousal control, sport psychologists are also interested in mental imagery as a method for learning and perfecting new skills. While there has been substantial documentation of the benefits of using mental imagery in sport situations, there are also significant methodological issues within the research that limit the generalizability of the findings. As with all research, the sport psychologist must exercise care when applying findings to individual clients.

The use of imagery to enhance performance by imaging skill performance without overt actions is referred to as *mental rehearsal*. It is theorized that mental rehearsal helps the athlete prepare to perform in two ways. The first is by recalling or priming the motor programs that will be used in the performance. Carpenter first proposed this psychoneuromuscular theory in 1894, asserting that lucid imaging produces minute enervation in the neural pathways that are employed during overt performance of the imaged movements. This rehearsal could serve to both prime the motor pattern and strengthen the neural pathway. The second theory, proposed by Sackett in 1934, suggests that imaging strengthens the cognitive aspects of the movement patterns through repetition. This repetition serves to advance the movement from a consciously controlled movement to the more unconscious, automatic action characteristic of advanced athletes (Onestak 1991).

Jack Nicklaus, Greg Louganis, and other athletes have publicly attested to the value they place on imaging a performance, or specific parts of a performance, before execution of the skill. There is also some documentation in the sport psychology research literature supporting athletes' anecdotal reports of enhanced performance when using mental rehearsal. A meta-analysis of 60 studies on the effects of mental rehearsal on motor skill performance by Feltz and Landers (1983) showed moderate improvement (effect size = 0.48) with the use of mental rehearsal over conditions with no rehearsal.

Another meta-analysis by Hinshaw (1991) reviewed 21 studies on the effects of mental rehearsal on motor skill performance. This meta-analysis also found significant increases in performance (effect size = 0.68) with mental rehearsal when compared to no practice. Further statistical analysis showed that certain characteristics of mental rehearsal supported greater improvements. Improvements were greater when the performer used *internal imagery*, which is imagining the performance as if the camera is in the athlete's eyes, compared with *external imagery*, in which the view is what would be seen if another person held the camera. The length of mental rehearsal sessions also affected its efficacy. Studies with mental rehearsal sessions of less than 1 minute and those with sessions between 10 and 15 minutes offered more benefit than studies with sessions of 3 to 5 minutes.

Jones and Stuth (1997) also reviewed the literature relating to mental imagery and performance enhancement. Their review of the research literature indicates that mental imagery has been found to enhance athletic performance when used alone, when combined with physical practice, and when combined with other cognitive strategies. They also state that although the studies of mental imagery to improve performance have resulted in mixed findings, the majority of the research supports the efficacy of imagery for this purpose (p. 103). Performance increases resulting from mental rehearsal have been found in multiple sports—hockey, basketball, darts, tennis, gymnastics, and golf—and increases have resulted when mental rehearsal is used by both novice and elite athletes, although elite athletes may benefit more because of their advanced skill levels and experience. Elite athletes have a distinct advantage in that they are more likely to mentally practice correct and efficient movements than novice athletes. The importance of mentally practicing the correct movements follows from the adage "Practice makes perfect, but only if you practice perfectly." While there is little research on imaging incorrect movements, there is support showing that negative practice—imaging a negative outcome in sport— leads to a deterioration in performance (Onestak 1991). Consequently, one must guard against mental practice of negative outcomes and help athletes reprocess or refocus an imagery session in which the putt fails to drop into the hole or the arrow misses the target.

If imagery can be used to improve performance of an acquired skill, might it also be useful in learning new motor skills? The use of imagery to acquire motor skills is referred to as *mental practice*. In the late 1960s and early 1970s, the motor learning research literature reported improved motor skill acquisition with the use of mental practice of movements. The imagery of mental practice is usually based on personal experience in performing the skill; however, mental practice can also be performed by observing models performing the target skill. These early studies showed that skill acquisition significantly improved with mental practice compared to a no-practice situation.

More recent studies have supported the efficacy of mental practice in skill acquisition, especially when combined with physical practice. In addition to facilitating the acquisition of new motor skills, mental practice is useful for transferring skills from practice situations to performance situations and in maintaining skills, making it useful for injured athletes. With skill maintenance, it is preferable that mental practice be augmented by physical practice—but in case of injuries in which the athlete must rest physically, mental practice can be employed to reduce loss of skill resulting from lack of physical practice.

Mental practice may promote skill acquisition in other ways. Acquisition of complex motor skills often requires that the skill be broken down into specific parts and that each part be mastered before combining them into the whole skill. This part–whole acquisition of complicated skills can be enhanced through the use of mental practice. Mental imagery of parts of a skill performance may facilitate integration of the parts into the whole routine (Jones and Stuth 1997).

The effectiveness of mental imagery as an intervention to improve skill performance and acquisition depends on the athlete's ability to image vividly and correctly and willingness to utilize imagery. Vividness and correctness of imagery are related to image quality, while use of imagery is related to quantity. Research on imagery training programs indicates that both quality and quantity of imagery can be improved with imagery training. Rogers, Hall, and Buckolz studied the effects of a 16-week imagery training program with figure skaters (1991). They found that both quality of imagery, as measured by the Movement Imagery Questionnaire (Hall and Pongrac 1983), and quantitative use of imagery, as measured by the Imagery Use Questionnaire (Hall, Rogers, and Barr 1990), improved. They also found an increase in performance when the imagery group was compared with a control group. While many questions remain, initial findings indicate that imagery training can facilitate quality and use of imagery and can be effective in improving performance.

Imagery is only one cognitive activity that affects skill acquisition. Among the other cognitive components of skill acquisition of interest to sport psychologists are problem-solving, decision-making, interpretation of feedback, and memory. With the explosion of knowledge in cognitive science, many of what were once considered to be stable and well-documented "laws" of motor learning have been modified. For example, in the area of feedback, motor learning textbooks have traditionally stated that augmented feedback is most effective when provided frequently and immediately after performance (Lee, Swinnen, and Serrien 1994). However, recent studies using retention and transfer of skill as the learning criteria suggest that delaying augmented feedback, so that the learner has time to "figure out" what the feedback will be, enhances skill production over time. As cognitive science creates new models of cognition processes, especially models based on complex, dynamic systems theory, we can expect that current knowledge related to the relationship of motor skill and cognitive processing will be challenged and reconfigured.

The Cognitive Model and Attention

The cognitive process of attention is another major topic in sport psychology. Attention has been studied both as its own concept and in relation to emotional control. The admonitions from coaches to "concentrate," "focus," and "pay attention" attest to the importance placed on selectively attending to important cues in the sporting environment. Additionally, many athletes report that they play "by feel," suggesting that they attend to internal states as well as environmental states. Nideffer's conceptualization of attention dominates the sport psychology literature on this topic (1976). Nideffer conceptualized attention in two dimensions—broad–narrow and internal–external. The broad–narrow scale describes how many stimuli are attended to simultaneously, while the internal–external scale reflects the degree of attention to self or the environment. Conceptualizing attention on a broad–narrow and internal–external matrix defines four distinct attentional styles. The broad–external style is optimal for performance situations where multiple external cues must be recognized. A football quarterback, for example, must read the defense, attend to multiple receivers and their defenders, and avoid blitzing linebackers using a broad–external attentional orientation. The broad–internal style might be used to design strategy for sport by recalling past information and organizing tactical plans to deal with projected situations. The narrow–external style is optimal for ball-striking efforts and might be employed by golfers executing a drive off the tee. The narrow–internal style would be advantageously employed by athletes in situations where they are attempting to center themselves, gain self-control, and relax during performances.

Nideffer designed the Test of Attentional and Interpersonal Style (TAIS) to measure individual strengths and weaknesses in attentional styles and as a predictor of performance. In addition to being able to employ all four categories of attention, athletes must be able to appropriately switch from one style to another as conditions change.

Nideffer's work promoted scrutiny of additional aspects of attention such as attentional overload and excessive narrowing of attention that excludes task-relevant cues. With regard to excessive narrowing of attention, an integral aspect of Nideffer's conceptualization of attention is the impact of anxiety on attention. He theorized that the ability to control attentional style and switch from one style to another is mediated by arousal level. This relationship has generally been supported in research that has confirmed that anxiety tends to involuntarily narrow attention.

Subsequent studies by other researchers employing the TAIS, including sport-specific versions like the tennis TAIS (Van Schoyck and Grasha 1981), suggest that the internal–external dimension of attention is not a strong factor in determining performance and that the broad–narrow dimension is more accurately conceptualized as multidimensional, with scan and focus as two of the components. Van Schoyck and Grasha define scanning as "the allocation of attention to many aspects of the stimulus field" (p. 159). Focus refers to the "integration of the objects of attention" (Schlesinger 1954, as cited in Van Schoyck and Grasha 1981, p. 159). Nideffer's attention matrix with scan and focus dimensions are portrayed in figure 3.3. There is little research on this aspect of attention in sport situations, however, and Nideffer's model continues to dominate the sport literature.

In addition to questions regarding the components of attention in sport, the attention literature has not addressed questions regarding which attentional styles are advantageous or detrimental to performance in specific sport situations, and whether attentional style is a stable personal trait or is influenced by situational determinants (Van Schoyck and Grasha 1981). It is possible that conceptualizing attention as a state–trait phenomenon, similar to the conceptualization of state–trait anxiety, will provide a clearer understanding of the role of attention in sport.

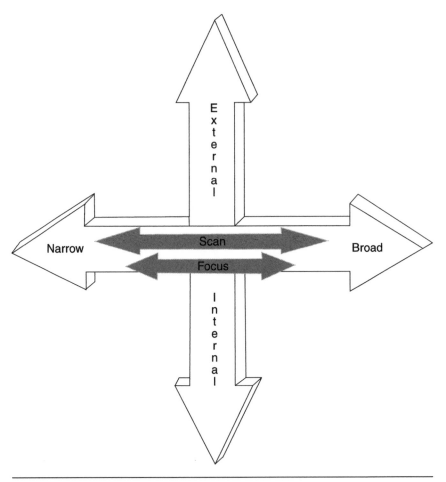

Figure 3.3   Nideffer's attention matrix (1976) with scanning and focus dimensions suggested by Van Schoyck and Grasha (1981).

The Cognitive Model and Sport Injury

New specialty disciplines, such as biobehavioral health and psychoneuro-immunology, have renewed emphasis on the body–mind connection in the field of health and medicine. This renewed interest in the influence of the mind on physical aspects of health and recovery has prompted interest in the role of cognitive techniques for all aspects of rehabilitation from injury and illness, including sports-related injuries. As a result of this phenom-enon, psychological interventions are becoming increasingly common in sport injury rehabilitation programs. In 1996, Larson, Starkey, and

Zaichkowsky reported that in a survey of a large sample of athletic trainers, 47 percent believed that every injured athlete experiences psychological trauma, 24 percent referred injured athletes for counseling related to their injuries, and 25 percent employ a sport psychologist on their sports medicine team (Crossman 1997).

Psychological interventions often employ imagery for both preventive and postinjury intervention. Jones and Stuth (1997) report that imagery has been employed to do the following:

- Facilitate relaxation, reduce stress, and reduce the potential for injury
- Facilitate the healing process and increase positive immune-system responses
- Control pain both by focusing attention away from pain (dissociation) and by focusing attention on the pain (association)
- Increase adherence to rehabilitation programs
- Maintain skill during rehabilitation through mental practice
- Block replay or rumination of the injury incident, which may have a negative effect on recovery

Other cognitive interventions for dealing with the trauma associated with sports injuries include positive self-talk to increase self-efficacy regarding coping and recovering from the injury, re-establishing sense of control over recovery, and reframing negative thoughts concerning the injury.

The Cognitive Model and Motivation

Motivation is the desire to engage and persist in sport, often despite disappointments, sacrifice, and discouragement. It is an important topic in sport because advancement to the highest levels of sport skill requires sustained dedication. One way the cognitive model addresses motivation is by conceptualizing it as an outcome of expectancy. *Expectancy theory* suggests that behavior is "pulled" by the person's expectations of desirable outcomes. These outcomes or incentives can be anything that is valued by the athlete—fame, money, personal satisfaction, gold medals, and so on. The person is motivated to exert effort in pursuit of incentives because he believes that this personal effort will result in attainment of the incentives. Assuming that incentives are provided and that the athlete is capable of performing the required skill, Bandura suggests that the athlete's actual performance will initially depend on self-efficacy (1977). As experience with the task increases, past performances will tend to increase or decrease self-efficacy and play a larger role in predicting future performance.

Self-efficacy, self-confidence, and personal competence are interdependent forces that contribute to one's motivation to initiate and persist in sport. In the sport psychology literature, these forces have been defined and investigated separately. *Self-efficacy* is the person's belief that she has the personal resources to succeed in attaining specific goals. It is the sense that the person has about personal competence in a limited realm, and it varies from one situation to another. *Self-confidence,* on the other hand, is usually viewed as a more global reflection of one's expectation of success across many realms. *Competence* is seen as a feeling of mastery or proficiency based on prior accomplishments. It is a reflection of one's skills and achievements.

Investigations of self-efficacy and its impact on physical performance have shown that it affects performance in weightlifting (Ness and Patton 1979), leg-endurance competition (Weinberg, Gould, and Jackson 1979), and arm-wrestling (Nelson and Furst 1972). Recognition of the importance of self-efficacy to performance has produced interest in methods of augmenting self-efficacy in athletes. Use of modeling, self-talk, imagery, environmental manipulations to create successful experiences, and verbal persuasion and support from significant others (such as the coach or teammates), are among the techniques suggested for improving athlete self-efficacy (Mahoney 1979).

Attribution, achievement motivation, and achievement orientation are three other aspects of motivation addressed in the cognitive model. *Attribution* refers to the athlete's beliefs regarding the causes for success or failure in a sporting event and how stable, controllable, and inherent these causes are in the athlete's perspective. Weiner's model of attribution divides it into causal elements and causal dimensions (1972). *Causal elements* are the different reasons people propose for success or failure—for example, ability ("I have innate athletic ability; therefore, I often win"), effort ("I always give 110 percent; therefore, I win"), task difficulty ("My opponent is not as good as I am; therefore, I will win"), and luck or chance ("Everything is going my way today; therefore, I will win"). *Causal dimensions* refer to whether the cause is

- internal (within the athlete) or external (outside the athlete);
- stable (consistent) or unstable (changeable); and
- controllable (under the influence of the athlete) or uncontrollable (outside the influence of the athlete).

The athlete's attributions regarding what caused success or failure are influential in determining subsequent actions and motivations. For example, attributing a winning performance to skill practice is likely to result in continued skill practice. Because practicing can be governed by the athlete, her success is also viewed as being connected to self (internal) and controllable. An athlete who attributes success to good luck, however, tends to view success as being generated by mostly uncontrollable, external factors that might be present one day but gone the next. Attributions, therefore, are important cognitive mediators of behavior as they influence the athlete's expectations of future performances and motivation to persist.

Since attributions influence the athlete's motivations and expectations, the cognitive practitioner encourages stable, internal, and controllable attributions for successful endeavors. For example, attributing a successful performance to "ability," which would encourage the client to be confident and work to develop his potential, is preferable to attributing success to "luck," which is external, unstable, and beyond the control of the athlete. Attributions for failure might differ depending on the circumstances. For example, attributing failure to an unstable, external, and uncontrollable factor such as a bad call by the officials can keep an athlete motivated and positive about the future. Likewise, attributing failure to a lack of practice, which is within the athlete's control and power to change, can be helpful for an athlete. Attributing failure to lack of talent—an uncontrollable, stable factor—must be avoided.

The need to achieve, or achievement motivation, is a cognitive factor that is related to attribution. *Achievement motivation* (McClelland, Atkinson, and Lowell 1953) refers to the person's propensity to either approach success or avoid failure. People who have a need to approach success tend to be high achievers, whereas people who need to avoid failure tend to be low achievers. The relationship between attribution and achievement motivation suggests that people with a high need for achievement tend to take personal responsibility and credit for their achievements by attributing them to their own ability and effort. Low achievers tend to deny personal responsibility for success by attributing it to uncontrollable, external sources.

Cognitive practitioners can use attribution retraining treatments (Dweck 1975) or achievement change programs (Weiner 1981) to impact clients' attributions and achievement motives. These programs encourage clients to attribute failure to a personal lack of effort rather than a lack of genetically based talent.

Guidelines for retraining programs include the following:

1. Select a task that the client can definitely accomplish if enough effort is exerted.
2. Emphasize the relationship between successful performance and effort before performance attempts.

3. Debrief the client after attempting the task. This debriefing includes asking the client why he succeeded or failed and reinforcing effort attributions. It can include instructing the client to engage in self-persuasion regarding the role of effort in attaining success.

4. As success at the task becomes more consistent, prompt the client to verbally acknowledge and celebrate both his success and effort.

5. Repeat the entire process with a new task. This retraining requires a long-term effort. Repetition of this process serves to change the client's attributions and achievement motivation. It may also influence a third aspect of cognition, achievement orientation.

Achievement orientation refers to an athlete's perceptions of the stability of personal ability—specifically, whether the athlete views ability as a malleable personal characteristic that can grow and develop through mastering tasks *(task approach)* or as a personal, stable trait *(ego approach)*. The ego approach often fosters the cognitive assumption of "my work or performance is equivalent to my self" (Robin 1993). This equation can be maladaptive for the athlete, and alternative, task-oriented perspectives may be presented by the cognitive practitioner for the athlete's consideration.

Summary

1. The cognitive model views mental processes such as thoughts, schemas, attributions, selective memory, self-talk, imagery, and attention as creators of the self's personal reality.

2. Systematic distortions in mental processes produce dysfunctional emotions and behavior in people. The solution is to change distorted cognitive patterns.

3. Distorted thinking presents itself in many forms. It is predominantly narrow, rigid, egocentric, and selectively biased toward negativity. Irrational beliefs, in which the person rigidly affirms that she "must" and "should" experience and live life in a specified manner, are a common form of distorted thinking.

4. Brief, active, collaborative treatment is designed to identify and change distorted cognitive patterns. Clients are taught to
   - monitor counterproductive thoughts;
   - recognize the connections among thoughts, feelings, and behavior;
   - examine evidence for and against distorted cognitions; and
   - replace distorted cognitive patterns with more reality-based thinking.

5. Combined with behavioral interventions, this is one of the most widely used models in sport psychology. Research on the efficacy of cognitive interventions has generally shown them to be effective in controlling anxiety, coping with recovery from injury, and improving skill level.

Process Plan for Lisa Irons's Case: Cognitive Perspective

As with the other psychological models, the first step in successful cognitive counseling is establishing a professional relationship with the athlete. Within each model, the practitioner–client relationship is conceptualized differently, but the relationship is always a prime concern regardless of the model. In the cognitive model, the practitioner serves as a guide who opens the client's mental processes to new horizons. In particular, the counselor provides the client with new perspectives and additional ways of viewing both self and the world. The cognitive sport psychologist attempts to expand the athlete's insights into the impact of her mental processes—thoughts, feelings, memories, and such—on performance. However, in order to accomplish such a lofty goal, there must be a relationship between the sport psychologist and athlete that engenders respect, confidence, and trust. Therefore, in my initial consultations with Lisa I must give consideration to establishing a trusting relationship.

Another early goal is to convey to Lisa the rationale of the cognitive model. I want to give her a clear understanding regarding how cognitive factors can both enhance and impede motor performances. I also hope to obtain some signs from her that confirm she is convinced about the methods we will use and committed to the process.

It is often helpful to explore the athlete's perception of the mind–body relationship while explaining the cognitive rationale. Athletes who believe that the mind and the body are two separate and independent entities, and also view sport as 99 percent physical, often have difficulty accepting the premise that their thoughts can dictate their mechanics. Demonstrations of mind–body connectedness are often necessary to instill this crucial link in the athlete. For example, I might simply ask Lisa to think of a particularly joyous occasion, describe it in detail to me, and then have her note the congruence between her thoughts and physical actions—posture, gestures, facial expressions, and so on—while telling me of this happy event. This could be followed by having her recreate a particularly sad occasion and noting how her physical actions change as she relates the event. Additionally, having Lisa describe in writing her performance in specific athletic experiences—what she was doing, what she was thinking, and what she was feeling during a good performance and a poor performance—may help her recognize the connection between mind and body.

At the other extreme is the athlete who believes that the mind must control the body, and therefore feels out of control when attempting to perform with a "quiet" mind (without constant internal dialogue). A golfer who tries to monitor and think about every part of the swing while performing, for example, may feel out of control if told to stop self-instructing and just swing through the ball. Information emphasizing the role of thinking during preparation for performance (the planning phase) and then trusting the body to carry out the action may need to be discussed with an athlete who has too much cognitive involvement while performing.

During our first meetings, I want to get to know Lisa and understand how she views her current situation. I am interested in her feelings and thoughts about her situation. As we are talking, I will note the explanations that Lisa gives to interpret her life events. I will note her use of absolute words—*every, always, never*—and other signs of irrational or dysfunctional beliefs. I will not challenge these beliefs at this time, as I want to listen to her view of the world long enough to get a complete and clear sense of how she thinks about herself and her life events.

Once I have enough information from Lisa, I will reflect back to her some of the "interesting" beliefs about herself and her life that I have heard. I want to confirm with her that my interpretation of what she has been professing appears accurate to her. My objective is that through our conversations, we will eventually identify two or three thoughts or feelings that are maladaptive for Lisa. For example:

Counselor 1: Lisa, I've noticed that in your autobiography, in our discussions about the possibility of retirement, and again when we talked about your current playing slump, you referred to the fact that you feel you have disappointed yourself and your parents, who have made significant sacrifices so you can play golf. Are you disappointed with your golf career?

Lisa 2: Personally, golf has been very fulfilling to me on some levels, and I can't imagine any other career I would prefer over being on the LPGA tour. But you are right in a way. I do feel that my parents made lots of sacrifices for my golf. They gave me the opportunity to be a great golfer, and I haven't produced. They would never impose on me and have always been my most loyal fans, but I feel an obligation to give them some sort of return on their investment. They always encourage me and tell me I can win another major. Part of being a successful golfer, for me, is being able to make enough money to buy my parents nice things for a comfortable retirement. Some top players on the tour have done this, and I want to do it, too. But I've been such a failure on the tour that I can barely keep myself financially solvent. My parents provided me with equipment, lessons, and playing opportunities when I was a kid—all things that cost lots of money, even though our family was never well off. I know they made sacrifices for me. They've been so supportive and I haven't come close to being able to pay them back or live up to their confidence in me. Even though my parents never expect anything back, I *want* to give back—I feel I should give back. It irritates me that I can't give back—I'm worthless.

Counselor 3: What makes you think you're worthless? What evidence do you have?

Lisa 4: Well, we could start by looking at my bank account. But that's not all of it. A golfer who can't win the majors is not a champion, and I started out to be a champion. I feel totally worthless because I can't win the majors. When I go out and play poorly, I know I have not achieved my personal best, and I feel totally worthless . . . and it's not that I don't try to do better. I worry all the time and I put so much effort into my golf, but I'm afraid that I just don't have what it takes. Sometimes I just can't stand it. It makes me crazy.

Through conversations like this, Lisa and I can uncover her performance-related irrational beliefs. In this particular conversation, several irrational beliefs can be identified:

1. Misapplication of the reciprocation rule (Cialdini 1993), which requires that we "give back" to others when they give to us. While the reciprocation rule works well in most relationships, it is impossible to apply to parent–child relationships because children cannot "pay back" their parents for all they do for them. Lisa may be putting undue pressure on herself in an attempt to reciprocate her parents' sacrifices for her.

2. Maximizing frustration into a global self-appraisal of total worthlessness.

3. A belief system founded on illogical equations. Robin identified three illogical assumptions, identifiable in Lisa's conversations, that affect performance (1993):

   - My work = my self.
   - My discomfort is unbearable and I cannot endure it.
   - Anxiety = effort, or worry is the same as effort.

4. Anxiety centered on concern with "What if I never win another major?" Lisa sees this as a criterion for success—for being a champion. She rates herself harshly on this criterion and fears that others (her parents) rate her in the same way. Strangely, she is irritated when others rate her in the same manner that she rates herself. At some

level, she feels it is unjust that she has to win major tournaments in order to be a "good daughter" or champion in her parent's eyes.

Additionally, Lisa's current tolerance for frustrations seems to be low—she "just can't stand it." Often, when people have low frustration tolerance they "perceive the physical and social discomfort they have experienced or expect to experience in a given situation as unbearable and intolerable" (Robin 1993, p. 161). This can result in an irrational demand from the athlete that the world not impose this or any other discomfort on her. In addition to feeling that it is "unfair" or "unjust" that she has to perform with these discomforts, Lisa may be concerned because she feels she does not have the resources to deal with these uncomfortable disadvantages. Complementing this line of thinking may be the belief that other golfers do not have to perform with these uncomfortable handicaps and/or do not suffer as much as she does from these handicaps. Her thoughts of retirement may be an attempt to avoid future encounters with her "intolerable" discomforts—in this case, back pain, anxiety about her slump, and questioning of her ability to succeed in winning major championships.

Before exploring Lisa's irrational beliefs, I will again take time to make certain that she understands the connection between these maladaptive assumptions and her golf performance. For example, we might discuss how excessive concern about further injuring her back could result in increased muscular tension during her swing, which would be destructive to her performance and may actually increase chances of further back pain. If Lisa cannot understand how her thoughts are related to her performance, the cognitive approach is undermined. She must comprehend how her assumptions about her work, her self, and her environment form the foundation for her self-efficacy and confidence, and that these qualities affect her disposition to trust her swing and her on-course decisions, and her ability to concentrate and emotionally support herself on the course. Our work will seem irrelevant to Lisa if these connections are not solid.

The available methods we can use to explore Lisa's maladaptive thoughts are direct disputation, Socratic dialogue (a questioning technique that the practitioner uses to lead the client to a logical conclusion), and empirical testing. In deciding on a primary method for working with Lisa, I will take into consideration her life experiences and personal characteristics so that the methods we use will complement her temperament. Lisa is a strong person, very competitive and quite intelligent. She is strong-willed and is convinced that she knows her own mind. Given these characteristics, I choose not to get into an adversarial position with her about her beliefs, as this may trigger her competitive characteristics and possibly promote resistance to me and to our work together. Therefore, we will initially depend primarily on Socratic dialogue and empirical testing rather than direct disputation from me. As Lisa becomes convinced about the maladaptive nature of some of her beliefs, we can shift into disputation of those beliefs, but I will encourage Lisa to take the lead in disputing her own dysfunctional beliefs.

Encouraging Lisa to scrutinize her own thought patterns, identify them, examine them critically, and then take action to modify or correct them is the ultimate goal. An important aspect of this goal is to provide Lisa with the tools and cognitive resources she will need to possess after our sessions are terminated. In order to accomplish this goal, I will set up a progression of experiences in which Lisa practices challenging and changing her maladaptive thoughts. The first experience in challenging her beliefs will be guided by me through questioning and use of Socratic dialogue. Subsequent experiences in challenging and changing belief patterns will each require more leadership and independence from Lisa. Before we end our sessions, I will want to see Lisa engage in actions and strategies to control her automatic beliefs. This will assure that she is able to maintain herself independent of my guidance.

A crucial decision that must be made early in our work together concerns the order in which Lisa's maladaptive thoughts should be examined. In most cases, clients are not aware of their dysfunctional beliefs, so it is unproductive to ask them where they want to begin. One strategy is to identify a "foundation" or "hinge" maladaptive assumption that seems to underlie several related problematic cognitions. This can be a very efficient strategy, because once the foundation belief is successfully challenged and altered, other beliefs that depend on the foundation belief are undermined and challenged more easily.

Care must be exercised in challenging and changing a foundation belief, however, as it might have the unintended consequence of toppling adaptive as well as maladaptive assumptions of the athlete. For example, if an athlete reported that when she plays poorly she believes it is a sign that God was displeased with her or punishing her, it would not be wise to set up challenges to the athlete's religion. This could undermine her spiritual life and introduce counterproductive chaos and angst into her view of the world. In this example, it would be prudent to limit the examination to the athlete's specific assumption that poor playing indicates God's displeasure with her rather than making a general challenge to her religion. The objective in this case is to accept the athlete's reality but dispute her inferences about that reality.

Another strategy for determining which dysfunctional belief to work with first is to select the belief that I think will be most easily challenged. The rationale is to select a maladaptive belief that can be changed in a relatively short amount of time so the athlete experiences some success and relief early in treatment. This is the strategy I would use in Lisa's case. I feel that Lisa's belief that she is "worthless" because she cannot "pay back" her parents for the sacrifices they willingly made to support her golf career is creating undue stress on her and perhaps contributing to her feelings of depression about her golf career. Providing Lisa with some relief from her self-imposed vise of being the "good daughter" by returning money she feels she "owes" her parents will free up some of her emotional resources and allow Lisa to be more relaxed about her performances.

In beginning to deal with Lisa's beliefs about "paying back" her parents for all the sacrifices they made for her, I might suggest some appropriate readings for Lisa, such as Robert Cialdini's *Influence* (1993). Cialdini's writings on automatic, fixed responses, which he calls "click, whirr" responses ("*click* and the appropriate tape is activated; *whirr* and out rolls the standard sequence of behaviors" [p. 3]), explain the advantages and disadvantages that we accrue from our automatic beliefs. This reading will reinforce my attempts to convince Lisa that her assumptions and feelings can affect her actions. Cialdini's chapter on the reciprocation rule, which fosters the feeling that we should try to repay in kind what another person has provided us, will cue Lisa to examine her internalization of this rule and question whether it is appropriate to apply it (play this tape) in her situation. Indeed, Cialdini specifically discusses the advantages of this rule to society, but suggests that it may be inappropriate to stringently apply this rule to family relationships. Through this reading assignment, I hope to have Lisa explore:

- how she acquired her ideas and feelings about reciprocation,
- how the reciprocation rule is beneficial in some situations—and that she is not "dumb" for believing in it,
- how it is sometimes misapplied by others to manipulate us,
- how we can misapply it with ourselves, and
- how we can defend ourselves from its misapplications.

I will discuss these issues and Cialdini's ideas with Lisa and ask her relate them to her own thoughts about what she owes her parents.

Using this reading as a springboard for further discussion, I will ask Lisa to consider a "what if" situation in which she has a child. What kind of reciprocal giving would she expect from her child for all the money she expended in child rearing? Viewing the reciprocation rule from this perspective, Lisa might begin to reflect on the truth that her parents are really interested in her love and respect as a daughter, rather than financial reimbursement for her childhood golfing expenses. I will encourage Lisa to engage in self-initiated thought-changing strategies to convince herself that providing her parents with money would be nice, but it is not a necessary condition for her to consider herself a loving daughter.

Assuming the challenge to Lisa's misapplication of the reciprocation rule is successful in providing Lisa with some release from her self-imposed pressure while performing, we would move on to challenging some other beliefs that interfere with her performances. Robin provides a basic outline of rational emotive therapy intervention strategies that I find useful (1993). Robin developed these strategies for use with performers such as actors, artists, and musicians, and they provide a starting point for work with athletes. As with all treatment of individuals, appropriate additions and modifications to the interventions based on the athlete's responses is part of the practitioner's responsibility to the client. Robin's outline of intervention strategies is reproduced in table 3.2. In addition to the cognitive interventions, you should be able to identify some behavioral interventions included in this outline of strategies.

Table 3.2   Robin's (1993) RET Intervention Strategies

RET Intervention Strategies

I. Disputes

  A. Empirical

    1. What is your evidence that...

    2. Where is it written that...

      a. You must succeed?

      b. You must not feel discomfort?

      c. People must see you as you wish to be seen?

      d. Things must be quicker/easier than they are?

      e. You are utterly worthless if you do poorly or experience any discomfort?

      f. Situations, people, or affects are toxic?

      g. You would fall apart, disintegrate, or in any way not stand it if you experienced failure, hassle, or discomfort?

  B. Pragmatic

    1. How will thinking...enable you to accomplish your goals?

      a. Any of the above

      b. Your own particular brand of mishagoss*

    2. How will (doing)...enable you to accomplish your goals?

      a. Procrastinating

(continued)

Table 3.2 *(continued)*

      b. Not rehearsing/preparing

      c. Not auditioning

      d. Not engaging in the activity

      e. Getting angry

      f. Worrying, getting anxious, panicking

  C. Philosophical

    1. Couldn't you still have (some kind of) a happy, productive life if...

      a. The worst happened?

      b. You always experienced discomfort?

II. Relaxation/Imagery

  A. "Quick & Dirty"

    1. Measure subjective units of discomfort (SUD).

    2. Take "good" breath.

    3. Hold for slow count of five.

    4. Let breath out through pursed lips.

    5. Resume normal breathing.

      a. Think "Calm" while inhaling;

      b. Think "Relaxed" while exhaling;

      c. OR visualize your favorite number riding the waves as you inhale and exhale.

    6. DO *NOT* follow any other stray, interesting, or defeating thought during this exercise.

    7. Repeat No. 5 and No. 6 for 1-5 minutes.

    8. Slowly return to regular activity.

    9. Retake SUD.

  B. Diaphragmatic Breathing

    1. Assessment

      a. Put one hand on upper chest and other on the abdomen

      b. Take a big breath

      c. Which hand moved?

        (1) If lower hand, then teach Rational-Emotive Imagery (REI) or meditative imagery.

        (2) If upper hand, then teach diaphragmatic breathing.

          (a) Inhale and expand abdomen.

          (b) Exhale and contract abdomen.

       (c) Lie down on flat surface with a tissue box, paper cup, or light book on your abdomen and "pop the box."

C. Relaxation scripts: A variety are available. I have used the ones by Arnold Lazarus to good advantage. I have also "tailor-made" tapes for specific clients.

D. REI**

  1. Visualize the "dreaded" situation.

  2. Strongly experience the negative dysfunctional affect.

  3. Try to change the dysfunctional affect into a functional one. Change anger to disappointment or frustration; change anxiety to concern.

  4. Examine the change in thinking (iB-rB ***) that preceded the change in affect.

III. Experiential exercises

A. Stay "in the moment"—stay process oriented, not product oriented.

B. Act *as if*—remember when Anna met the King of Siam? She pretended bravery and convinced herself as well as others.

C. "Desacredize" the observer.

D. "Who is your audience?"

E. Self-acceptance exercises

  1. "Warts and All"

  2. "Tissue Box Dispute"

F. Give yourself "permission" to screw up.

G. Symptom rehearsal/symptom permission

IV. Homework

A. Cognitive

  1. Work on changing your thinking.

  2. Do REI.

B. Behavioral

  1. *Try* to practice, prepare, etc.

  2. Do relaxation exercises.

---

*mishagoss = Yiddish term for one's own unique brand of "craziness"

**REI = Rational Emotive Emagery

***(iB-rB) = irrational belief to rational belief

(Robin, M. 1993. Overcoming performance anxiety: Using RET with actors, artists and other "performers." In *Innovations in rational emotive therapy*, edited by W. Dryden and L. Hill. Pages 172-173, copyright © 1993 by Sage Publications. Reprinted by permission of Sage Publications.)

The first strategy involves disputations. Employing Socratic dialogue, I use more empirical and pragmatic challenges of athlete assumptions than philosophical challenges, but it is necessary to consider the predisposition of the athlete. Some athletes connect very well with the philosophical approach, particularly if they are very spiritual or scholarly. For them, accepting the belief that a happy, successful life does not depend on winning or rising to a self-chosen level of sport provides a great emotional relief, reduces performance anxiety, and results in improved performances. However, athletes like Lisa, who are anxious over the fact that they have not risen to the level of sport that they aspire to, can be threatened by just considering the implications of the philosophical arguments. Lisa seems very pragmatic, and although she is introspective, she is not inclined to "seek the meaning of life" with her sport psychologist. Lisa's goal is to perform better, and she demands the most direct route to improved performance. This tendency toward pragmatism is reflected in Lisa's impatience to move out of her current uncomfortable, painful state. Using pragmatic and empirical disputations, I will try to gradually move her to a more comfortable position. Later in our work, we can return to more philosophical challenges to bolster the change in her assumptions.

The experiential exercises suggested by Robin can be very powerful for athletes who prefer an action-oriented approach to their problems (1993). These exercises expand the athlete's perspectives through active learning. The tissue box dispute is an example of a metaphoric method of introducing challenges to the injurious assumption that "I am my performance." In this technique, the athlete is given a full box of tissues and asked to list her strengths and weaknesses. As she lists each positive and negative trait, she pulls one tissue from the box. When the athlete runs out of traits, she is asked to identify "which tissue was the box: that is, which trait is the person" (Robin 1993, p. 175). This can be a very effective technique to introduce the concept of the self being more than any one trait or skill. Additionally, if some tissues remain in the box, that can be used to remind Lisa that we can probably never know all of our strengths and weaknesses.

Other techniques suggested by Robin that I might use with Lisa are desacredization, particularly in relation to her approach to major championships, and "acting as if" she were the champion she hopes to be. *Desacredization* involves reframing the major championships to make them less important in Lisa's mind. Viewing the majors as important, but not sacred or sacrosanct, may help Lisa's performance by reducing the anxiety associated with this goal. The *act as if* technique will encourage Lisa to adopt a more positive attitude and play with more confidence. It might also help her to realize that even if she wins the major championships that have eluded her, she will still have some stresses and worries. In this way, she can begin to view some stresses as normal and universal rather than abnormal and particular to herself.

Another issue that we will explore is the chronic lower back pain Lisa is experiencing. It is not uncommon for this to plague golfers, and given Lisa's age and medical history, the pain is something she will probably experience a good part of the time. I will confirm with Lisa that she has consulted her physician, physical therapist, and swing coach to explore all the medical and biomechanical interventions that might alleviate her pain. I will also confirm with her that she has not been told to stop playing golf because it is causing physical damage to her body tissues. Pain is a protective device for the body, and it would be unethical to encourage an athlete to play against medical advice.

It is often helpful to use cognitive techniques as an adjunct to medical treatment, and that will be the strategy suggested for Lisa. We will explore several issues in relation to Lisa's back pain. The first constellation of issues concerns the nature of her injury. Does Lisa have diagnosed damage to her back that is appropriate to her pain? Or does she have diagnosed damage that is not commensurate with her reported pain? Or is there no identifiable damage, but she still complains of pain in such a way as to convince medical personnel that real damage has occurred? Or is her pain purely psychological in nature, perhaps with malingering due to secondary gains the pain brings her—such as an excuse for poor performance, or sympathy from significant others (Rothschild 1993)? Other information, such as Lisa's perceived level of pain and pattern of pain (when is pain worse, when is it better?) will also be discussed. Rothschild suggests several common irrational beliefs related to chronic pain that can be explored with Lisa (1993, pp. 101-107):

"I must feel good all the time."

"The pain is the most important thing in my life."

"I must never be thwarted."

"I must never be helpless."

"I shouldn't be in pain."

"I can never be happy with this pain" or

"I can never play well with this pain."

"It is awful to have to change my lifestyle
to accommodate this pain."

Discussions with Lisa regarding her back problem—both its history and present manifestations—will reveal whether she holds any of these underlying assumptions. If her back is not bothering her presently, but she indicates that she worries that crippling pain might return every time she plays, then this concern will be the focus of our efforts. In this instance, pragmatic disputing of her fear of re-injury would include recognition that the worry itself may cause her to alter her swing, resulting in not only poorer scores but also incorrect biomechanics that may exacerbate her back pain.

Throughout our sessions, I will ask Lisa to keep a journal of her thoughts, feelings, and actions on issues we discuss in our sessions. Progress will be evident from her writings and from her assessments of her golf performances during this season. Continuation of this journal will be useful to Lisa in monitoring her own control over the mental side of her game. As maladaptive thought patterns are challenged, Lisa will work on replacing them with positive thoughts and feelings. These new thoughts and attitudes can be blended into her precompetition routine. Lisa may also benefit from including some individualized activity-mood phrases ("I'm relaxed and I love hitting this shot"), affirming self-talk ("I'm good at this shot"), and task-related reminders ("Hit through the ball") to her routine. We will discuss not only the content of these self-talk cues, but also the appropriate time to "think" during her golf round (between shots) and the appropriate time to have a quiet, uncluttered mind (during shots). Symptom relief, including improved performance, and demonstrated ability to recognize, challenge, and alter her own cognitive material are signs of Lisa's progress and will suggest when she is ready to terminate.

Additional Case for Discussion

Sport psychologists need to address the needs of athletes in a variety of contexts. This includes working to enhance performance of athletes at various skill levels, in various sports, and with different challenges, such as Special Olympians and Masters athletes. This case study presents the issues of a Masters athlete, a 59-year-old marathoner. How might the cognitive practitioner view this athlete's performance issues? What are Fran's enhancing and detrimental thoughts? What prejudicial thoughts about aging might the practitioner need to guard against in his own belief/thought system? Would your approach to this case change depending on whether Fran was a man or a woman?

"I know other people think I'm foolish. You know what they say, 'There's no fool like an old fool.' But I can't stop running. It gives me life, and when I have to stop or slow down to the point that I'm not competitive, I think I'll die," Fran said, half-joking but with a tinge of seriousness.

"I used to be fast—very fast. But then I used to be a lot of things," Fran said with resignation. "Like I used to be able to remember things, and I definitely used to look a lot better in Lycra," Fran laughed. "Or at least I would have looked better in Lycra if it had existed back then."

Fran is a young 59-year-old—a few wrinkles around the eyes and mouth, mostly laugh lines, but she appears to be in great shape, still slim and sturdy. Fran continued:

"I played lots of sports as a youngster. We didn't have all the organized children's sports that exist now; back then we had to make our own fun. All the neighborhood kids played the sport of the season—baseball in the summer, football in fall, hockey in winter, and basketball in spring. There was always a pickup game for me to play in. I played recreational ball in high school and college and was always one of the best players because of my quickness. After college I started teaching and raising a family, so I got out of shape for a while.

"When I turned 30 I decided to get back in shape, and I started jogging. Gradually I started running 5Ks and then 10Ks. I always placed well in those road races, and I liked the challenge and competition. I decided to run a marathon on my 40th birthday to mark my 'over-the-hill' milestone. I trained for eight months and was able not only to go the distance, but to place fourth in my division. Since then I have been training for long distances and doing two to three marathon competitions per year.

"Lately, however, I have cut my training and have become more fearful of the risks of long-distance running. I am particularly concerned with being able to handle the heat on race day if the temperature is over 85 degrees. I never used to even consider the heat factor until one of my friends, another top Masters runner, collapsed from the heat in Atlanta. Now it's always in the back of my mind. I start checking the weather forecasts days before a race, and I know that if it's over 85 degrees or if it's very humid, I will hang back and not give my full effort, even though I know I am in top condition.

"I keep playing this scenario in my head in which I am running and collapse from the heat. The other runners just keep passing me by, shaking their heads in pity. People along the road are staring, too. They're saying, 'Look at that old idiot. Some old folks don't have the sense they were born with. What's that old gray head trying to prove anyway? Go back to your rocker.' Then the first aid people come and carry me off the road. I'm embarrassed to be so weak.

"I never used to worry about heat, injury, or risks, but as I get older, I think I've become more cautious. I can't seem to just open it up and run with abandon like I did before. This worry and caution have plagued my training and performance times in races. My times haven't just been gradually declining—they're in a free fall. I'm finishing at the back of the pack, and it's not fun."

Suggested Readings

Beck, A. 1988. *Love is never enough.* New York: HarperCollins.

Ellis, A. 1988. *How to stubbornly refuse to make yourself miserable about anything—yes, anything!* Secaucus, NJ: Lyle Stuart.

Meichenbaum, D. 1977. *Cognitive behavior modification: An integrative approach.* New York: Plenum.

Wubbolding, R. 1991. *Understanding reality therapy.* New York: Harper and Row.

Chapter 4

THE HUMANISTIC MODEL

Martin Seligman coined the term *positive psychology* to describe a "psychology dedicated to building the best things in life as well as healing the worst" (Seligman 1998, p. 2). This emphasis on positive growth and development—*to be the best you can be*—occupies center stage in humanistic models of psychology. Whether the terminology is *positive psychology* from Seligman, *self-actualization* from Maslow, or *person centeredness* from Carl Rogers, the humanistic models elevate holistic development of individual human potential as the primary concern of psychology. Although the humanistic model has not received as much attention as cognitive and behavioral models in sport psychology, its emphasis on superior functioning fits well with many athletes' aspirations to "be the best." Popular works such as Timothy Gallwey's *The Inner Game of Tennis* (1974), Michael Murphy's *Golf in the Kingdom* (1972), and Mariah Burton-Nelson's *Embracing Victory* (1998) have added to public recognition of this perspective.

As with the other models, there is no single accepted humanistic theory, rather there are many variations based on humanistic principles. One of the best-known humanistic approaches is the person-centered or client-centered perspective developed by Carl Rogers. Representative of the humanistic model, it exemplifies many of basic concepts shared by the different styles found in this category and will be used as the primary example of the humanistic approach.

Basic Concepts

The humanistic model celebrates the individual. Its basic concepts reflect the importance of development of the whole person. Developing one's potential through self-actualization and respecting personal experiences as an integral part of the development of self are key characteristics of this model. Empathy, genuineness, and nonjudgmental caring distinguish the client–practitioner relationship, reflecting the respect and high regard offered to the client at all times.

Self-Actualization

Humanistic theory views human nature as a benevolent force that seeks to grow, develop, and acquire competencies that will raise the self to the highest levels of personal attainment and accomplishment. The force that drives each individual toward the lofty goal of self-fulfillment is referred to as *self-actualization,* and it is the central concept in the humanistic model. It is seen as an innate force that drives human development, as well as a prime motivator of human behavior. The term *self-actualization* was coined by Maslow and defined as "an episode, or a spurt in which the powers of the person come together in a particularly efficient and intensely enjoyable way, and in which he is more integrated and less split, more open for experience, more idiosyncratic, more perfectly expressive or spontaneous, or fully functioning, more creative, more humorous, more ego-transcending, more independent of his lower needs, etc. He becomes in these episodes more truly himself, more perfectly actualizing his potentialities, closer to the core of his Being, more fully human" (cited in Gundersheim 1982, p. 187).

This self-actualizing force has the property of self-organization—that is, it comes from within the individual and is specialized for each person. It is the birthright of all human beings and guides each individual toward the realization of personal full potential. In *A Way of Being* (1980), Carl Rogers described self-actualization "as part of a *formative tendency,* observable in the movement toward greater order, complexity and interrelatedness that can be observed in stars, crystals and microorganisms, as well as in human beings." In some ways, Rogers's ideas are precursors for the more recent tenets of complexity theory, which holds that biological life is based on complex adaptive systems that are self-organizing, nonlinear, dynamic, and interdependent.

In practice, this assumption of a self-actualizing force that guides the individual toward high-level functioning and personal fulfillment translates into trusting the client, and her self-actualizing tendencies, to set her own goals, seek her own path to fulfillment, find her own insights, and control her own interventions. With such trust and emphasis on the resources of the client, it is apparent why humanistic models in psychology are often referred to as *client-centered* or *person-centered* psychologies.

While self-actualization occupies a central position in human motivation, it is not seen as the only motivating force for behavior. In *Motivation and Personality*, Abraham Maslow (1954) outlined a hierarchy of human needs that motivate people to act (see figure 4.1). In Maslow's theory, those needs that are lowest in the hierarchy, such as physical survival needs, must be satisfied before needs higher in the hierarchy are attended to by the individual.

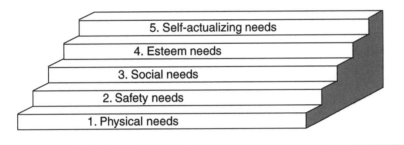

Figure 4.1   Maslow's hierarchy of human needs.

At the top of Maslow's hierarchy is self-actualization. While Maslow's conceptualization of self-actualization relegates it to one of the last motivators, other humanistic approaches, like Rogers's, attribute much greater importance to self-actualization, viewing it as a force directing development of basic competencies. Rogers used the example of a child learning to walk to illustrate the intrinsic nature of self-actualization and its importance as a determining force for behavior. He notes that the initial attempts of a one-year-old to walk are often painful for the child, but still the child persists until the skill is mastered. Rogers attributes the child's persistence at the task, in spite of pain and discouraging setbacks, as the force of self-actualization at work in the child.

The Client–Practitioner Relationship

The relationship that develops between the client and the practitioner is often recognized as a major force in the efficacy of psychological interventions. This relationship itself—often referred to as the *therapeutic alliance*—can be viewed as an integral cause of change in the client. Therefore, the shaping and nurturing of this alliance is part of the practitioner's responsibility. The psychologist must never sexually, emotionally, or financially exploit the client. In addition to doing no harm, however, the practitioner must be proactive in building a relationship based on trust, caring, and respect (Hales and Hales 1995). While all psychological models stress the importance of the relationship between the client and the practitioner, few specify the nature of this relationship as completely as the humanistic model. Within this model, self-actualization of the client must be fostered and stimulated by the relationship with the practitioner (Raskin and Rogers 1995, p. 128). The qualities of this relationship provide "sophisticated support" for the client, enabling him to tap into personal self-actualizing forces that improve his ability to function and bolster well-being (Hales and Hales). Rogers's original idealization of the therapeutic alliance identified three characteristics that the therapist must bring to the relationship—genuineness, nonjudgmental care, and empathy.

Genuineness

Genuineness requires the therapist to be authentic, honest, and sincere in the relationship with the client. The therapist does not put up a professional façade and is congruent in feelings, thoughts, and behavior toward the client. Rogers uses the term *congruence* to describe the necessity of a point-to-point correspondence among the therapist's words, body language, voice quality, and facial expressions. (He also uses *congruence* to refer to "the conscious integration of an experience to become a part of the self" [Chaplin 1985, p. 99], which can be confusing.) While the humanistic practitioner is ideally genuine with the client, this honesty does not translate into negativity, displays of disgust, or criticism of the client due to the necessity of nonjudgmental caring, the second quality of the therapist.

Nonjudgmental Caring

Nonjudgmental caring refers to the therapist's attitude of complete, uncensored acceptance of the client as a person. Rogers described it as "unconditional positive regard" for the client. Such an attitude engenders an atmosphere of nonpossessive warmth in the client–practitioner relationship and provides a nonthreatening and secure environment in which the counseling relationship can flourish.

This security within the relationship is necessary if the client is to become vulnerable to the practitioner through self-disclosure. Because the humanistic perspective is centered in the human experience of the client, and that phenomenological experience can only be conveyed to the therapist through the client's willingness to be open and disclosing, the client must be assured of unconditional positive regard from the practitioner. The client must be secure in the knowledge that her vulnerability will not result in rejection or other consequences that might be destructive to the self.

Establishment of a "safe" environment for clients to open up their internal world is only a first step in unconditional positive regard. The practitioner must also be proactive in supporting clients in their self-actualizing efforts. This requires that the practitioner demonstrate that she prizes the client's efforts and is grateful for the client's willingness to share his internal world. The counselor demonstrates through actions, words, facial expressions, and all other forms of communication that the client's unfolding of his real self is valued by the counselor, and the exposed self will be cherished.

Empathy

Empathy is an expression of communion with the client. Through accurate, empathetic understanding of the client, the counselor communicates that he is able to "be with" and share the client's experience. Empathetic displays establish rapport with the client by demonstrating a desire to affiliate with the client's ways of experiencing the world. Empathy demonstrates interest in the external circumstances of the client's life and, more important, an interest in the client's internal experiencing.

The counselor attempts to share the client's experience as a fully functioning person. This includes acknowledging that since no two people experience the world exactly alike, we can never know precisely how one experienced the whole of a situation. However, in our common human heritage there is enough significant correspondence among our experiences to share in each other's experiences. This commonality is employed by the counselor, who makes every effort at joint participation in the client's experiences in order to understand her fully. The counselor is not an impartial observer and does not diagnose or direct the client's growth, but rather tries to live with active attention to the whole phenomenon of reality as experienced by the client (Raskin and Rogers 1995).

In practice, demonstrations of empathy can be verbal restatements of the client's emotions; facial expressions of acceptance, such as smiling; body language that shows interest in the client, such as leaning forward toward the client; and use of eye contact. Other signals denoting human communication and acceptance, such as nodding and a soft, pleasant tone of voice, communicate empathy between the counselor and client.

It is most important that these techniques for establishing rapport be genuine and honest. Attempts to fake empathy undermine the therapeutic process by violating the genuineness of the alliance between the client and the counselor. If the counselor cannot genuinely provide nonjudgmental caring and empathy with a client, then the client should be referred to another qualified counselor. In this model, genuineness, nonjudgmental caring, and empathy are "necessary and sufficient" conditions for successful change in the client. If the counselor cannot provide these qualities within the counseling environment, it is unethical (fraudulent) to pretend that help is being provided.

Attention to Human Experience

While the psychodynamic interest is in unconscious dynamics, behaviorists focus on external stimuli, and cognitive practitioners concentrate on thinking, humanists are interested in the human organism as a whole entity. Specifically, humanistic psychology centers on the client's human experiencing of life. In direct opposition to the mechanistic biases of behaviorism, in which specific environmental stimuli determine human behaviors, the humanistic perspective views the complexities of human experiencing as the key to personality and personality change. Rather than viewing reality as the happenings in the external world that affect the person, humanists view reality as a personal, internal phenomena. External happenings are of interest only after they have been experienced or processed by the whole of the human organism. In this way, people create their own realities, and this personal reality feeds back to alter its creator—the person. This is a process that continues throughout the life of the individual, reflecting the model's interest in life-span development.

An important component of one's phenomenological internal world is one's concept of self. *Self* refers to our personal "patterns of perception and/or values that are experienced as 'I' or 'me'. The 'self' develops as a result of the organism's interaction with the environment as it strives to maintain and enhance itself . . . " (Ibrahim and Morrison 1976, p. 68). How the individual views self ("myself") is crucial to the humanistic model. Ideally, individuals should hold their self in high regard, and their presentation of self should reflect this sense of high self-regard.

Self-regard flows from several sources. One important source is the individual's perception of some correspondence or congruence between the self as experienced at the present time and one's ideal self. Congruence between one's experiencing self and one's ideal self naturally produces high self-regard. If there is little match between one's experiencing self and one's ideal self, the disparity leads to disappointment and self-criticism.

Self-concept in the humanistic model is related to the issue of locus of evaluation. If one holds the self with high regard, then the basis of evaluation and self-evaluation should come from one's internal criteria and not from external entities. Judging oneself in relation to others is referred to as *social comparison* (Festinger 1954). When we judge ourselves against individuals who are less fortunate, less skilled, or less accomplished (downward comparison), it temporarily makes us feel better about ourselves. Downward comparisons provide a favorable yardstick with which to measure self. While downward comparison may temporarily improve how one feels about self, it is a poor long-term strategy because it fails to provide the self with appropriate role models and information about how to improve one's condition. Upward comparison, on the other hand, often makes one feel inadequate and unhappy with self.

While many questions remain unanswered regarding the phenomenon of social comparison, Rogers and other humanists note that unhappiness results when individuals judge themselves by other people's standards. Therefore, it is considered important in the humanistic model to promote the individual's tendencies toward using internal criteria, criteria valued by the self, when making evaluations and decisions. Self-measurement should be based not on social comparison but on internal values and judgments in the fully functioning person.

Moving the client's locus of evaluation from external to internal criteria can be approached by encouraging an increase in task orientation and a decrease in ego orientation in the client. Task orientation defines success in terms of getting better (process) and trying hard (effort). Ego orientation, however, defines success in terms of winning and outperforming others (outcome). Encouraging a client to be task oriented supports the humanistic goal of self-actualization and encourages an emphasis on narrowing any discrepancy between one's present experiencing self and one's ideal self.

Another important component of one's phenomenological internal world is the nature of how one experiences the world. The process of *experiencing* is itself subject to alteration in the humanistic model, and there is emphasis on high-quality "experiencing," which is viewed as being open and flexible. It is characterized by conscious living in the here and now. It is a conscious incorporation of the present, with all its complexities and textures, into the "fully awake" self. The fully functioning person mindfully incorporates sensations and perceptions of worldly happenings when experiencing is at its best. Unfortunately, fringe components claiming association with the humanistic movement have sometimes advocated the use of "mind-expanding" drugs such as LSD to enhance experiencing. This is not the norm, however, and the process of natural, open, flexible, present-oriented encounters with life events is viewed as a major characteristic of the fully functioning person in this model.

The relationship between the components brought to the therapeutic alliance by the counselor and the client's human experience is summarized by Raskin and Rogers (1995). They state that:

There is considerable evidence that when clients receive congruence, unconditional positive regard and empathy, their self-
concepts become more positive and realistic, they become more
self-expressive and self-directed, they become more open and free
in their experiencing, their behavior is rated as more mature, and
they deal better with stress. (p. 130)

Goals and Procedures

The goals of the humanistic model are derived directly from the humanistic conceptualization of human nature. Emphasis on becoming a fully functioning person through conscious experiencing of life is a meta-goal. The
client is seen as rightly seeking to realize the full potential of his human
existence. As the client's human potential is realized, the client will demonstrate a high degree of self-regard, which results in the client seeing himself as a competent, worthy, and inventive person. The client's concept of
self changes so that the client feels greater resonance between his current
self and his ideal self. This congruence results in the client viewing himself
as a more capable, deserving, and creative person who desires to live life
fully through willful experiencing of the present. The client will also become more independent and self-referencing in making judgments, particularly about his own life. He is more confident about his own personal
insights and becomes more self-directed in expanding his awareness of
internal and external aspects of life.

These attitudinal, perceptual, and behavioral changes occur within the
individual. The counseling goals are internal changes that will produce
external changes. Interpreting relationships between past and present or
changing environmental stimuli is not perceived to be as powerful as changing the client's sense of self. It is through the change of self and confidence
in one's own self-actualizing forces that the client can reorganize her experiences and act to change her external circumstances.

One aspect of the change in self that is seen as desirable in the humanistic model is an improvement in the client's current personal experiencing.
This experiencing is a private and individualized creation of the individual.
It is the primary mechanism for each person's creation of his own reality,
values, attitudinal outlook, and, most important, self-view. Humanists see
openness to experiencing life's phenomena, heightened awareness of these
experiences, and flexibility in interpreting experiences from multiple perspectives as positive aspects of personal experiencing. Consequently, counseling supports and encourages the client's efforts in these directions.

The definition and exact qualities of a "fully functioning person" exist
as generalizations in the humanistic philosophy of human nature. The de-

tails of defining the fully functioning person must be determined primarily by the client. As a result of genetic makeup, experience, and disposition, each client is viewed as an individual with a specific conception of her "ideal self"—the person she strives to be. This ideal self, as conceptualized by the client, is an important formulation because the goal of counseling is to help the client realize more congruence between her current self and this ideal self. The client consequently determines much of the direction of counseling, including the topics, direction, and specific goals of counseling sessions.

Rogers refers to this quality as *nondirective counseling*. In nondirective counseling, the practitioner supports and follows the lead of the client. The counselor does not support the client's efforts by simply being reassuring, but rather offers support by actively seeking to understand the client's whole experience and staying with the client through empathetic displays of sharing the client's sense of the experience.

The counselor's effort is directed toward trying to understand the client's world. This is done in each session by encouraging the client to first share his experiences and then to expand on his statements, delving deeper into his internal phenomena. While some humanistic interview sessions make use of direct questioning, others, such as Rogerian interviewing, rarely use questions. Rogers felt that questions, by their nature, indicate that the counselor is not "present with" the client and not connecting (Raskin and Rogers 1995). Whether questioning is used or not, the counselor must make every effort to attune himself with the client from the initial minutes of the session and follow him through all the experiences and emotions that the client expresses throughout the session. Both the client and the counselor engage in fully experiencing this counseling session in the "here and now." Solutions for the client's issues are viewed not as the responsibility of the counselor, but rather as a natural outcome that will appear as a result of the client and counselor both trusting and having faith in the superior force of the client's self-actualizing tendencies.

Some physical techniques used to convey trust, empathy, nonjudgmental caring, and genuineness are reflection, eye contact, and mirroring of physical expressions of emotions. *Reflection* refers primarily to verbal recounting by the counselor of what the client is saying. The counselor attempts to echo the content and feelings expressed by the client, though not necessarily using the same words. Eye contact, leaning toward the client, and other physical signs of intimate, understanding communication are also displayed by the counselor. Mirroring of the client's body language is another technique used to demonstrate empathy with the client and his present condition. The mirroring should not be mechanistic, although it may seem artificial when counselors are first learning nondirective counseling. Non-directive counseling in its highest form is not mechanistic or manipulative. It is more like a dance between the counselor and client in which the client leads and the counselor follows. The pair moves together, engaged by the tempo of a common experiencing of the client's situation. The manifestation of this shared experiencing of the client's universe involves acceptance of the client's view, and affirmation of the client's values, desires, and sense of self, which all serve to implement the counseling goals.

Assessment and evaluation of progress are also centered in the client in this model. Because one of the goals of the humanistic model is to encourage the client to make evaluations based on her own personal criteria rather than basing them on what others think, it is inappropriate for the counselor to use psychological testing for purposes of diagnosis or assessment. Evaluation of progress in sessions is also the prerogative of the client, and the client's willingness to express and act on her own self-evaluations is in itself a positive indicator of progress. The counselor may encourage self-assessment by advising the client to keep a journal for the purpose of self-understanding, but assessment techniques that result in outside evaluation, such as testing, are not employed.

Client-centered counseling assumes that self-understanding and development can be achieved if the client learns to trust his personal judgments, ideas, feelings, and decisions. Encouraging the client to trust the self, and the use of nondirective counseling, requires that the counselor trust the self-actualizing tendencies of the client and have faith in both the client and the process. This trust is demonstrated through the therapist's practice of genuineness, nonjudgmental caring, and empathy within the therapeutic relationship. The client–counselor relationship serves as a nurturing environment for the client's personal change as well as serving as a model for other relationships in the client's life.

The Humanistic Model in Sport Psychology

We have seen how the basic concepts and goals of each theoretical model determine how the athlete's problems are defined and the type of interventions used to solve the client's issues. Theory not only influences practice when working with athletes in applied settings, but also influences the research methods used to assess the efficacy of interventions. For example, the psychodynamic model's perspective that one's past, especially childhood, establishes present personal dynamics lends itself to using case studies for research; while behavioral perspectives, with their emphasis on observable behavior and environmental influences, are inclined toward empirical methods of research. Likewise, the humanistic view's emphasis on the value of the person and self-actualization have promoted qualitative research methods in sport psychology.

In addition to shaping research methods, theory also leads the practitioner to attend to particular aspects of the client's person and situation in helping him with performance issues, and it suggests ways to explain the client's issues. Research grounded in the humanistic model is disposed toward investigations of themes central to the model—self-actualization, meaning in the experience of sport, self-development, and peak moments in sport.

Research Methods and the Humanistic Model

The quest for acceptance as "scientific" disciplines has dominated both of sport psychology's parent disciplines, psychology and physical education. This valuing of the "scientific" has resulted in adoption of empirical methods as the gold standard for research in these disciplines. Emphasis on "objectivity" via empirical studies fostered the illusion that human beings can be accurately studied as objects or things without regard to the complexity of the entirety of human nature.

As the humanistic perspective gained credibility, it challenged the underlying assumptions of the empirical model. It challenged the objectivity and generalizability of the empirical paradigm (Wilber 1996) in addition to challenging the notion that quantification of human behavior through empirical experiments is the only path to knowledge about human beings. The humanistic movement is one of several that supported alternative methods of inquiry centered on treating individuals as unique human beings rather than as objects. Qualitative methods of inquiry were developed that conceptualized the individual not as a subject, but as a participant in cooperative inquiry. These alternative research paradigms encourage participation of the individuals being studied as "co-investigators" and argue that research should be of value and use to all participants, including those who are the center of the inquiry.

The new research paradigms support investigations of personal meaning and values as well as phenomenological descriptions of personal actions. Phenomena that cannot be observed and measured in quantified units, such as personal stories, are legitimate topics for investigation in qualitative paradigms because they advance knowledge by revealing the richness of the human experience. By expanding the scope and methodology of research, the humanistic perspective is making significant contributions to human knowledge. However, recognition of this contribution is both recent and localized rather than universally accepted.

Consequently, while the volume of qualitative, humanistically oriented research is growing, it has not reached equal proportions with empirical studies in peer-reviewed journals. An electronic search of the PsychInfo database in which the descriptor "sport psychology" is combined with the descriptor "qualitative research" returned zero entries before 1985. After 1985 there are several research studies, such as Scanlan, Stein, and Ravizza's studies of sources of enjoyment and stress in figure skaters (1989a, 1989b, 1991), and Gould, Finch, and Jackson's two 1993 studies of coping strategies and stress in figure skaters. At least three articles specifically addressing the place of qualitative research in sport psychology have been published since 1985—Dale 1996; Krane, Andersen, and Strean 1997; and Strean 1998. While this is only a rough indication of research trends supported by the professional journals, it does indicate the strong influence of empirical research in the sport psychology literature until the late 1980s and a recent trend toward recognizing the legitimacy of qualitative research. These articles indicate growing interest in expanding research methodologies in sport psychology to include qualitative methods reflecting the humanistic perspective of studying the whole athlete and investigating sport from a phenomenological perspective (Dale 1996).

Many paradigms of research are encompassed by the qualitative label, and qualitative studies employ diverse approaches. However, there are two humanistic tenets that are common to most of the varieties of qualitative research. One is an emphasis on studying the "whole" with all its complexities and various perspectives. Unlike most quantitative studies, which seek to isolate variables so they can be manipulated and measured, qualitative investigators are interested in entire, intact phenomena. As Strean points out, "much of qualitative inquiry is based on a coherence theory of knowledge, which suggests that there are multiple maps of the world as it is experienced. The transformational move (from quantitative to qualitative methodologies) is that we are no longer in the business of trying to discover the one correct map. Rather, we are seeking to construct a useful one" (1998, p. 334).

The second humanistic tenet reflected in qualitative studies is a concern with individual human experiences in specific contexts. There is a recognition that each athlete gives meaning to his experiences and that those meanings are shaped by individual perceptions and social constructions. Examination of both internal processes of the individual athlete and the external social milieu are important to most qualitative studies. In discussing this issue in context of the phenomenological interview, Dale writes, "proponents of existential phenomenology would view an athlete as being indissolubly linked to his or her world whether it be in practice or competition. The two (athlete and world) do not exist apart from each other and each individual and his or her world are said to co-constitute one another, which is another way of saying you cannot really talk about an athlete without talking of his or her world" (1996, p. 309).

While several authors have argued for increased acceptance of both qualitative studies and diverse methodologies within this rubric, acceptance of qualitative work in sport psychology is evolving slowly. There are several reasons for this slow evolution. One is the time-consuming nature of conducting qualitative studies, and another is questions regarding validity and reliability of these studies. Acceptance in professional journals is also an issue, and while there is certainly more acceptance of qualitative studies now than in the past, there seems to be a strong bias for quantitative studies in the literature.

This bias has resulted in qualitative studies having to justify the rigor of nonempirical approaches as part of the submitted manuscript. Krane, Andersen, and Strean suggest that this trend of providing detailed justifications for employing qualitative methods is unnecessary, not practiced in other disciplines, and detrimental to publication of qualitative research in sport psychology (1997). Lengthy defenses and justifications of qualitative procedures substantially increase the length of manuscripts that have to compete for limited space in journals. These authors acknowledge that studies must present adequate descriptions of methodology, but if qualitative studies are to expand, their presentation should be streamlined to exclude detailed justification for employing qualitative methods. The fact that researchers are calling for an end to defending and justifying qualitative methods indicates increased acceptance of these studies as legitimate paths to knowledge in the discipline of sport psychology.

Qualitative research techniques contribute to the applied practice of sport psychology as well as to its research. In the realm of applied professional practice, the need for both objective, technical knowledge and subjective, reflective knowledge are seen as critical competencies (Harris 1993). A competent sport psychologist must have the technical knowledge necessary to design an athlete's mental training program based on empirical research, as well as the skills to engage athletes in reflective introspection of their performance experiences. The skills necessary to access athletes' subjective experiences are critical to the task of personalizing mental skills training programs to serve individual athletes.

While there are common elements in many mental training programs, sport psychology is not a "one program fits all" profession. Professional practice is both a science and an art, and excellence in practice requires competency in both the objective and subjective realms. Formal study of the subjective experiences of athletes is a necessary foundation for understanding the variety of experiences, and methods for revealing those experiences, encountered in athletics. Sport psychologists must study the subjective experiences of other athletes to expand and balance the sport psychologist's own subjective experience in athletics. Recognizing that it would be a mistake to assume that one's clients' subjective experiences mirror the practitioner's experience, the formal study of the vast range of subjective experiences reported by athletes in different sports, at different levels of competency and of various personal characteristics (gender, race, and so on), becomes evident. Qualitative research provides practitioners with insight into another person's meaningful experiencing.

The study of athletes' experiences is also useful to the sport psychologist in acquiring the communication skills necessary to tap into a client's experiential world. Attention to the nuances of language, the art of asking questions, listening, and interpretive skill sets can be enhanced by study of the subjective aspects of sport revealed in qualitative research. Study of exemplary qualitative studies by itself will not necessarily translate into improved skills in the reader, but analyzing the questioning techniques and interpretive skills presented in qualitative research is a good way to become acquainted with various approaches to accessing the inner world of the client. It can expand the practitioner's repertoire of ways to assist athletes in reflecting on their experiences.

Ravizza's research on peak experience, especially in baseball, is a prime example of the blending of art and science—of subjective and objective—in sport psychology (1990). His work is based on an educational philosophy that blends both the humanistic and behavioral traditions. He says that "researchers investigating peak experience have relied primarily on a two-step research strategy, the first step involving detailed athlete interviews which described these psychological phenomena. In the second step, the researcher rigorously analyzed the content of the interviews and attempted to extract its major characteristics. . . . This type of phenomenological technique for studying psychological experience works best when used as a preliminary research technique, followed by behavioristic measures such as standardized psychological inventories" (p. 459). Serial employment of selected aspects of both the humanistic and behavioral models in research and practice offers an interesting, nondoctrinaire approach to sport psychology. In his work, Ravizza successfully approaches research and practice by touching both the subjective and objective bases.

Meaning, the Sporting Experience, and the Humanistic Model

Historically, the discipline of psychology is the child of two older areas of study, philosophy and physiology. From physiology, psychology captured Freud and Pavlov, among others. The connection between physiology and psychology is evident, for example, when we trace the discovery of classical conditioning, a basic tenet of the behavioral model, directly to Pavlov's studies of digestion.

In contrast to the behavioral and cognitive rooting in physiology, the humanistic model expresses more of the philosophical origins of psychology, with its emphasis on meaning, experience, and the nature of human beings. One of the legacies of the philosophical orientation of the humanistic model is the development of a distinctly humanistic philosophy of sport that forms a foundation for the humanistic model of sport psychology. This philosophy views sport as an expression of the human spirit. It is more concerned with the sporting experience as a meaningful process than an outcome. Humanistic views of sport emphasize the game more as a path toward fulfillment, joy, and the playful expression of human happiness than as a path to self-aggrandizement, winning at all costs, or financial betterment. Balance is sought between the instrumental and expressive aspects of the game, as well as a prioritization of quality-of-life issues, self-fulfillment, and liberation of the individual spirit ahead of trophies, fame, and superiority over one's opponents.

In the humanistic tradition, the essence of sport, competition, is defined in a specialized way. Rather than conceptualizing competition as a "war" with one's adversary, it is looked upon as a cooperative venture in which "associates" (Simon 1983) agree to provide each other with the necessary resistance to catalyze development of each other's human potential. Competitors agree to respect each other's human worth and dignity by striving for excellence; to strive for equality of rights and opportunities by respecting the contest's rules; and to seek self-determination and growth by giving full effort (Burton-Nelson 1998). At the conclusion of the contest, both parties profit from the game, even though only one is the "winner." The humanistic contest has two scorecards, and the most important one is the reckoning of gains in the player's human potential. Individual advancement in skill and improved individual performance result from this conspiratorial struggle.

This conceptualization of competition flips the Western tradition of competition inside out. The contest and training for the contest are part of the process path leading toward the goal of skill advancement. Skill advancement is not seen as the process path toward the illegitimate goal of winning for winning's sake, but rather as a path toward self-actualization.

A corollary of this definition of competition is that success is self-determined and is not necessarily based on the final score of the contest. Putting forth one's best effort and improving on one's personal best performance or an aspect of that performance defines success in this context. A player is viewed as successful if her self-determined aspirations are met during the play, regardless of the final score. As a result of continued success in meeting one's self-determined goals, over time the final scores start to fall more and more in the player's favor. Each player plays the contest against herself as well as against the other side. This allows the individual athlete to set her own standards for judging the contest, and she is not judged solely by the mathematical standards of the scoreboard.

Self-Development, Sport, and the Humanistic Model

Self-assessment based on standards set by oneself is but one aspect of self-development promoted by humanism. The philosophical orientation of athletic competition, in which excellence is accessed through the struggle, logically leads to viewing sport as a tool for affecting many aspects of self-development and self-actualization. Due to the domination of empirical research methods in physical education, as well as sport psychology publications, most investigations of the relationship between development of self-concept and self-actualization through sport have attempted to quantify changes in self resulting from participation in sports. The application of quantitative empirical research methods to humanistic concepts is inherently difficult for two reasons. First, humanistic philosophy emphasizes "individual experiencing" and the personal meanings assigned to experience, while quantitative research is designed to identify patterns and differences among groups. Quantitative methods are designed to examine aggregate data, not specific data points. In fact, the power of quantitative studies rises with increasing numbers of subjects and declines as "N" moves toward one.

A second philosophical break between quantitative research methods and the humanistic model exists in the emphasis on isolation of variables. Quantitative methods are most elegant when the variables under study can be isolated and those extraneous to the study can be controlled or held constant. The humanistic model, however, is invested not in isolation of parts, but in wholeness. It is the complexities of the interacting parts of the whole that provides the focus of the humanistic perspective. This is not to say that empirical studies should not be done on humanistic constructs. However, empirical studies should not be the only research methodology used.

In spite of the philosophical discrepancies between humanism and empirical research, most of the research relating to sports participation, self-development, and performance has pragmatically employed quantitative methods in order to get published. It is hoped that future qualitative studies will be done to add to our knowledge of the complexities of self-development through sport.

The earliest empirical work on the relationship between self and performance was done by Fitts (1965, 1972). He designed an instrument called the Fitts Tennessee Self-Concept Scale (TSCS) to test changes in self-concept and provide norms for different populations. In his studies, he found that a favorable self-concept correlates positively with effective performance, and that when two individuals have equal ability, the one with the higher self-concept will perform better. The positive relationship between self-concept and performance was ascribed to increases in positive expectations for a successful outcome and to decreases in negative emotions, such as anxiety. A positive self-concept can be viewed as both a precursor and a consequence of effective performance in that it can mediate negative thoughts and tension, thereby promoting better performances. Better performances then serve to increase and reinforce self-concept, setting up an interactive spiral that enhances the self through positive experiences (Howard and Reardon 1986).

Empirical investigations of self-actualization most often employ Shostrom's Personal Orientation Inventory (SPOI), a paper and pencil test designed to measure Maslow's concept of self-actualization. Studies employing the SPOI to measure self-actualization in sports participation have produced mixed results. Magill (1975) found that male college baseball players scored significantly higher than the SPOI norms for college students, indicating that they were more self-actualized than the general population. Subsequent studies by Ibrahim and Morrison (1976) and Gundersheim (1982) revealed a different and more complex story. Ibrahim and Morrison compared 100 male and female athletes to 100 male and female nonathletes on the TSCS measure of self-concept and the SPOI test of self-actualization at both the high school and college levels. This study concluded, "athletes in general . . . tend to be less than average in their concepts of their physical self, moral-ethical self, personal self, family self and social self. On the other hand, they tend to be either average or above average in their self-actualizing traits" (p. 78). However, there seemed to be no significant differences in self-concept or self-actualization between female athletes and nonathletes at the high school level, and between male athletes and nonathletes at the college level. Significant differences were found between high school male athletes and nonathletes in both self-concept and self-actualization, with the nonathletes testing closer to the tests' suggested norms. Significant differences between college female athletes and nonathletes on the self-actualization scales showed the female athletes to be closer to the tests' standardized norms on the inner-directed, self-actualizing values, flexibility in applying values, sensitivity to personal needs, view of humans as essentially good, and appreciation of the synergy of opposites scales.

Gundersheim's 1982 self-actualization investigation compared male and female athletes in several different sports, as well as comparing them with male and female nonathletes ($N = 399$). He found no differences in self-actualization of male or female athletes based on participation in different sports. Additionally, while the total female sample (athletes and nonathletes) was more self-actualized than the total male sample, further analysis suggested that the difference was primarily due to the difference between female and male athletes, with the female athletes being more self-actualized. Comparisons between male athletes and nonathletes and between female athletes and nonathletes showed no differences, suggesting that athletic participation did not promote or restrict self-actualization.

Schindler and Waters (1986) also used the SPOI to examine whether there are differences in self-actualization among males and females who engage in different levels of athletic activity. Their study compared college male and female team athletes with recreational athletes and nonathletes. Results indicated that in general, females were more self-actualized than males, regardless of athletic involvement. Furthermore, while male athletes scored better than male nonathletes, athletic involvement did not seem to affect female self-actualization. In opposition to Gundersheim's conclusion that there is not sufficient evidence to show that athletes are more self-actualized than nonathletes, Schindler and Waters claim that the research generally shows athletes are more self-actualized. As the debate on this important issue continues, empirical researchers will have to tighten up their operational definitions of "athletes" and "nonathletes," as well as employ multistudy strategies to tease out the significant differences. At this point, the "one-shot" studies offer conflicting stories regarding the impact of sport participation on self-actualization. Qualitative studies may also shed some light on this issue and generate more hypotheses regarding the relationships between sport and self-actualization.

While the self-actualization and sport empirical studies are contradictory, there is considerable scholarly discourse in the literature regarding the relationship between sport participation and self-development. Many scholars, including Martens (1975), Orlick (1975), Kleiber (1983), and Shields and Bredamier (1995), have written about the capacity of the sporting experience to both enhance and degrade the self, depending on the characteristics of the experience. Salient aspects of the sporting experience that affect whether the self will be positively or negatively affected include parental behavior (Shields and Bredamier 1995), coaching behavior (Smoll and Smith 1984), and degree of athlete control over the contest (Kleiber 1983). The prevailing view is that while sports participation, in and of itself, does not assure positive self-development in any sphere—physical, moral, cognitive, or emotional—sport can be a powerful and effective means to develop the self if it is organized with emphasis on development of athletes. Sport as an activity has the requisite characteristics—intense emotional involvement, capacity for social connection, sense of importance, and mass popularity—to be a powerful venue for both positive and negative aspects of self-development (Oglesby 1987; Frost 1974).

Although attempts to quantitatively prove that sport is a positive path toward self-development and actualization have not been successful, the hypothesis that self is impacted in lasting ways by sports participation remains viable. Qualitative investigations of this question may yet confirm the experiences and anecdotes reported by hundreds of athletes regarding the impact of sport on self. Future research will likely uncover both positive and negative relationships between sport and development, including information that will identify specific sport practices necessary for sport to be an enhancing experience.

Emotional Experiences in Sport and the Humanistic Model

Because the humanist views the athlete as a whole being, emotional arousal is viewed in terms of the Gestalt phenomenological experience of the athlete. In the humanistic model, emotions are not isolated from physical, cognitive, or spiritual aspects of the performance. Conceptualization of emotional arousal in the humanistic model tends to be broader and more inclusive of aspects of the totality of the sporting experience, including aspects of the context and environment. Additionally, the humanistic emphasis on self and individuality is reflected in conceptualization of emotional arousal in sport. Two conceptualizations of emotional arousal that employ humanistic principles are Kerr's reversal theory (1997) and Hanin's individual zones of optimal functioning (1994).

According to Kerr, reversal theory "(a) is a *general theory* applicable to diverse areas of psychological investigation; (b) is a *phenomenologically based* theory concerned with subjective processes, cognition and affect, and the experience of one's own motivations; (c) is *structural* in the sense that phenomenological experience is thought to be influenced by certain structures and patterns; (d) posits that human beings are *inherently inconsistent* in their behaviour; and (e) argues that alternation or *reversing* between paired *metamotivational states* forms the basis of human personality and motivation" (Kerr 1997, p. 9). These reversals between metamotivational states can be triggered by environmental events, personal frustration regarding lack of satisfaction, and satiation. Reversal theory views arousal as "the degree to which an individual feels him- or herself to be worked up or emotionally intense about what one is doing" (Apter 1989, as cited in Kerr 1997, p. 90). It is termed "felt arousal" because it is based on the individual's subjective experience. Studies of arousal based on reversal theory suggest that "successful performance is characterized by high levels of felt arousal which are experienced by the performers as positive, pleasant, and nonstressful. In addition, those who performed successfully were consistently more able than less successful performers to achieve and maintain their preferred levels of felt arousal when performing" (Kerr, p. 92).

Hanin's (1994) individual zones of optimal functioning (IZOF) conceptualization of athletes' emotional experiences in sport is another example of a humanistically oriented perspective of arousal. IZOF emphasizes individuality. It views each athlete as possessing an optimal range of emotional arousal for individual peak performance. For some athletes the zone of optimal arousal may be low, but for others it may be moderate or high. The main determinant is the individual athlete, rather than the task or situational variables, and there are no "universal" levels of arousal that apply to groups of athletes. Exploration of each athlete's personal experience with different levels of arousal and subsequent performance is necessary to determine optimal arousal for specific sports tasks. Once peak performance emotional states are identified for the athlete, methods to induce those ideal states are devised.

Research on IZOF generally takes the form of asking athletes to recount how they felt during their "greatest experience" in sport. Delving into reminiscences of an athlete's "greatest experience" in sport is often followed up with exploration of his "worst moment" in sport to contrast the emotional climates of these experiences. Investigations using this technique have shown that while athletes do have individual profiles of their emotional experiences in sport, there are also some common denominators—qualities that recur in many descriptions of peak athletic experiences.

"The Zone"

The humanistic emphasis on individual uniqueness, self-actualization, and unity of person is reflected in its approach to state-of-consciousness components of athletic performance, particularly peak moments in sport. Athletes commonly refer to exceptional sport experiences as "being in the zone." *The zone* is a fuzzy, nebulous term that exemplifies the inherent problem of attempting to use language to convey the essence of a subjective experience. The words athletes and researchers rely on to convey the qualities of these subjective experiences are often imprecise by scientific standards and possess connotative meanings specialized to the individual speaker. Consequently, there is a certain amount of imprecision and "wiggle" in research about exceptional performance because the words used to describe it are not "locked" into place. Efforts to define the terms describing exceptional moments in sport—*peak experience, peak performance,* and *flow*—have been only partially successful in sorting out the research in this area. McInman and Grove suggest that researchers adopt the umbrella term *peak moments* to describe this general area of research (1991). While distinct definitions of each of these terms are evolving as the research expands on this topic, the terms continue to be used interchangeably by athletes, the press, and, sometimes, by sport psychology researchers. Unfortunately, this lack of standardized definitions confounds the literature on this topic, but it is worthwhile to attempt to sort out these three concepts (McInman and Grove 1991).

Peak Performance

Peak performance is viewed as "behavior in any activity that transcends what normally could be expected in that situation" (Privette 1981, p. 51). It is characterized by full focus on the task and a strong sense of self succeeding in a challenge. The focus on self and success in the struggle is the primary focus of peak performance, and the importance of other people to the outcome of the transaction is relegated to the background of the athlete's attention (Privette and Bundrick 1987, p. 317). Peak performance refers to a high *level* of functioning rather than a *type* of experience. Therefore, its phenomenological characteristics may vary from one activity to another. For example, the phenomenological characteristics of peak performance when giving a speech may vary from those experienced during peak performance when playing a musical instrument. Privette identified the following peak performance characteristics (1981, p. 51):

1. Clear focus on the task
2. Intrinsic interest in or fascination with succeeding at the task
3. Intentionality
4. Self-absorbed involvement
5. Spontaneity
6. Superior performance

Peak performance represents behavior that is among the personal best performances of an athlete in a given situation. It is not limited to an athlete's absolute best performance, but rather describes superior performance within a given context. An athlete might count her best performances in a national competition and her best performances in an international competition as peak performances. Similarly, a golfer might have a peak performance experience for match play that is distinct from his peak performance in stroke play. Consequently, an athlete can have peak performance experiences in different contexts, as well as serial peak performances in each context as she establishes new personal bests.

While it is the high level of accomplishment that distinguishes peak performance from peak experience by definition, there are also other components that characterize peak performance. Privette (1983) offers a topology of peak experience, peak performance, and flow. Selected characteristics of each peak moment are presented in figures 4.2, 4.3, and 4.4. In this topology, clarity of focus is unique to peak performance. This focus includes maintaining a strong sense of self, along with focus on the task.

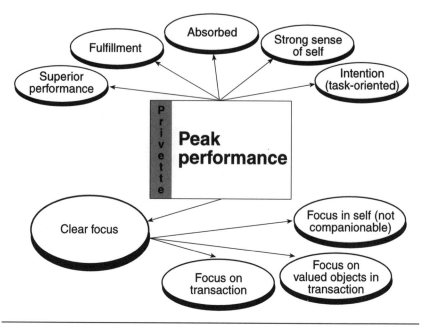

Figure 4.2 Privette's components of peak performance (1983).

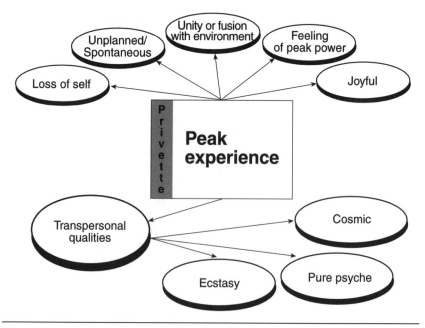

Figure 4.3 Privette's components of peak experience (1983).

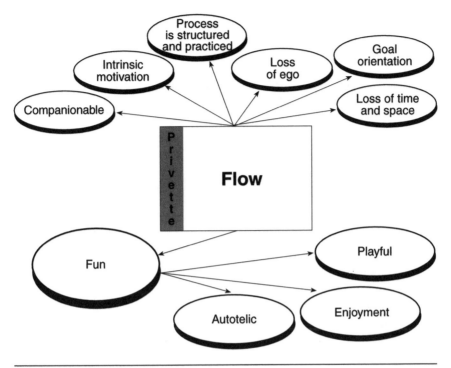

Figure 4.4   Privette's components of flow (1983).

Peak Experience

Peak experience is operationally defined as "a subjective experiencing of what is subjectively recognized to be one of the high points of life, one of the most exciting, rich, and fulfilling experiences which the person has ever had" (Thorne 1963, p. 248). It has an unique "mystic or transpersonal quality associated with fusion and loss of self" (Privette and Bundrick 1987, p. 317). Descriptors of peak experience include joyfulness, transcendence, and heightened awareness that result in personal integration, growth, and expansion of personal identity. The experience can be described as an emotional or spiritual high point that can override concerns about the results obtained.

Controversy exists in the research literature regarding two important aspects of peak experience. The first is whether peak experience must be accompanied by optimal performance, and the second is centered on the frequency of peak experience in athletics. Anecdotally, some athletes have reported "zoning out" that did not result in their best performances. However, Ravizza (1984) implies that during peak experience "the participant is performing optimally" (p. 453). Additionally, most descriptions of peak experience by athletes also tend to imply that the experience accompanies a high level of performance (Privette 1981; Jackson 1992). Most models recognize that peak experience can occur with or without peak performance. Thorne's model of peak experience recognizes multiple categories of peak experience that allow for peak experience phenomena both with and without personal best performance. He classifies peak experience into the following six categories (1963, pp. 249-250):

1. Sensual peak experiences that include optimum satisfaction of the senses, such as eating a gourmet meal
2. Cognitive peak experiences or adventures of the mind, such as creating, inventing, understanding, and intellectual discovery
3. Climax peak experiences, such as mystical spiritual experiences
4. Self-actualizing peak experiences in which people sense that they have been all that they can be
5. Emotional peak experiences, such as falling in love and feelings of euphoria and elation
6. Conative or growth peak experiences that include personal best performances

Within this model an athlete could have a self-actualizing peak experience while performing with or without a conative peak experience involving best performance.

Privette and Bundrick's 1987 model of feeling and performance also allows distinction of peak experience with and without peak performance (see figure 4.5). This model uses two intersecting scales to model peak and nadir episodes. The vertical scale is an affective or feeling scale with ecstasy on the north pole and misery on the south pole. The horizontal scale is a performance scale with "total failure" on the west pole and "personal best" on the east pole. In this model, the upper left quadrant represents a positive affective state accompanied by low performance, while the upper right quadrant represents a positive affective state accompanied by high performance.

The frequency with which peak experience occurs in sports is also an open question. Ravizza (1984, p. 453) refers to them as "rare moments," while athletes such as NFL player David Meggyesy claim that "not only are zone experiences common among athletes, but they become more common the higher the level of play" (Cooper 1998). There is some agreement, however, that peak experiences in sport become more frequent as skill level increases, so that elite athletes have more peak experiences than novice athletes. Ravizza states that a precondition to a peak experience is mastery of the basic skills of the sport, and there seems to be some consensus in the literature on this point (1984).

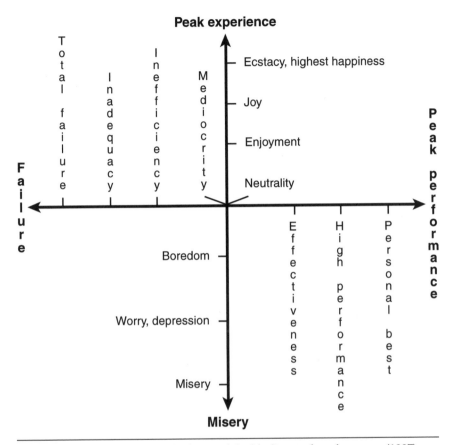

Figure 4.5 Privette and Bundrick's model of feeling and performance (1987).

(Reprinted by permission, from Privette, G. and C. Bundrick. 1987. Measurement of experience: Constructs and content validity of the experience questionnaire. *Perceptual and Motor Skills* 65: 315-332.)

Related to the issue of frequency of peak experience is whether athletes can be trained to induce peak experiences on demand. There is no research directly addressing this controversy, and sport psychologists occupy positions on both sides of this issue. For example, Keith Henschen, an applied sport psychologist at the University of Utah, has developed a program using techniques from the martial arts, psychology, and meditation designed to help athletes enter "the zone" more frequently. Bob Rotella, a respected sport psychologist specializing in golf, disagrees with Henschen's premise and claims peak experience "happens when it happens," and trying to force it makes it less likely to happen (Cooper 1998).

Components of peak experience include: a focused awareness that is present centered and narrow; a sense of unforced control of self and the environment that includes self-confidence; and a transcendence of self-reflecting harmony, nonjudgment, and effortlessness (Ravizza 1984). Figure 4.6 illustrates characteristics associated with peak experience in sport from Ravizza's 1984 research.

Flow

Flow is a concept employed by Csikszentmihalyi to describe immersion and pleasured involvement in a task that is intrinsically rewarding. The examination of flow in sport is an outgrowth of Csikszentmihalyi's larger research agenda on human happiness. In discussing flow in sport, Jackson and Csikszentmihalyi (1999) declare that flow is "a state of consciousness where one becomes totally absorbed in what one is doing to the exclusion of all other thoughts and emotions. So flow is about focus. More than just focus, however, flow is a harmonious experience where mind and body

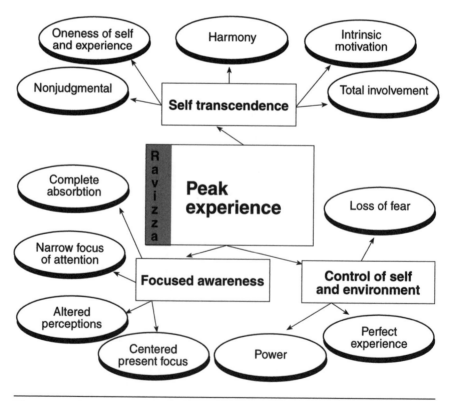

Figure 4.6 Ravizza's characteristics of peak experience (1984).

are working together effortlessly, leaving the person feeling that something special has just occurred. So flow is also about enjoyment" (p. 5). The terms *enjoyment* and *optimal experience* are used synonymously with the term *flow* in Jackson and Csikszentmihalyi's writings, indicating the importance of both pleasure and gratification in the flow experience.

Jackson and Csikszentmihalyi identify nine prerequisites or components of the flow state (they are also represented in figure 4.7):

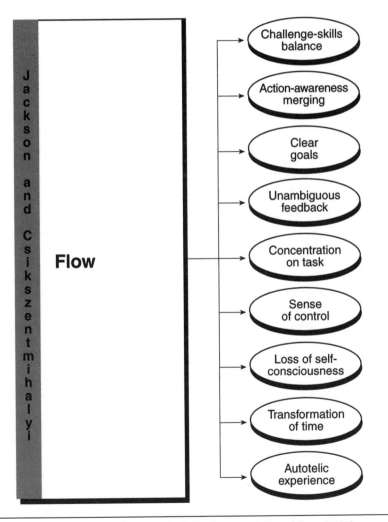

Figure 4.7 Jackson and Csikszentmihalyi's characteristics of flow (1999).

- *A balance between the athlete's perception of the challenge of the situation and the athlete's skills or resources.* This challenge–skills balance, or C–S balance, is characterized not only by a perceived equilibrium between the task and resources but also by a perception that both the task and the skills necessary for success will require the athlete to expand her personal limits and "push the envelope." This expansion of the limits of one's current talent produces a stress that is necessary for the flow experience. However, the C–S balance, as perceived by the athlete, makes the experience eustressful and positive, rather than distressful and fearful.

- *The merging of action and awareness.* In flow there is a blending of the body's movements with the mind's consciousness that produces a sense of total unity. The mind is so totally absorbed in the immediate activity that self-consciousness ceases to exist. All thought processes are immersed in the activity and movement, as the mind's eye becomes the body's eye. There is more than just a sense of totality of the self, however. The merging of action and awareness produces a blending of body, mind, and spirit of self with the immediate environment. The self and the situation are embedded in each other so that the immediate environment seems like an extension of one's self. The athlete's equipment and the sporting arena are enveloped within this sense of self.

- *Clear goals.* The focus so necessary for the flow state results in part from the athlete's total commitment to clear, specific goals. Goals allow the athlete to devote full attention to implementing his intentions, and he can be confident that he knows what to do. They reduce the need to think about decisions regarding what should be done and focus on getting the job accomplished. Optimal goals are not just verbalized. They are assimilated by the athlete to the point that he can visualize himself performing the exact actions that are needed to accomplish his goals. Goals also provide a regulating mechanism for moment-to-moment feedback by allowing the athlete to match his goal vision with what is happening in real time. If what is happening in the competition matches the athlete's goal vision, the athlete is reassured that all is going according to plan, and confidence is reinforced. If there is a mismatch, the athlete will be alerted to it early and can adjust to bring the performance back to the goal vision.

- *Unambiguous feedback.* Athletes cannot discern progress toward their goals without objective, concrete feedback. This feedback can come from many sources, and the athlete is aware of the different sources of feedback available during performance, although she may not attend to all of them. The two primary sources of feedback during performance are *kinesthetic feedback* from the athlete's own body and *outcome feedback* from the competition itself. Coaches, spectators, and teammates provide additional sources of feedback for the athlete. Qualities of the feedback, such as continuous or discrete, immediate or delayed, and specific or general, vary from situation to situation, and athletes must learn how to respond to different types. Athletes must have a plan for utilizing feedback that includes which feedback will be attended to and how to respond to negative feedback. Not all feedback, even during flow episodes, will be positive, and negative feedback can be useful to the athlete if she knows how to process it so it enhances rather than detracts from her performance.

• *Concentration on the immediate task.* Concentration is the ability to devote all of one's attention to the pertinent cues needed to accomplish the task at hand. It requires the athlete to focus on relevant events in the present and be alert to "now" or the present moment rather than the past or future. It requires total immersion in only those aspects of the present that are germane to accomplishing the task at hand. Athletes are often required to concentrate for long periods of time, so it is a skill that must be practiced. Paradoxically, while the athlete must concentrate while performing, concern or worry about being able to concentrate is counterproductive. Focusing and refocusing plans that bring the athlete's consciousness into engagement with pertinent stimuli of the task are more likely to produce concentration than verbal orders from the coach, self, or others to "concentrate!"

• *Sense of control.* Athletes who experience flow have total confidence that their efforts will produce the results they desire. This sense of being in control of self and all aspects of the situation is founded on the athlete's "knowing" that his skills are sufficient for accomplishing the task. Athletes most often describe this sense of control as being "effortless," and while there is a real sense of being instrumental in the flow of events, there is no sense of "forcing" things to go as planned. While the athlete's sense of control over self and the situation are complete, perfectionism is not a part of the sense of control. Perfectionism is more likely to make the athlete feel inadequate than in control. Obtaining control includes knowing what aspects of the performance are "controllable" and what aspects must be "let go." The athlete must have a sense of trust that those aspects of the performance that are uncontrollable will not harm him or derail progress toward his goals.

• *Loss of self-consciousness.* Athletes who have experienced flow often speak about losing themselves in the action. Loss of self-consciousness is best described as an absence of worry or concern for one's self. The athlete is nonjudgmental about herself and is not concerned about others' judgments of her performance. Self-doubt is absent because confidence in the self is strong. Loss of self-consciousness and self-judgment does not mean that the athlete is not self-aware. Paradoxically, while in flow, athletes report that they are totally in tune with their bodies and their movements. They are aware of how the performance is unfolding, and they continually observe the match or mismatch between their performance goals and the moment-to-moment unfolding of the performance. However, this mindfulness is not accompanied by negative emotions or fears about their personal worth. There is no concern or threat to the athlete's ego. Loss of self-consciousness is closely aligned with other components of flow, such as the merging of action and awareness, clear goals, and sense of control. These components blend together to create an immersion in the process of the performance and a sureness or sense of trust that the outcome will be favorable.

• *Transformation of time.* The total task absorption characteristic of flow also contributes to a sense of time distortion for the athlete. During flow, time can be either slowed down, causing the athlete to feel unhurried even in the frenzy of the competition; or it can be sped up, causing the athlete to feel that a four-hour marathon passed quickly. Athletes often report other distortions during flow such as enlargement of a target (for example, the basketball hoop or golf hole seems bigger). These distortions are not easily understood, but it is hypothesized that they may be a by-product of total concentration (Jackson and Csikszentmihalyi 1999, p. 29).

• *Autotelic experience.* An *autotelic experience* is a happening that is so pleasurable that it is worth doing simply for the enjoyment it brings to the athlete. Above all, athletes report that flow episodes are fun, rewarding, and enjoyable. The experience of flow is self-reinforcing, and once it is experienced, the athlete will seek the pleasure of that experience repeatedly. The sheer enjoyment of the activity motivates the athlete to continue practicing and playing. The activity itself is intrinsically motivating, and external rewards are reduced to a position of secondary motivators.

While these nine characteristics have been isolated and identified as factors of the flow state, they do not operate independently. They appear to be synergistic, although the exact nature of their interactions is unknown at this time. Identification of these characteristics is an important first step in understanding flow state of consciousness. Research to identify techniques for nurturing these characteristics in athletes, so that flow can be experienced more often and by more individuals in sport, is the next step in enhancing the athletic experience.

In the completed research that attempted to distinguish among peak performances, peak experiences, and flow, there appear to be connections or interactions between these concepts. Cooper examined "the zone" as part of his exploration of the spiritual dimensions of sports (1998). In his discussion of the zone, he reports that Jackson's 1992 investigation of the flow concept among elite athletes indicates that "optimal subjective experience is key in the enhancement of an athlete's performance" (p. 32). A majority of the 28 world-class athletes in Jackson's study believed that flow was necessary for peak performance, although they had difficulty distinguishing between flow and peak experience. Additionally, while they acknowledged that the flow state is elusive and cannot be attained on command, the athletes felt that they could predispose themselves for flow experiences through their mental and physical preparation (Cooper 1998).

Patterns of High Performance

Given the humanistic model's emphasis on individuality and sport's requirement for consistently high performance, it is surprising that the topic of individual patterns of high performance has received so little attention in sport. *High-performance patterns* are personal success patterns in which consistently high levels of performance are maintained over time by paying attention to individual and environmental qualities that foster high performance for an individual. High performance differs from peak performance in that it is a level of performance that is of high quality *and* sustainable. Peak performance, by definition, is not consistent. One builds toward the peak and hopes to "peak" at the most important competitions. But peak performance is not sustainable over long periods of time and certainly does not occur for every competition in a season. High performance, on the other hand, is necessary at every competition in a season in some sports in order to make it to postseason play. High-performance patterns attempt to identify components that contribute to optimal sustainable performance over the course of a sport season.

Uncovering an individual's high-performance patterns can be accomplished by asking the person to recall times in her life experience when a task or project worked better than expected. These experiences do not have to be experiences in sport, and it is often helpful if the experiences are drawn from various aspects of the individual's life. Three or four high-performance experiences are recorded in detail and then examined for common elements. It is the processes depicted in the stories rather than the content of the stories that is of interest. Once specific processes have been identified in each story, the results are compared and common elements are noted. These common elements become the basis for the individual's personal pattern of high performance.

Fletcher provides examples of the use of this technique in business, but the technique is applicable to sport as well (1993). One of the advantages of discovering one's patterns of high performance is that these patterns can be applied to all aspects of life. Fletcher states: "Each person has only one High Performance Pattern. Regardless of the nature or context of the activity in which the individual is engaged, he or she follows a consistent and unique sequence of specific actions when achieving his or her personal best. Each person's pattern is as unique as a fingerprint. Since it is so consistent, once the individual's pattern has been identified, it is a highly effective guide to future action. It maps out how the person can produce outstanding work consistently" (pp. 16-17).

High-performance patterns describe processes that have repeatedly worked for the individual in the past in different contexts. High-performance patterns map out how an individual gets drawn into an activity, how he handles the start-up, how he sustains momentum, and how he concludes or finishes a successful endeavor. These topics are not foreign to sport psychology, but the humanistic approach of viewing these topics in light of an individual's personal pattern that extends into other aspects of life is an unexplored aspect of the discipline.

Summary

1. The humanistic perspective focuses on the client as a self-actualizing human being. Self-actualization is viewed as a force within the individual that produces a striving for self-fulfillment and promotes efforts to become a fully functioning person. Humanistic theories tend to view human nature in a positive light. However, theorists such as Rollo May and others have also addressed the darker sides of human nature.

2. The *self* is a central concept in humanistic models. The self is a holistic conceptualization of the client and includes her thoughts, feelings, values, expectations, and ways of understanding the world. Of particular importance is how the individual views herself, or her self-concept. Humanists believe that peoples' behavior is influenced by their self-concept or self-image. Congruence between the behaving self and one's ideal self is an important goal of humanistic counseling.

3. Humanistic psychologists look at human behavior not only through the eyes of an observer, but also through the eyes of the person doing the behaving (Bustamante, Howe-Tennant, and Ramo, 1999). Consequently, how the client experiences the world is a major focus. Increasing openness, attentiveness, and flexibility of experiencing is a path toward fuller personal functioning. This emphasis on the perspective of the client logically results in the client having a major role in directing interventions.

4. Among the important characteristics to be nurtured in each client are self-awareness (including the ability to consciously experience life), free will to make decisions and judgments, and sociability.

5. The client's efforts toward self-actualization are nurtured by the counselor's expressions of genuineness, nonjudgmental caring, and empathy.

Process Plan for Lisa Irons's Case: Humanistic Perspective

It is difficult to outline an *a priori* process plan in much detail with this model because the client controls and directs most aspects of the counseling process. Decisions regarding what issues are to be discussed and how they should be resolved must be made by Lisa. She is also the authority regarding assessment of the benefits of different interventions. The practitioner provides confidence, trust, and support of Lisa's decisions and encourages her to trust herself.

The humanistic model is most attractive to individuals who are seeking a personal growth experience as well as relief from specific problems. This model is a person-centered approach rather than a problem-centered approach. Consequently, athletes who are only interested in solving a single, discrete problem may become impatient with humanistic emphasis on holistic explorations. Athletes who value holistic approaches and view problems as having personal contexts and connections to other aspects of self will value the humanistic emphasis on personal experience, self-development, and actualization.

Humanistic Interests in Lisa's Case Material

While Lisa must determine the direction of the counseling process, her case material suggests several general areas of interest to the humanistic counselor. A close reading of Lisa's autobiography suggests that she could benefit from a humanistic approach by reorienting her definition of personal success from others to herself. In her autobiography, she frequently judges herself by comparing herself to other athletes on the tour rather than setting her own criteria. Adoption of a task orientation to her golf performance rather than an ego or outcome orientation would assist Lisa in avoiding the disadvantages of social comparison and help her set her own criteria for self-evaluation. Additionally, changing her self-presentation style from depreciating to enhancing by acting more like her ideal self may encourage her to "fulfill" or live up to this more positive image of herself, resulting in more confidence and better performances.

Another general area of interest is Lisa's sense of self. Her autobiography presents a very narrow view of self, and consulting sessions might help expand Lisa's sense of self, identify her "ideal self" in greater detail, and examine ways to move her self toward her ideal self. Expanding her sense of self could include adding dimensions to her view of her self, as well as bringing aspects of her self into sharper focus. Most of her references to self in her autobiography are centered on her athletic self and herself as a daughter. There is little information on herself in relationships with others—as a friend or in romantic relationships. Sharpening the focus of her athletic self might include examining herself as a competitor, particularly her views of who or what she is competing against. How does she view herself out on the course? Is she a warrior, artist, or something else? Does she see herself as competing against the other players, or competing against the course? These are all questions she might ask herself in search of a self-definition that is in synchrony with her best performance state.

Another aspect of Lisa's athletic self is her view of her talent. Does she describe her talent as malleable and expandable, subject to growth through effort, or does she view it as a fixed, inherent ability that is out of her personal control? Expanding and focusing Lisa's athletic self can stimulate self-confidence by giving her an expanded vision of her potential and renewing her efforts to grow and self-actualize through her sport. Working toward more metaphysical life issues could give Lisa the impetus she needs to persist, make sport more valuable to her, and paradoxically lead to improved performance by concentrating on broader self issues.

Sample Interview with Lisa in the Rogerian Style

The humanistic model uses various interview methods as both interventions and as a component of qualitative research methodology. Interviews are the main approach used for capturing the experiential totality of the client's world. Rogers often presented his case studies and research in the form of verbatim dialogues and demonstration interviews. In keeping with this practice, the following script is presented as an example of person-centered interviewing. The script is adapted from a script quoted in Raskin and Rogers's presentation of person-centered counseling (1995). It has been adapted to Lisa Irons's case to demonstrate the interviewing approach of the humanistic perspective. When possible, I have used Rogers's exact words (designated by quotation marks), hoping to portray the tone of his technique accurately. Even though his comments are out of their original context, they are in a similar context and in keeping with the humanistic model. When it was necessary to change his words, I have tried to stay as close as possible to his original transcript.

Counselor 1:"OK, I think I'm ready. And you ... ready?"

Lisa 2: I think so.

Counselor 3: "I don't know what you might want to talk about, but I'm very ready to hear. We have half an hour, and I hope that in that half an hour we can get to know each other as deeply as possible, but we don't need to strive for anything. I guess that's my feeling. Do you want to tell me whatever is on your mind?"

Adapted by permission of the publisher, F.E. Peacock Publishers Inc., Itasca, Illinois. From R. Corsini and D. Wedding, *Current Psychotherapies*, 5th ed., 1995 copyright, pp. 144-147.

Lisa 4: My poor play is what's constantly on my mind. It's been going on for too long now, and I'm afraid I'm washed up as a professional golfer. I keep thinking about quitting—retiring. But I'm afraid of that, too. I feel guilty about being a quitter . . . and somewhat afraid of what to do after I leave golf.

Counselor 5: "A need to hang on to your golf career so you can kind of make up for the things you feel guilty about—is that part of it?"

Lisa 6: Yes. That's some of it. Letting my family and myself down because I have not been more successful. But as frustrating as playing badly on the tour is, I'm afraid that if I do retire, there will be this big void in my life. I know I can do other things, but I think the excitement will be gone.

Counselor 7: The old vacuum, sort of, when the competition's not there?

Lisa 8: Yes. I would like to just be able to retire, let go, and move on, but it's really hard when I have these doubts and guilty feelings.

Counselor 9: "It's very hard to give up something that's been so precious in your life, but also something that I guess has caused you pain when you mentioned guilt."

Lisa 10: Yes, I have devoted all of my life, it seems, to golf. And it has given me a lot, but I still need more from it. Part of me can see that it's unreasonable for me to expect that all my needs would be met from my career, but that doesn't make it any easier. I get angry, and in some ways I feel I have a right to get what I need because I have sacrificed so much and worked so hard.

Counselor 11: So it may be unreasonable, but still, when you don't get your needs met, it makes you mad.

Lisa 12: Yes I get angry . . . angry and scared and guilty, all at the same time.

Counselor 13: You're also feeling a lot of tension at this point, I guess.

Lisa 14: Yes, lots of conflict.

Counselor 15: Lots of conflict. Can you say anything more what that's about?

Lisa 16: Conflict in the sense of I don't know if I would be thinking about retiring if I were playing better. Yet I am 39, so maybe I am ready. My back pain is chronic; maybe I'm too old to play competitively—even though others are doing it. And it's hard to give up my dreams, to disappoint my parents.

Counselor 17: "It sounds like a very double feeling there." Part of it is "Damn, I want to play better and win." The other part of it is "I want to let go because golf is costing me too much in the form of pain and disappointment. It's not meeting my needs."

Lisa 18: Umm-hmm, yeah, I should be stronger—more determined. I should grow up and be a mature adult about making these decisions.

Counselor 19: But instead, sometimes you feel like a child.

Lisa 20: Yes, sometimes I just want someone to tell me what to do—to end my turmoil so I can get on with it. Other people seem to deal with their lives so easily, most people seem glad to retire. But this is hard for me.

PAUSE

Counselor 21: "But you place a lot of expectations on yourself: 'I should be different.'"

Lisa 22: Yeah, I should be more mature. I should have my needs met by me so that I don't have to get them met from golf.

Counselor 23: "You should find other ways and other sources to meet your needs, but somehow that doesn't seem to be happening?"

Lisa 24: Well, I'm confident that I can get lots of my needs met outside of golf. I mean, I'm having financial difficulties, but I'm not worried that I won't be able to eat and support myself outside of golf. But the things I get from golf are special … and very strong. I can't seem to get those needs met anywhere else.

Counselor 25: There are some things that you want that are just from golf.

Lisa 26: Yes, just from my career on the tour.

Counselor 27: But you haven't had any satisfaction for a time now; that's a very painful experience.

Lisa 28: Yes, that really hurts. It hurts deep.

PAUSE

Counselor 29: It looks like you're feeling some of that hurt right now.

Lisa 30: Yes, I feel I'm losing my golf—a big piece of me seems to be slipping away.

Counselor 31: "Umm-hmm. Umm-hmm."

PAUSE

Counselor 32: "Pulling away from you."

Lisa 33: Yes. Going away.

Counselor 34: "You feel it sort of slipping away and you … and it hurts … and—"

Lisa 35: Yeah, I'm just sort of sitting here alone. I guess, like you know, I can feel that it's gone and I'm just left here.

Counselor 36: Umm-hmm. You're experiencing it right now. That golf is gone, leaving you here all alone.

Lisa 37: Yeah, yeah. Yeah. I feel really lonely. [Cries]

Counselor 38: Umm-hmm. Umm-hmm. If I understand right, not lonely in every respect, but lonely for what your golf gives you.

Lisa 39: Yeah, yeah, lonely for all that.

Counselor 40: "I'm not a good therapist—I forgot a box of Kleenex, but ... I think I've got ... " [Laughs]

Lisa 41: Thank you. [Laughs] I feel I could cry a lot about that. [Laughs]

Counselor 42: "Umm-hmm, it feels as if the tears could just flow and flow on that score."

Lisa 43: Yeah, never stop.

Counselor 44: That you'll just have to leave, pull away from the tour, is just more than you can take.

Lisa 45: Yeah, it will be hard to go on without it.

Counselor 46: "It sounds as though that is almost the center of your life."

Lisa 47: It's very close to that, you know. My friends, my career, my success. There's something about my heart that's connected to golf.

Counselor 48: And there's a real ache in your heart at the thought of leaving.

Lisa 49: Yeah. [Cries] I just don't want to leave.

Counselor 50: I want to stay, keep on playing.

Lisa 51: It's what I am—an athlete, a competitor, a winner.

Counselor 52: You want to keep that part of you active—the athlete, the winner.

Lisa 53: Yes, the strong "me." Once that's gone, I feel scared. Scared about going out into the world. I don't want to go out into the world and have to figure everything out again. Face new problems and not know where I am going.

Counselor 54: You did that once and now you'll have to figure everything out again.

Lisa 55: Yeah, it'll be a struggle.

Counselor 56: "It's a hard world ... "

Lisa 57: Yeah, very hard ... unknown.

[Middle section of interview omitted]

Counselor 58: Does that mean that you feel no one cares, no one accepts?

Lisa 59: No, I feel like now that there are people who do accept and value me even when I'm losing. But there's something ... someone ...

Counselor 60: So that the person who can't accept and value you is you.

Lisa 61: Um-hmm, yeah, it's mostly me.

Counselor 62: The person who sees those bad shots and losses as unforgivable is you.

Lisa 63: Yes, nobody else is as hard on me.

Counselor 64: "Umm-hmm. Nobody could be that cruel to you, or make such awful judgments."

Lisa 65: [Sigh]

Counselor 66: "Or hate you so."

Lisa 67: Or hate me so. Yeah.

Counselor 68: "Sounds like you're the judge, the jury, and the executioner."

Lisa 69: Yeah, my own worst enemy.

Counselor 70: You pass a pretty tough sentence on yourself.

Lisa 71: Yeah, yeah, I do. Not a very good friend to me.

Counselor 72: "No." You're not a very good friend to yourself.

Lisa 73: Um-hmm.

Counselor 74: "And you wouldn't think of doing to a friend what you do to yourself."

Lisa 75: That's right. I would feel terrible if I treated anyone the way I treat me.

Counselor 76: "Umm-hmm, umm-hmm, um-hmm."

PAUSE

Counselor 77: "Because to you, your self is just unlovable."

Lisa 78: Well, there's parts of me that are lovable ...

Counselor 79: "OK, OK."

Lisa 80: Yeah.

Counselor 81: "OK. So in some respects you do love yourself."

Lisa 82: Yeah. I love and appreciate the strong, talented part of me—the athlete.

Counselor 83: Umm-hmm—

Lisa 84: That's the part of me that has struggled and come through—

Counselor 85: Umm-hmm—

Lisa 86: And survived—

Counselor 87: Umm-hmm—

Lisa 88: An awful lot.

Counselor 89: Umm-hmm. A really strong athlete.

Lisa 90: Yes, really special.

Counselor 91: Umm-hmm—

Lisa 92: That part of me will go away if I leave golf.

Counselor 93: "Uh-huh."

Lisa 94: I want to stay strong.

Counselor 95: And the athlete is the strong part of you that you want to hold onto.

Lisa 96: Yes, I want to keep that part of me. I love that part of me.

Counselor 97: Your athlete is a survivor, and she's strong, and she's been through a lot, but she's OK.

Lisa 98: Yes, she is. She is special, very special.

Counselor 99: Yeah. Yeah. She is. She's real special.

PAUSE

Counselor 100: It must be nice to have such a special person in your life.

Lisa 101: Yes it is, she's very nice.

Counselor 102: Can she care for the other parts of you? Away from the golf course?

Lisa 103: Yes, I think so. She's strong and determined. In a way, she's started to.

Counselor 104: She's started to.

Lisa 105: Yes, it's her strength and determination that keeps me going, trying to come to grips with this slump.

Counselor 106: Um-hmm—

Lisa 107: She's determined, but also more understanding and committed to me.

Counselor 108: Um, committed to you, will stick with you no matter what.

Lisa 109: Yes, I guess now I feel like she will always be with me. She will be me even when golf is gone.

Counselor 110: So the strength, determination, and love of your athletic self will stay with you—will not abandon you.

Lisa 111: Yes, she'll never go away. Always be there for me.

Counselor 112: Yeah, yeah.

Lisa 113: [Chuckles] That feels better. I'm more sure that I won't be "missing" the part of me that I love if I retire. I feel better . . . that the strength of my athletic self will stay with me no matter what. That strength will get me through.

END

This script is only a small portion of one meeting, but it illustrates some of the techniques compatible with the humanistic model, and specifically the person-centered approach. It is evident that Lisa is initiating the content of the interview. The counselor does not attempt to lead or insert direction, even when the client is quiet. Pauses are allowed to exist as the counselor waits for the client's lead. While the client does lead with the choice of content, the counselor's mirroring of content encourages more in-depth examination of some content and de-emphasizes other content. For example, in lines 105 and 106, the counselor's use of "um-hmm" does not mirror Lisa's initiation of her "slump" into the content. Instead, the counselor concentrates on the theme of "self" and Lisa's "strong, athletic self staying with her." This is in concert with the humanitarian perspective of the importance of self, and once Lisa introduces the "self" into the session, the counselor stays with it, ignoring, for the present time, the reference to the slump. Throughout the interview, the counselor is confident that the client's direction will identify the important issues and find the appropriate path to their resolution.

Reading the script of this type of interview, it is sometimes difficult to understand the extent to which the counselor attends to the client using body language and facial expressions. Great effort is made to connect on every level—cognitive, emotional, and behavioral—with the client to demonstrate empathy. The human sharing that occurs as the counselor uses self-deprecating humor to connect with Lisa is apparent in the transcript, as are the counselor's efforts to reflect back to Lisa what she is saying and feeling to document their strong connection. This mirroring is not mechanical, but rather it demonstrates a focused attention on the client's situations. The counselor does not try to change the client's feelings or thoughts and indicates openness to whatever Lisa says. As Raskin and Rogers point out, the counselor demonstrates that "he is a reliable, understanding partner who stays with the client as she lives with her various negative feelings and accompanies her as she finds the strength to rise above them" (1995, p. 148).

Because the humanistic model views Lisa as a whole person and does not compartmentalize her into isolated segments, dealing with Lisa's concern about retirement is also an intervention for her current playing problems. In dealing with her retirement issue, the session focuses on Lisa's sense of trusting in herself, which is an important component of performing out on the golf course. Bolstering Lisa's sense of always "being there for herself" enhances her sense of security and gives her confidence in her strength. This confidence and trust in herself is necessary for her performance as well as for her postretirement plans. Much has been written regarding the crucial role that self-confidence and trust play in golf performance. Lisa's sense of her "strong self" always being available to her transfers to enhance her performance by allowing her to commit to her shots and trust her swing on the golf course.

Additional Case for Discussion

The relationship between sport and pain is varied and complex. All athletes must endure a certain amount of discomfort in order to train. The training process is dependent on pushing the body a little farther, closer to its limits, with each training session, and this is often painful. Training and practice must also be frequent, which can promote overuse injuries, not to mention the pain associated with traumatic injuries in sport. In addition, specific sports, such as boxing, football, and ice hockey, have an element of pain built into the contest with each punch, tackle, and body check. These sporting cultures sometimes encourage the athlete to define what might be considered an "unhealthy" characteristic as part of self. How might a sport psychologist operating in the humanistic perspective deal with the problems presented in the following case of a professional hockey player?

Jacques DuBois moved slowly and stiffly toward the chair in my office. The left side of his forehead and temple were swollen. Underneath his swollen forehead, he sported a purplish black eye topped by a one-inch cut held together with black sutures and dried blood. It was evident that the symmetry of his face disappeared long ago and that even after the swelling of his current injuries went down his features would remain off-balance. Jacques took several minutes to find a tolerable position in the chair. With every adjusting move he winced slightly, but finally he began to speak. His head hung down and his voice was muffled as he started: "I'm afraid I'm losing my rep in this game," he said dully, "and I'm not sure I can muster the energy to fight for it—the pain is getting to me."

I had some idea of what Jacques meant. In the culture of hockey, the sport and pain are almost synonymous. Michael Farber described it best in a *Sports Illustrated* article aptly named "Stitches in Time": "The hockey ethos that exalts playing with pain is no more complicated than a kid's refusal to say *uncle* in the schoolyard. At times your manhood is up for grabs. Montreal assistant coach Dave King says, 'Playing hurt is a status thing. It's the simplest way of getting the respect of teammates, opponents, coaches. As coaches, we're always judging players. After a hard check or big-time slash, is he the kind of guy who gives up on the play and heads to the bench or does he stay with the play? After a guy blocks a shot, does he lie on the ice or get back up? Pain is one of hockey's measuring sticks. . . .'" (Farber 1998, p. 94).

I looked at Jacques and replied, "You're afraid you're losing your rep?"

"Yeah, yesterday I got double checked, high and low. It flattened me on the ice. I didn't want to get up. I wanted to just stay there. I've stayed down before . . . I've had this feeling before, but never this strong—I couldn't, wouldn't move. After what seemed like a long time, I just groaned, struggled up from prone to kneeling, and wobbled to the bench. I sat alone on the bench with my forearms on my knees, head hanging, trying to be cool about aches and pain far beyond what most people consider bearable. Sweat was mixed with blood from the cut over my eye. My chest was heaving. Worse than my external condition was how I felt inside. The helpless rage of victimization rocked in my chest. My physical condition was both shaming and infuriating. It was embarrassing not to have put up a better fight. Deep inside I knew I gave up the fight when I decided to stay down on the ice. The team knew it too. When I was down, guys on the bench wouldn't let the trainer come out. They held the gate shut and just let me lie there until I got up. In the locker room before the game they told me they were going to do it if I didn't get up, and they did."

DuBois recounted how he used to play with great abandon, flinging his body at full speed into other players when he first started in the NHL six years ago. The inevitable injuries didn't faze him then. He even welcomed them because they gave him status as one of the tough guys in a game of hard men. As the years progressed and his injuries multiplied, he mostly toughed out the pain. He used lots of ice and pain pills, but mostly he got through on grit. When the injuries were too bad and started limiting his play, he had the trainer freeze them during the game, but for the most part he just gutted it out. Toward the end of last season and for all of this season, however, he has lost the sense of pride he used to have in his pain. To be sure, the pains had changed too. It was taking him longer to recover, and recovery didn't seem to be complete.

"I want to make it clear," DuBois said convincingly, "I'm not ready to quit. What I want is respect—from my teammates and myself. I need to get my drive back, I want to get up. I want to re-establish myself. How can I do that?"

Suggested Readings

Levant, R. and J. Shlien. 1984. *Client-centered therapy and the person-centered approach.* New York: Praeger.

Raskin, N. and C. Rogers. 1995. Person-centered therapy. In *Current psychotherapies,* edited by R. Corsini and D. Wedding. Itasca, IL: F. E. Peacock.

Rogers, C. 1951. *Client-centered therapy.* Boston: Houghton Mifflin.

Rogers, C. 1961. *On becoming a person.* Boston: Houghton Mifflin.

Chapter 5

NEURO-LINGUISTIC PROGRAMMING: A COMPOSITE MODEL

From the previous discussion of the psychodynamic, behavioral, cognitive, and humanistic models, it is evident that each model suggests a different perspective on Lisa's situation. Which model is the "right" one? The truth is that no one model has a monopoly on veracity. There are many paths to helping athletes develop their potential and perform their best. While the models do offer different approaches, they are not mutually exclusive. In fact, the models often complement each other, as in the case of the behavioral and cognitive approaches.

This chapter presents an example of a composite model called *Neuro-Linguistic Programming* (NLP). You will recognize selected components of the psychodynamic, behavioral, cognitive, and humanistic models in NLP. For example, you will see that NLP incorporates the unconscious–conscious dichotomy from the psychodynamic perspective. It also stresses the importance of thinking processes, as represented by language and imagery, along with an emphasis on sensation and perception, which are central to cognitive psychology. The behavioral perspective provides a foundation for modeling, anchoring, and aspects of learning found in the NLP model, and the NLP emphasis on developing human potential and expertise are congruent with the humanistic perspective.

It is not surprising that NLP encompasses aspects of all of these models, for John Grinder and Richard Bandler, the creators of NLP, studied the work and techniques of psychologists who employed different approaches, such as Fritz Perls (Gestalt therapy), Paul Watzlawick (psychodynamic), Virginia Satir (family therapy), and Milton Erickson (hypnotherapy). Bandler and Grinder also studied the linguistic theories of Noam Chomsky and structured NLP on selected aspects of transformational linguistics. The influences of Bandler's background in computer science and systems theory are also evident in NLP. Consequently, the NLP model draws its theses from various sources and can be viewed as a conglomerate of concepts that are related to ideas found in other perspectives. Knight (1995) states that "NLP brings together many techniques that have been around for years, and combines them with discoveries that are new. It is both a study of masters of change [the aforementioned psychologists], some of whom are no longer alive, and a recognition of the talents that exist within each person" (p. 10). As you are reading this chapter, you might want to note the relationship between aspects of NLP and the other four perspectives by placing a "P" (psychodynamic), "B" (behavioral), "C" (cognitive), or "H" (humanistic) next to NLP concepts that are congruent with these other models.

It is not just the adoption of concepts from other models that you should note. It is the *selection, integration,* and *modification* of these various components that is of interest in this model. NLP will provide you with an example of how concepts borrowed from other perspectives and different disciplines can be blended into a unique approach to helping people change. While composite models are drawn from other models, they are more than just a collection of their parent perspectives. The truism "The whole is more than the sum of its parts" applies here. The selection of aspects of other models and the integration of these selected parts results in a unique product.

As with the other models, NLP has many variations, but because it is relatively new (1970s), it is sometimes difficult to identify what is "new" and what is a "continuing development" of Bandler and Grinder's original model. The continuing evolution of NLP and its interpretation by new disciples is generating a stream of new assumptions, techniques, and uses of the model. In the following description of NLP, I have relied mainly on the writings of Bandler and Grinder, as well as on authors who have used their works as a basis for their research.

Basic Concepts

Controversy surrounds several aspects of NLP, including agreement on a precise definition. NLP has been labeled the "beginnings of an appropriate theoretical base for the describing of human interaction" (Bandler and Grinder 1975, p. ix), a "meta-model, a model of the modeling process itself" (Dilts, Grinder, Bandler, and DeLozier 1980, p. 5), a "meta-model for therapy" (Bandler and Grinder 1975, pp. 57 and 180), an "explicit set of tools" (Bandler and Grinder 1975, p. 2), an "epistemology" (Dilts 1996), and "a pragmatic school of thought" (Dilts 1996). Bandler's *First Institute of Neuro-Linguistic Programming and Design Human Engineering* (1996), defines NLP as: "the study of the structure of subjective experience and what can be calculated from that and is predicated upon the belief that all behavior has structure. . . . Neuro-Linguistic Programming™ was specifically created in order to allow us to do magic by creating new ways of understanding how verbal and non-verbal communication affect the human brain. As such it presents us all with the opportunity to not only communicate better with others, but also learn how to gain more control over what we considered to be automatic functions of our own neurology." In other writings, NLP is defined as a "discipline whose domain is the structure of subjective experience. . . . It offers specific techniques by which a practitioner may usefully organize and re-organize his or her subjective experience or the experiences of a client in order to define and subsequently secure any behavioral outcome" (Dilts, Grinder, Bandler, and DeLozier 1980, foreword). Bandler considers NLP to be an "educational tool," not a form of therapy. He states: "We don't do therapy. We teach people some things about how their brains function and they use this information in order to change" (Bandler 1997). In *The Structure of Magic*, Bandler writes, "what we are offering here is not a new school of therapy, but rather a specific set of tools/ techniques which are an explicit representation of what is already present to some degree in each form of therapy" (Bandler and Grinder 1975, p. 40). While Bandler rejects the notion that NLP is a new school of therapy, it seems to have expanded beyond being just a "set of tools and techniques." The NLP literature includes presuppositions about human nature and the human condition, a rationale for human behavior and how it can be changed, and a set of organized and interrelated concepts that explain isolated facts regarding human behavior, just as the major theories do.

The Nervous System, Language, and Programming in NLP

The elements of NLP are many and not easily catalogued. A theme common to most writings on NLP is "learning to use your mind to develop excellence." Examining each of the components of its name provides a logical way to introduce NLP.

- *Neuro* refers to the nervous system as a regulator of feelings, generator of thinking processes, and mediator between the body and the environment. NLP is interested in the sensory nervous system (visual, auditory, creating representations or models of reality and accessing those representations for use as a basis of behavior is a central area of study in NLP. While all humans create models of reality, and parts of our representations are similar due to similarities in the human nervous system, each individual's models have unique variations. Consequently, individual models or representations of reality differ from person to person, and all human-generated models are different from the world itself. These differences stem from the fact that our nervous systems selectively filter information coming in from our environments. The human nervous system distorts, generalizes, and deletes signals from the "real world." The human nervous system is just one "filter" affecting our representations of reality. Individual history and social constraints, such as language, also shape our representations and therefore are important aspects of NLP (Bandler 1975, p. 9).

- *Linguistics* is the study of language structure and function. NLP initially built on concepts found in transformational linguistics and the work of Noam Chomsky concerning language surface structures and deep structures. The linguistic aspects of NLP examine the client's use of language to encode reality. Language is viewed as a tool for communicating personal representations or models of reality to others and to oneself. Analysis of an individual's language provides a method for examining the person's representations of the world. Pathology and unhappiness can be attributed to impoverished representations of reality, which are detected through this analysis of the client's language patterns. Altering the client's impoverished representations is a pathway to personal change in NLP.

- *Programming* is a term from computer science that is used in NLP to refer to the practice of coding change and excellence into one's nervous system. This coding involves *modeling*, the practice of copying strategies used by experts, as well as *anchoring*, which is related to classical and operant conditioning in that it involves associating a behavioral anchor with specific feelings and actions.

Presuppositions of NLP

In order to understand the NLP model, it is important to identify the assumptions that NLP makes about human nature and the world. Bandler (1997) identifies eight presuppositions of NLP:

1. "The ability to change the process by which we experience reality is more often valuable than changing the content of our experience of reality."
2. "The meaning of the communication is the response you get."

3. "All distinctions human beings are able to make concerning our environment and our behavior can be usefully represented through the visual, auditory, kinesthetic, olfactory and gustatory senses."

4. "The resources an individual needs in order to effect a change are already within them."

5. "The map is not the territory."

6. "The positive worth of the individual is held constant, while the values and the appropriateness of internal and/or external behavior is questioned."

7. "There is a positive intention motivating every behavior, and a context in which every behavior has value."

8. "Feedback vs. Failure—All results and behaviors are achievements, whether they are desired outcomes for a given task/context, or not."

These presuppositions provide a foundation for NLP components. The first presupposition is an underpinning of NLP's emphasis on studying the structure of subjective experience. It postulates that discovering the processes that experts use to attain high levels of performance and then learning the process is more advantageous than examining what the expert thinks—the content that is produced. While NLP acknowledges that human behavior is complex, it also postulates that there is structure within the complexity. The uncovering of the structure of one person's talent allows that structure to be taught to others and provides them with a foundation for that same talent. A basic concept of NLP is to discover or uncover "processes" or strategies that produce excellence and install the processes in others. NLP is interested in changing how the client interacts with the world by replacing the client's diminished processes with expert processes. It does not seek to simply change what individuals think about the world; rather, it promotes a change in how they process the environment with their central and peripheral nervous systems. In examining the process of excellence, one can look at the processes used by acknowledged experts, as well as examining the process used by oneself at a time when performing exceptionally well. Bandler and Grinder adhered to this presupposition when they studied the processes used by expert therapists— Satir, Perls, and Erikson. Their goal was to uncover the processes used by these experts and formalize them into meta-programs that could be taught to others.

A corollary to this emphasis on defining and transferring expert processes is a concept borrowed from systems theory called the *Law of Requisite Variety*. This law states that "in order to successfully adapt and survive, a member of a system needs a certain minimum amount of flexibility, and that flexibility has to be proportional to the potential variation or the uncertainty in the rest of the system" (Dilts 1998, p. 9). This law justifies the primacy placed on flexibility in NLP. This emphasis encourages individuals to develop multiple strategies for meeting their goals and to continually add to their personal repertoires of skill-building processes to prepare for future needs.

The second presupposition, "The meaning of the communication is the response you get," illustrates the importance of communication in NLP, as well as providing a criterion for interpreting communication efforts. All interactions between individuals are dependent upon communication skills, and these skills are emphasized in NLP. Techniques to develop rapport with, persuade, and effect change in others are important tools of NLP practitioners. Regardless of one's intent when communicating or the content of the communication, it is the receiver's response that is the criterion for determining the meaning of the communication. Bandler and Grinder state that "words . . . are nothing more than arbitrary labels for parts of your personal history" (1979, p. 15). They continue, "there is an illusion that people understand each other when they can repeat the same words. But since those words internally access different experiences—which they must—then there's always going to be a difference in meaning" (p. 16).

Many of the communication techniques used in NLP are designed to promote congruence between the message sent and the message received. Communication in NLP is not limited to language. It also includes body language, gestures, tone of voice, facial expressions, and other forms of nonverbal communication. Like the other models in this book, NLP is interested in how individuals communicate with themselves, including processes for accessing, employing, and modulating stored representations of their internal and external environments.

The third presupposition reflects the emphasis placed on the role of the sensory nervous system in accessing and filtering information from our environment and creating representations of the world. While we all use our senses—vision, hearing, touch, smell, and taste—to know our environment, as individuals we have preferred patterns for using our sensory systems that affect our thinking patterns. NLP divides the senses into primary senses (visual, auditory, and kinesthetic) and secondary senses (olfactory and gustatory).

Studying how people use their sensory systems to understand their world and create their reality is an important component of NLP. Understanding how others make use of their sensory modalities can also enhance effective communication and modeling. For example, if one is communicating with a person who has a strong preference for auditory input, matching her preferred sensory style can enhance communication. One might choose to phone her rather than writing her a memo and to use "auditory" references in the message (for example, "Does that *sound* good to you?" rather than "How does that *look* to you?"). The study of sensory modalities and how experts employ them is also of interest in delineating and modeling the processes of expert performance. For example, NLP practitioners believe that certain eye movements indicate which sensory representational systems a person is using at a given time and that eye movements provide clues to the structure of the processes in which the person is engaged (Bandler and Grinder 1979, p. 18).

NLP's perspective on human nature is revealed in the presumptions that "the resources individuals need in order to effect a change are already within them" and "the positive worth of the individual is held constant, while the values and the appropriateness of internal and/or external behavior is questioned." These statements support a positive view of human nature and unconditional respect for the individual as a person. The presuppositions are optimistic about human capacity for change and the benevolence of human intention. There is an assumption that behavior is not synonymous with the self and that individuals are more than the sum of their malleable behaviors. Individual behaviors are driven by motives that enhance the personal self in some way and correspond to the individual's representation of the world. The seventh presupposition addresses motivation and suggests that understanding the value of a behavior to the individual, and identifying the sometimes hidden intention behind the behavior, is a necessary condition for understanding the person's motivation. The key to understanding the value of a behavior to an individual lies in understanding how he represents reality.

The presupposition that "the map is not the territory" is one of the most frequently quoted statements in NLP writings. It is an acknowledgment that our personal perceptions of "the world" or "reality" are the result of mental processing that depends on selective attention, sensory interpretation, and contamination or alteration by past experiences. These and other elements of sensation and perception shape and distort our internal representations of the outside world. Some of these distortions are advantageous and some harmful. Bandler and Grinder (1975) state that ". . . there is an irreducible difference between the world and our experience of it. We as human beings do not operate directly on the world. Each of us creates a representation of the world in which we live—that is, we create a map or model which we use to generate our behavior. Our representation of the world determines to a large degree what our experience of the world will be, how we will perceive the world, what choices we will see available to us as we live in the world" (p. 7). Recognizing that our representations are self-created, and not necessarily immutable realities, allows the possibility of discarding an impoverished map of the territory and replacing it with one that is more helpful, accurate, and useful.

The last presupposition prevents premature judgment of failure by reframing unwanted outcomes as feedback. It encourages a neutral view of negative outcomes and discourages judgmental approaches to outcomes. Knight presents the following story to illustrate the value of being nonjudgmental.

> "A father and his son owned a farm. They did not have many animals but they did own one horse. One day the horse ran away.
>
> "'How terrible, what bad luck,' said the neighbours.
>
> "'Good luck, bad luck, who knows?' replied the farmer.
>
> "Several weeks later the horse returned, bringing with him four wild mares.
>
> "'What marvelous luck,' said the neighbours.
>
> "'Good luck, bad luck, who knows?' said the farmer.
>
> "The son began to learn to ride the wild horses, but one day he was thrown and broke his leg.
>
> "'What bad luck,' said the neighbours.
>
> "'Good luck, bad luck, who knows?' replied the farmer.
>
> "The next week the army came to the village to take all the young men to war. The farmer's son was still disabled with his broken leg so he was spared. Good luck, bad luck, who knows?" (Knight 1995, p. 149)

The assumption that "there is no failure, only feedback" is found in many Eastern and New Age philosophies and is advantageous in that it promotes persistence in moving toward a goal. This presupposition is aimed at allowing the mind to quiet its constant evaluation of events as being right or wrong, good or bad. Viewing outcomes as feedback encourages an emotionally detached perspective and allows for a wider range of creative responses.

Feedback is also a major component in the modeling process. The NLP modeling process employs a component developed by Miller, Gallanter, and Pribram (1960) known as the *TOTE process*. TOTE stands for *test-operate-test-exit*, and a TOTE is a "sequence of activities in our sensory representational systems that become consolidated into a functional unit of behavior" (Dilts, Grinder, Bandler, and DeLozier 1980, p. 27). An example of a TOTE is the behavior of adjusting the volume on your television set. If you turn the television on and the sound is too low (*test* = sound does not correspond to what I need in order to hear it), then you hit the remote control volume button several times (*operate* = hitting the button to increase volume). Then you test it again (*test* = is it too soft or too loud), and if it corresponds to your criteria, you stop adjusting the volume (*exit* = stopping the volume-adjusting behavior). A TOTE is essentially a feedback loop used to compare initial conditions with one's outcome goals during modeling. Even simple behavioral programs can have multiple TOTE feedback loops, some of which may be nested within other TOTEs. Feedback loops in NLP's concept of behavioral programs are conceptually similar to loops in computer programming code and reflect the cybernetic nature of NLP's conceptualization of the human nervous system.

Overall, NLP promotes an optimistic view of the human condition and is positive in its assessment of human capacities in relation to accomplishment and change. This optimistic position has led some proponents of NLP to make rather fantastic claims for NLP techniques and has generated criticism of NLP regarding its objectivity.

Goals and Procedures

The goal of NLP is to provide a set of tools that can be use to produce desirable change in self and/or other people (clients). These tools provide the client with the ability to define and change his representational models of the world. It is the change in the client's processing of environmental stimuli and representational models that results in a change in behavior, enhanced creativity, and flexibility of response to environmental situations.

Defining and Changing Representational Models: Meta-Model of Linguistic Analysis

As mentioned earlier, NLP is based on the presupposition that humans make representations of their experience and environment by processing signals through the channels of sensation and perception. These representations are the individual's models of reality. They are a depiction of the world as interpreted by the person's sensory and cognitive activities rather than exact replicas of what actually exists in the world. An individual's representations or models are powerful because they direct behavior. One way that humans express their representations is through language. NLP practitioners analyze language to understand an individual's representations of the world, including both the processing strategies used to create the representations and the content. They then seek to enhance those representations that are impoverished, restrictive, or destructive.

The methods of linguistic analysis employed in NLP are based on selected aspects of transformational linguistics, especially the writings of Noam Chomsky, regarding surface structures and deep structures (Chomsky 1957). Chomsky is best known for his theory that humans are born with innate language capabilities that enable infants to hear speech, organize it, and derive the basic rules of language. According to Chomsky, humans have an innate ability to formulate and process language. Chomsky also postulated that language communication has two layers, referred to as *surface structure* and *deep structure*. Surface structures are the words and sentences spoken or written by the individual. They are what the person says verbatim. Deep structures refer to the meaning elements and underlying complexity of meaning represented by the surface structures. When individuals translate the entirety of their meanings and experiences into representations, they symbolize them in deep structure. This deep structure is then transformed into words to communicate their experience to other people. The processes of transforming all the signals from our environment into our individual phenomena of deep and surface structures necessarily results in deletion, distortion, and generalization of all worldly events into first our phenomena, or deep structure, and then our language, which describes our phenomena.

Figure 5.1 illustrates the results of these processes, in which the set of all events or signals in the world at large contains a subset of the signals that each of us as individuals actually contacts. Processing through each individual's nervous systems reduces and distorts all the signals in an individual's immediate environment into a subset of signals that have meaning for us as part of our individual phenomenology, labeled in NLP as our deep structures. These deep structures are not always known to the individual and can be unconscious as well as conscious. The process of translating our deep structures into surface structures is accomplished through language and nonverbal behaviors such as gestures and body language. Because the process of putting our deep structure into language results in the subset, surface structures, NLP postulates that examination of a client's language surface structures allows a counselor to access the client's deep structures. Additionally, NLP supplies a format for challenging a client's deep structures and reconnecting them with the person's experience in order to foster change. Bandler and Grinder state: "For the therapist to challenge the Deep Structure is equivalent to demanding that the client mobilize his resources to reconnect his linguistic model with his world of experience. In other words, the therapist here is challenging the client's assumptions that his linguistic model is reality" (1975, p. 46).

The Process of Linguistic Analysis

Understanding the client's deep structures through analysis of language surface structures is dependent on the counselor's alert recognition of certain surface structure characteristics. These characteristics can be identified by semantically ill-formed surface structures. Characteristics that are particularly important are linguistic indicators of deletions, distortions, and generalizations.

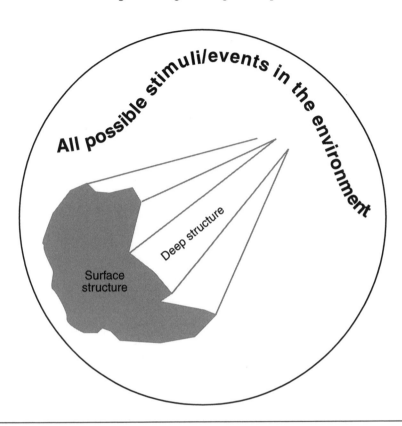

Figure 5.1   Bandler and Grinder's conceptualization of personal reality as surface structure and deep structure (1975). NLP views human experience as the result of a selective process in which surface structure, as expressed in language and nonverbal indicators, is a subset of deep structure, or sensory experience. Deep structure is a subset of the universe of world events or signals that surround us. Each level is affected by generalization, deletion, and distortion of the previous level.

Deletion

As defined by Bandler and Grinder, *deletion* is "a process which removes portions of the original experience (the world) or full linguistic representation (Deep Structure)" (1975, p. 59). Surface structure deletions indicate that the client does not have a rich, complete representation of his experiences. They are a sign that the client's model is missing important components. Grammatically, deletions can be recognized as sentences in which the object of the verb is unstated. For example, the statement "I'm nervous" is incomplete in that it does not identify who, what, where, or why the speaker is nervous. Further probing by the counselor is necessary to understand the nature of the client's nervousness. Asking the client, "What is making you nervous?" and receiving the response, "I am nervous about appearing foolish," adds more information but still contains deletions (appearing foolish to whom?). Further questioning is necessary to delineate the deep structure of "I am nervous about appearing foolish in front of the television cameras when I miss a 3-foot putt." Assisting the client in composing a fuller linguistic representation (surface structure) of her nervousness not only explicates her deep structure for the counselor, but also clarifies it for the client, who might not have consciously identified her own deep structure regarding her nervousness.

In addition to object deletions, there are other linguistic surface structure markers that indicate deletions in the client's surface structures and possibly in his deep structures as well. Some of these are the use of comparatives and superlatives, use of -ly adverbs, and modal operators such as *should* and *must*. For example, if an athlete says, "I must win this match," the sentence reflects deleted material concerning why the athlete feels he "must" win the match. NLP practitioners learn to recognize these markers, explore them with the client, and enhance them to reclaim what was lost in their representations. Bandler and Grinder explain, "once the therapist has recognized that the Surface Structure the client has presented is incomplete, the next task is to help the client recover the deleted material. The most direct approach we are aware of is to ask specifically for what is missing" (1975, pp. 63-64). For example, if the athlete says, "Obviously, I'm playing horribly," the counselor would recognize that the surface structure is an incomplete representation of the deep structure from which it came. The statement is a reduced version of the athlete's deep structure regarding how or to whom this is "obvious" and how it is "horrible." To recover the missing material the counselor asks the athlete direct questions, such as "To whom is this obvious?" or "How is it horrible?" This type of questioning restores the surface structures so they are a full portrayal of the athlete's deep structures. This restoration allows the athlete to operate in the world with a clearer and more complete model of his reality.

Distortion

Distortion also affects an individual's representational process. Distortion occurs because of selective attention—human inability to attend to all of the event signals from the environment—and human perception, the organization and interpretation of raw neural energy signals by the brain. Fortunately, most perception follows a common basic process for all humans, so that we can agree on a common reality. However, some aspects of the perception process are unique to each individual, and some are unique to specific cultures. Whether perceptions are shared or unique, they do involve additions, deletions, and combinations of signals that make our representations different from the raw energy signals in the environment. Once representations have been established, there is a perceptual tendency to favor signals that fit with one's existing representations. This results in a bias toward bolstering existing representations that makes it more challenging to alter or replace established representations. However, with enough meaningful and repetitive experiences, representations that are limiting can be altered.

As with deletions, NLP practitioners observe the client's language for certain linguistic markers that indicate specific types of distortions. One of these markers is *nominalization,* a transformation in which a verb or action word is distorted into a noun. Nominalization indicates that the client has transformed an active, ongoing process into a static, unchangeable event. In the client's representation of the world, a dynamic and alterable action has been distorted into an immutable occurrence. Nominalization makes the client's perspective less flexible.

An example of nominalization in surface structure is "My decision to stay on the tour is causing me grief." In this sentence, the act of deciding has been nominalized into a noun, which gives it a sense of permanence. The language reflects a deep structure that distorts the decision-making process into a fixed constant. Challenging the deep structure allows the client greater flexibility because the ongoing process of decision-making allows for continual updating of "a decision" based on changing circumstances. The client is encouraged to recognize that she has flexibility in the decision-making process that is fluid and continuous rather than fixed and immutable.

Other categories of distortion that are of interest to NLP practitioners are presuppositions, implied cause–effect relationships, and mind reading. *Presuppositions* are underlying assumptions that support, and sometimes limit, the client's representations. They are unstated in the client's surface structure, and the goal of the NLP counselor is to detect and expose them for the client. The client can then confirm that the presupposition is supported in his experience, or he can modify the presupposition, thereby enriching his representation. Cause–effect relationships are another aspect of representations that often go unnoticed by the client. For example, an athlete who comments that "his bad calls made me lose the match" assumes that his tennis match was lost because the chair umpire made unfavorable calls. This cause–effect relationship in the athlete's representation is limiting because it makes the athlete's ability to win dependent upon getting favorable calls. This severely limits the athlete's choices of ways to

respond and win in situations where he receives some unfavorable decisions from the umpire.

When one person assumes that she knows the internal feelings or
thoughts of another person or group of people, she is engaging in *mind
reading*. An example of a mind reading surface structure is the statement
"Everybody on the team hates me." This statement indicates that the speaker
knows the feelings of all members of the team. The NLP counselor deals
with indications of mind reading by explicating exactly how the client
knows that everyone on the team hates her—what evidence is she using to
draw this conclusion? Bandler and Grinder state: "Since it is highly im-
probable that one human being can directly read another's mind, we want
details about how this information was transferred. We view this as being
very important, as in our experience the client's assumed ability to read
another's mind is the source of vast amounts of inter-personal difficulties,
miscommunication and its accompanying pain" (1975, p. 105).

Distortions are identified by their semantically ill-formed surface structures, and once they are exposed the counselor has several options of how
to address them. One option is to allow them to remain unchanged for the
present. Clients typically have multiple distortions, and it is not possible to
address all of them simultaneously. A second option is to confirm the distortion with the client and ask her to clarify it and explain it more fully.
This allows the client to place qualifiers on the distortion and recognize its
limitations. The third alternative is to challenge the distortion, allowing
the client to replace it or delete it from her representation. Changing the
client's representations to less distorted models that allow more flexibility
enhances the behavioral choices of the client and improves her situation.

Generalization

Generalization is the third universal characteristic of human representations.
It is a "process by which a specific experience comes to represent the entire
category of which it is a member" (Bandler and Grinder 1975, p. 216). For
example, a child who is unable to hit a ball with a bat during gym class
may generalize that specific event into a representation expressed with the
surface structure "I'm not good at sports." In this case, as with all generalizations, specific details of the actual event are lost and a single event is
expanded to include the entire universe of "sport." The NLP model identifies generalizations and then challenges them. The purpose of challenging
the client's generalizations is to

- reconnect the client's representation with the actual experience;
- recast the permanence and breadth of the generalization into a specific instance that the client can address; and

- restore detail, circumstances, and vividness to the client's representation in order to create choices based on distinctions that were not previously available to the client (Bandler and Grinder 1975, p. 80).

Generalizations can be expressed by many forms in the client's surface structure. Table 5.1 outlines some of the linguistic markers for generalizations in the client's surface structure.

Examination of verbal communication is only one way to access an individual's representations of the world. While linguistic analysis is a mainstay in the NLP model, the meta-model generalizes to other modes of creating and expressing representations, such as body language, facial ex-

Table 5.1 Linguistic Characteristics of Generalization in the NLP Meta-Model

Linguistic structure	Definition	Example
Missing referential indices	Noun or noun phrases that do not refer to a particular person, place, or thing	"Nobody cares about me when I don't make the cut." In this statement, the word *nobody* does not refer to a specific person or group.
Symmetrical predicates	Predicates that describe a relationship in which it is implied that their converse is true	"John is arguing with the umpire." If John is arguing with the umpire, then the umpire must also be arguing with John.
Disguised if–then statements	Statements that imply an unstated consequence	"I have to be nice to other people." This comment implies that if I am not nice to other people, then some consequence will follow.
Equivalence	Two statements made together in which the client indicates that he equates the first statement with the second	"My coach doesn't like me . . . he never speaks to me in the dugout." In these statements, the client equates not being spoken to with the coach not liking him.
Incompletely specified verbs	Use of verbs that can have multiple meanings	"My coach hurt me." In this sentence, the verb *hurt* might refer to physical or emotional pain.

pressions, and tone of voice. These behaviors are also surface structures. Like language, they can be examined for their relationship to deep structures and changed to provide the client with more useful representations of reality.

Techniques for Changing Representations: Modeling

Identifying surface structure markers of deep structure inadequacy is the first step in the NLP model. The second step is to challenge inadequate deep structures and expand them to broaden the client's representations. Dilts states that "one of the goals of NLP is to identify problematic generalizations, deletions or distortions through the analysis of the syntax or form of the surface structure and provide a system of tools so that a more enriched representation of the deep structure may be attained. Another goal of NLP, represented by the modeling process, is to be able to create better links and pathways between surface structures and deep structures" (1998, p. 15). NLP's interest in how individuals create their subjective experience focuses on the processes, or strategies, that individuals use to create their representations. Answering the question, "How do people model their world?" is as important as, perhaps even more important than, determining "What is the model?"

What processes do people use to create their representations? NLP proposes that the processing strategies for creating subjective experiences, including our mental concepts, core beliefs, emotional responses, and behaviors, emanate from the human nervous system. Specifically, our subjective experience is a product of the processing done in the sensory and perceptual aspects of our nervous systems. Sensory aspects of human nervous systems include vision, hearing, smell, taste, and kinesthesia (touch/feeling). Perceptual aspects include the complex neural network processing performed by the associative areas of the brain cortex and other brain structures. NLP focuses more on sensation-related aspects of processing strategies than on perceptual aspects, although perception is addressed in a generalized manner. This is understandable given the current lack of knowledge in the neurosciences concerning the structure and function of perception.

The five senses control our subjective experiences by utilizing patterned representational strategies to process energy signals from the external world. Anything that exists in the external world can only be "known" by a person through sensory processing. Therefore, in NLP, sensory processing is the key to understanding an individual's subjective experiences in any activity, whether it be swinging a golf club, falling in love, building a bridge, or preparing a sermon. Most sensory processing occurs unconsciously. It is implicit to the individual and operates automatically. NLP seeks to make this implicit processing explicit and bring it into consciousness for the purpose of understanding it, modulating it if it is deficient, or transferring it to other people if it is useful. NLP provides a set of tools and techniques for accessing the sensory processing used by individuals to create the models of the world that generate their subjective experience and behavior. NLP is a model of how humans make the models of the world that guide virtually all their activities.

In order to instill a new representational strategy or supplement a deficient strategy in clients, it is necessary to have an unambiguous, detailed description of the new representational process and be able to communicate it to clients so that they can adopt it and use it to produce the desired skill. The NLP model of how humans model identifies specialized techniques to elicit, utilize, design, and install any given representational strategy. Each of these phases—elicitation, utilization, design, and installation—are major areas of interest in the NLP perspective, and specialized vocabulary, notation, and tools exist within NLP to accomplish these necessary steps for making representational strategies explicit and therefore transferable.

Elicitation

Elicitation refers to the "procedure the neurolinguistic programmer uses to gather the necessary information to make explicit the ordered sequence of representational system activity that constitutes a particular strategy" (Dilts, Grinder, Bandler, and DeLozier 1980, p. 60) Representational systems, as mentioned before, are the five human senses—vision, audition, kinesthesia, smell, and taste. These representational systems are notated in NLP by using capital letters: "V" for visual, "A" for auditory, "K" for kinesthetic, and "O" for olfactory/gustatory. Superscripts and subscripts are used to indicate specific qualities of each representational system, such as "i" for internally generated and "e" for external. For example, V^i indicates an internal visual, such as when an athlete uses imagery—as opposed to V^e, which would indicate actually looking at an object. In addition to internal and external characteristics, other commonly used superscripts and subscripts are "c" for a constructed image (imaging a person with six arms), "r" for remembered images (imaging your first bicycle), "+" for a positive feeling, and "−" for a negative feeling. These symbols are combined in sequences known a "4-tuples," which resemble mathematical sets, to describe representational strategies. A 4-tuple for typing the word "the" might be $<A^i V_r K^e/K_r>$ where the individual first internally hears the word "the" (A^i) and then visually images the remembered letters (V_r). Next there is a comparison between the feel of hitting the correct keyboard keys in the present with a remembered internal feeling of the motor program for hitting the keys (K^e/K_r). If the K^e matches K_r then the behavior is completed and the performer exits from the strategy. This sequence might continue with a comparison of the visual external word "the" as seen on the computer screen with an internally remembered visual image of what the typed word should look like.

In this example, there is a special content (the letters "t," "h," and "e" in sequence, for example) that processes through the representational strategy ($<A^i V_r K^e/K_r>$). NLP recognizes this content as important in the modeling process but is equally interested in the processing strategy because it applies to other content material. For example, the strategy for typing the word "first" will be the same as the strategy for typing "the," except that the content has changed. This is a simple example of the type of sensory coding common in the NLP elicitation process. The goal is to have a complete, detailed recipe for performing the target skill.

More recent NLP literature emphasizes the characteristics of the representational systems within a strategy. Characteristics, or *submodalities,* of the representational system are believed to determine the impact of a representational system in a sensory strategy. Submodalities, such as brightness, clarity, color, and size for visual representations, or tone, volume, and tempo for audition, affect the power that the particular representational system exerts in processing information from the "real" world. If a client's visual processing in a particular strategy includes large, bright, colorful images but auditory images are soft and fuzzy, this might indicate that the visual representational system exerts more influence in the process than the auditory representational system. Examining and manipulating these submodalities offers one method for defining and ultimately changing a strategy.

Strategies are elicited through interviewing and asking the client or expert to explain his strategy, and having the client perform the strategy while being observed. Various formats of these two basic approaches can be used to identify representational strategies. For example, if it is not possible to directly observe the person while performing a strategy, having the person act "as if" he were performing the strategy in context or reproducing only a portion of the context of the strategy can help in identifying it. NLP maintains that "all behavior is a transform of interior neurological processes and carries information about those processes" (Dilts, Grinder, Bandler, and DeLozier 1980, p. 77). Therefore, observing the person perform (or pretend to perform) a skill provides cues to what sensory representational strategies are being employed. Neuro-linguistic programmers also believe that *people do what they are talking about.* Consequently, when a person talks about how he performs a specific skill, he will demonstrate in his verbal and nonverbal activities the same strategies that he is describing (Dilts,

Grinder, Bandler, and DeLozier 1980, p. 61). Detailing a particular strategy is done by examining multiple indicators of strategies and observing the accessing mechanisms used by the performer of the strategy to detail or "unpack and chunk" the conscious and unconscious aspects of a strategy. In addition to language, some of the indicators that neuro-linguistic programmers attend to are

- eye movements,
- tonal and tempo vocal qualities,
- breathing characteristics,
- skin color changes,
- posture, and
- muscle tone.

NLP asserts that there is a correspondence between these behavioral indicators and internal sensory processes that can be discerned as patterns. NLP practitioners are taught to recognize these patterns and use them to elicit the details of the underlying strategies.

Among the other techniques used to elicit the strategies of a particular behavior, NLP modeling also utilizes multiple descriptions of the behavior being modeled. Exploring the talent from three different perspectives creates these multiple descriptions. The first perspective is to view the behavior from one's own point of view; the second is to examine it from the performer's point of view; and the third is from the position of a neutral, outside observer (Dilts 1998, p. 48). Examining a behavior from different positions allows a fuller description of the talent to emerge by providing additional information about the strategy.

Utilization

Dilts, Grinder, Bandler, and DeLozier describe *utilization* as "the process of applying an existing strategy, one that you have elicited, for the purpose of assisting a client (individual, family, group or organization) in achieving some desired outcome, or in securing some outcome for yourself. Using this process, the NLP practitioner assists clients by running new content through the formal representational sequence of an existing strategy by packaging or repackaging the client's experience in terms of the existing structure of that strategy" (1980, p. 105). *Pacing* is the major technique used in NLP to apply a strategy to a client's problem by running new content through it. In this process, the NLP practitioner mimics the client's behaviors and strategies. The format of the practitioner's presentation to the client, "matches, step for step, the sequence of representations the person cycles through in that strategy" (Dilts et al. 1980, p. 107). This matching or mirroring of the client's strategy will resonate with the client because it is a photocopy of his own strategy, and rapport between client and practitioner will be enhanced.

Strategy Design

Pacing is a useful technique for processing new content through a client's strategy to change her representations, but what if it is the strategy that is depleted and not just the content? For example, if a client's strategy for making decisions about eating behavior (what and when to eat) is only represented in visual external (it looks good) and olfactory (it smells good) representational systems without input from the kinesthetic representational system ("Am I hungry?") or auditory internal dialogue ("Will this food benefit my health?"), the strategy is missing important information because it is not processing data from all of the person's sensory channels. In this situation, a new strategy must be designed and installed for the client's use. A client's need for new strategies occurs when she lacks a strategy for a desired outcome, when she is using a strategy that does not fit the situation, or when a strategy is deficient, as in the eating situation. NLP strategies are designed using four basic principles.

1. Strategies are designed to include input from all major sensory representational systems—vision, audition, and kinesthesia. This allows for the fullest possible input of information both from the environment and from the client's life experiences.

2. Strategies are designed to be elegant. *Elegance* refers to having the least possible number of components to get the job done.

3. Strategy design should take advantage of existing strategies. New strategies should build on the client's current strategies when possible. New strategies should be based on tested, effective strategies of others when possible. If another person, such as an "expert" in the target behavior, has developed an appropriate strategy, it is more efficient to elicit that strategy and teach it to the client than to start from scratch.

4. Strategies should meet the conditions for well-formedness—that is, they should conform to a series of criteria established for efficient and effective strategies. These criteria are detailed in Dilts (1998) and Dilts et al. (1980, p. 204) and include guidelines for sequencing, using representational system modifiers, looping, and inserting decision-making points in 4-tuples.

Strategy Installation

Once a new strategy is designed, it must be adopted, learned, and practiced by the client. This process is referred to as *strategy installation*. Two basic methods of installation are employed in NLP. One method is anchoring, and the other is rehearsal. These installation methods can be used separately, but operate best when used together.

Anchoring refers to the process of associating a representation or a strategy (or part of a strategy) with an action that triggers the representation or strategy. Conceptually, anchoring is similar to the stimulus-response conditioning in the behavioral model. Dilts et al. distinguishes between behavioral conditioning and anchoring, though, claiming that anchors can be established in one trial, reinforcement is not required, and internal experiences are considered to be behavior and can be anchored (1980). However, the behavioral model does recognize one-trial conditioning and conditioning of internal experiences, like emotions. Consequently, the most significant difference is the claim that anchoring can be accomplished without any type of reinforcement. Anchors are established by creating a correspondence between representations in two different sensory systems. The correlation is established by associating the representations in time and space. Knight offers the following directions for establishing an anchor (1995, p. 153).

- Make yourself comfortable in a quiet place where you will not be disturbed.
- Select a subjective experience or resourceful state that you have encountered in your life that you would like to be able to access at will.
- Recall a time when this resourceful experience or feeling was most powerful. Try to recreate all of the sensations of this experience in your mind using all of your senses. Focus your attention on each representational system in both its internal and external modes to assure that all of the representations are recreated. Imagine that you are re-experiencing the situation in full, rich detail. As your sense of being in the experience reaches its strongest magnitude, touch your little finger and thumb together for as long as you can recreate the experience in your imagination. As your sense of reliving the experience begins to fade, release your fingers.
- The touching of your little finger and thumb should now trigger a return to the subjective experience that you have just anchored. The process can be repeated several times if the anchor is not well established.
- Test the anchor to ascertain that firing the anchor triggers the desired state.
- Imagine a future situation in which you would like to re-experience your anchored state. As you imagine the future situation, fire the anchor to confirm that it connects you to your resourceful experience.

Establishing an anchor in another person or client follows a similar routine. A signal is established prior to the client entering his recreation of the resourceful state. The signal communicates to the practitioner when the client's feelings are beginning, getting stronger, and finally diminishing. The practitioner then applies an anchor, such as squeezing the client's wrist from the beginning to the end of the recreated state, to set the anchor for the client.

In addition to using anchors to cue representational processes, strategies can be installed through rehearsal. *Rehearsal* involves having the client practice each representational step in the strategy in sequence until it can be accessed automatically. The practitioner, who performs functions similar to those of a theater director, usually guides rehearsals of strategies with clients. Strategies can be rehearsed by having the client process many different contents through the strategy, or by repeatedly practicing the strategy in a step-by-step fashion. The practitioner's role is to be an informed observer, noting the client's accessing cues, and correcting mistakes of deletion or improper sequencing. If the strategy being rehearsed is not working for the client, the practitioner must determine why it is not working. This requires a problem-solving approach that examines the contextual characteristics of the strategy, the client's past learning that might interfere with the strategy, and characteristics of the strategy itself—(Is it complete? Is it sequenced properly?). Often, this problem-solving will require going back through the elicitation, utilization, and design phases to check for breakdowns in the modeling process.

NLP in Sport Psychology

NLP's strong emphasis on the use of the five senses in creating phenomenological experience is a very interesting and attractive approach to sport psychology because of its physiological grounding, short-term duration of treatment, and pragmatic approach to the athlete's immediate problem. However, there is very little literature regarding NLP in sport, even though the general NLP literature frequently refers to sport as an area in which NLP can be applied. One reason for the lack of studies and professional literature is the NLP position on research. The founders of NLP have repeatedly stated that NLP is not about the "truth," but is concerned only with what is useful (Dilts et al. 1980, foreword). Bandler and Grinder prefer to call NLP a *model* rather than a *theory* because "a model is simply a description of how something works without any commitment regarding why it might be that way. A theory is taxed with the task of finding a justification of why various models seem to fit reality" (Dilts et al. 1980, foreword).

Unfortunately, pronouncements of this nature, and the grandiose claims made by some NLP practitioners, have contributed to a discounting of NLP and have discouraged research on NLP's uses in sport. The implication that theories are subject to justification, and models are not, is spurious. Both models and theories are open to inquiry, and ethical considerations require professionals to test their efficacy. While NLP may not lend itself to empirical research because it is a study of subjective experience, qualitative research designs could be employed with NLP. Mackenzie rejects the use of experimental designs for testing NLP in sport but suggests that the effectiveness of NLP as a counseling system can be examined (1984). He suggests using "a) athletic performance records; b) feedback (self-reports) from athletes about changes in their lives and their judgment about which techniques have helped accomplish those changes; c) observable, postcounseling sensory data which are related to the athlete's mood and self-esteem; d) feedback from coaches, friends and relatives about the athlete's performance, moods and changes in behavior; and e) detailed chronological notes of the counseling techniques use in relation to specific outcomes" (p. 132) to investigate the efficacy of NLP interventions. In light of the current favorable climate toward qualitative investigations in sport psychology, further research on NLP's application to sport issues should be supported.

A search of the SportDiscus and PsychInfo databases offers few returns on the descriptors "NLP" and "Neuro-Linguistic Programming" in connection with "sport." There is more research on NLP in the broader field of psychology, although it is not plentiful. Some of the investigations of the techniques of NLP found in this broader domain are of interest to NLP researchers in sport. Research questions regarding whether eye movement is an indicator of sensory components being employed by the individual, for example, would be transferable to the sporting domain. As is the case with imagery and a host of other research topics, the research results are mixed on this issue. Eye movements as an indicator of visual-constructed (V_c) or auditory-remembered (A_r) in an imaging task, and eye movements' relationship to sensory processes while answering open and closed questions, were not supported in studies by Monguio-Vecino and Lippman (1987) and Bliemeister (1988), respectively. However, a study by Buckner, Meara, Reese, and Reese (1987) did find support for the visual and auditory, but not the kinesthetic, aspects of the eye-movement paradigm in a thought concentration task.

Ingalls's 1988 doctoral dissertation investigated the NLP principle of congruence between sensory system employment, eye movements, and predicates in athletics with a small sample ($N = 8$). Ingalls's study is unique in that it included consideration of an NLP concept called *synesthesia*, a process in which two or more sensory systems operate together in a task. Ingalls concluded that "from the point of view of an empirical test, they (the results) are supportive if [*sic*] the NLP assumption, however, considerd [*sic*] from a theoretical point of view, a model which provides an explanation of any result, as does the NLP model with the concept of synesthesia, obviates data that does not support the model" (Ingalls 1988, abstract). Ingalls suggests that future research of the NLP congruence assumption and synesthesia should employ a hermeneutic (explanatory) paradigm.

Sharpley (1984, 1987) reviewed the experimental literature on NLP and concluded that "the effectiveness of this therapy was yet to be demonstrated" (p. 103). In response to Sharpley's review, Einspruck and Forman (1985) raised six categories of design and methodological errors in NLP empirical studies and called for an improvement of the quality of research on NLP before drawing conclusions regarding its efficacy. One of the crucial methodological issues is use of individuals trained in NLP. Studies using judges and raters formally trained in NLP seem to produce results supporting NLP more frequently than studies that employ untrained examiners.

In the sport domain, NLP studies are rare. Stanton reported that three NLP techniques—ego-state reframing, changing personal history, and symptom prescription—have been used with success as single-session interventions in sport (1989). This study employed a case-study methodology rather than an experimental protocol.

Mackenzie published a descriptive article on NLP as a counseling system for athletes and coaches (1984). This paper outlines the NLP assumptions about human behavior, presents a cybernetic model of behavioral regulation, and discusses sequential steps in the counseling process. This work also contains examples of how NLP can be used with athletes and coaches. Mackenzie has also published several books describing the NLP approach to specific sports such as tennis, skiing, and golf.

While the scholarly investigations of NLP conducted primarily in the 1980s produced mixed results, the 1990s witnessed an explosion of books on NLP for popular consumption. Recent books and audiotapes applying NLP to sport seem to center on golf as a sport that can be improved with NLP (Mackenzie and Denlinger 1990; Rosa 1998; and Adler and Morris 1997). Consumers' and clients' increasing interest in NLP should propel more research of this model.

Summary

1. Humans create representations of the real world that they use to guide their behavior. These representations are different from all that exists in reality because our senses and cognitive processing of information necessarily delete and distort signals from the environment. These representations of the world are not only different from the world itself, but they are unique to each individual because we each have our own "filters" that we employ as we experience the world. NLP is a model based on how humans create and use these representations of the real world.

2. Representations are created by the senses—vision, hearing, touch/feeling, and smell/taste—which are called *representational systems* in NLP nomenclature. These representational systems provide the building blocks for the strategies or processes that people use to create their representations.

3. Unhappiness and limitation can be attributed to impoverished representation of the world. These impoverished representations blind us to alternative behaviors and solutions to problems.

4. Impoverished representations can be analyzed by examining the language and images used to communicate representations to others and to ourselves. Analyzing the surface structure and deep structures of the language, body language, gestures, facial expressions, and eye movements that a client uses to describe her representations of the world allows the counselor to identify aspects of distortion, deletion, and generalization that have occurred in the client's processing. Surface structures also reflect the strategies that the client uses to process information from the world.

5. There is an emphasis in NLP on unconscious behavior, but it differs from the psychodynamic role of the unconscious. In the psychodynamic model, symptom relief results from insight into unconscious material. In NLP, interest in the unconscious is centered on the importance of representations and the unconscious strategies used to create representations. Alterations that enhance and enrich these mostly unconscious strategies are the force for symptom relief in NLP.

6. The processes that individuals use to create their representations have structure. Enriching a client's impoverished representation is accomplished by teaching new ways of processing experience—there is a change in the processing structure as well as a change in the content of the client's representations.

7. There are many NLP techniques designed to expand the manner in which the client processes the world and to enrich the representations created by this processing. The NLP practitioner uses these techniques to elicit, utilize, design, and install new processing strategies. Anchoring and modeling are two major techniques used to change and enrich clients' processing structures.

Process Plan for Lisa Irons's Case: NLP Perspective

The NLP approach to Lisa's problems is direct and pragmatic. It is not necessary to provide Lisa with a detailed description of NLP, as it will be effective whether she is aware or unaware of NLP techniques. My personal preference, however, is to have an informed client, so I will spend some time in our initial sessions explaining NLP techniques and concepts. This will allow Lisa to understand and consciously participate in elicitation and modification of her sensory strategies.

The establishment of rapport with Lisa is my first objective in her process plan. During her initial consultation, I carefully observed her use of sensory representational systems by noting her language patterns—especially her use of predicates, as well as her accessing cues, gestures, and eye movements. For example, Lisa's body posture (head and shoulders slumped down) and breathing pattern (deep and slow) indicates use of her kinesthetic representational system. Her eye movements, down and to the right, were congruent with use of the kinesthetic senses. Her language—especially in her autobiography, where she repeatedly uses the words "feel," "felt," and "feeling" along with descriptors such as "burning desire" and "drop me"—also indicates that she relies on kinesthetic input. Lisa also has strong indicators in her language for the visual representational system. For example, her statements "I also started keeping a journal to *see* if I could figure out what's going wrong in my game," "I have a lot of nervous energy, but I can't seem to *focus* it," and "I hate to quit before *seeing* more success on the tour" indicate use of the visual representational system.

In order to establish and keep rapport with Lisa, I will mirror her use of representational systems, employing more visual and kinesthetic indicators in my own language and body language. Using representational systems that match Lisa's will generate a sense of connectedness between us, enhance communication, and make Lisa feel comfortable that I understand her representational view of her situation. Building rapport is an ongoing process, and throughout our work I will periodically test to make sure that I have not broken rapport and slipped back into using my own preferred representational systems.

To establish the focus of Lisa's program, we must determine exactly what specific outcomes she desires. The meta-model of language analysis will be a primary tool for clarifying exactly how Lisa views her current situation and what types of changes she wants for her future. NLP dialogue is often presented in two or three columns to portray important aspects of the client's communication. The first column usually contains verbatim language spoken by the client, while the second and third columns record eye movements, gestures, body language, and other nonverbal surface structures that reveal information about the client's sensory representations.

For example, the opening of Lisa's case study can be presented thus:

"I'm going to cause you all sorts of trouble."	Smiling (facial expression) Strolling (slow movement)
"I'm Lisa Irons."	Slumped into chair. Head and shoulders down and forward

| "I don't know if you can help me or not, but I'm desperate. I've tried everything else and nothing works, so I figure this can't hurt." | Sigh (deep, slow breathing pattern) |

By closely observing both language and nonverbal indicators, I will collect information about Lisa's surface structures that will help in revealing her deeper structures. I will also look for congruence between her verbal and nonverbal signals when determining which sensory representations system she is using to produce her representations. In this case, Lisa's indicators seem to be congruent with kinesthetic representations. Her body language (head and shoulders slumped and deep breathing) and comment that "this can't hurt" are primarily kinesthetic indicators ("this can't hurt" also contains deletions that could be explored with Lisa).

For simplicity's sake, let's consider only Lisa's language surface structure, but keep in mind that nonverbal indicators, such as eye movements, would also be used throughout the counseling process. In working with Lisa's language surface structure, I will look for instances of generalization, deletion, and distortion. For example, in her initial consultation Lisa commented, "My game is not consistent—or maybe I should say it is consistent—consistently bad! Each day it seems like I have a different problem with my game. I never know what's going to be working for me when I go out on the course." Within these three sentences, there are several examples of deletion, distortion, and generalization that could be addressed. I note these:

- "Consistent" is an ambiguous term, and I might ask Lisa to tell me what a consistent game entails. I might ask her to tell me how she knows when a golfer is consistent (what criteria she is using).

- "Bad" is also ambiguous. How can she tell whether a game is "good" or "bad"? Is it the score, or money won, or being able to shape her shots? Does it mean never hitting into trouble, or being able to make creative shots from less than perfect situations?

- "Each day I have a different problem" deletes specific information regarding the nature of the "problems." What are some of the problems? Is it inability to concentrate? Poor putting? Wayward drives?

- "I never know what's going to be working for me when I go out on the course." Never? Has there ever been a time when she knew what would work? How did she know?

It is evident that there are many directions that could be explored with Lisa based on just three of her comments. I will select the last comment to illustrate how the language meta-model can be used to help Lisa through her slump. I will challenge Lisa's distortion that she "never knows what's going to be working" by asking her if there was ever a time when she did know what was working. Because I know that Lisa has experienced success in her game in the past, I want to draw on that successful experience. I view Lisa as a golf expert who at one time had a successful, working model for winning golf tournaments. This model consisted of sensory strategies that guided her expert behavior. Within the past two years, she has inadvertently changed her model, perhaps by deleting or adding sensory representations that are not effective for the task of playing her best.

A second explanation for Lisa's slump that needs to be explored is whether there has been a change of context or environment resulting in Lisa's previously successful model being inappropriate for the new context. An example of a change of context that might incapacitate Lisa's previous model for winning is her back problem. If Lisa's strategies for successful play had a kinesthetic element that is no longer available because her back pain prevents her from making a full turn in her swing, then new strategies will have to be developed and installed. In talking with Lisa about contextual issues, she reports that she started having back troubles right after college and had them during her most successful phase on the tour. Consequently, it does not appear that her back pain is a new contextual element.

My approach now is to examine with Lisa all the contextual factors that might affect her strategies. We will try to determine whether her current strategies are not working because of a change in context by comparing her performance context today with what existed when she was successful. If there are contextual differences, then we must elicit and install new strategies that will be effective given Lisa's new context. For instance, if Lisa's back pain were a new context for her, we might find an expert golfer with back pain who is playing well and elicit her strategies to use with Lisa.

If we cannot find any contextual differences between Lisa's successful experiences and her current situation, then we will compare her strategies from her successful past episodes with the strategies she is using at the present. This comparison requires that we first elicit both Lisa's past successful strategies and her current strategies.

Eliciting Lisa's past and current golf performance models requires some detective work. We will explore Lisa's past model, the one that produced her success on the tour, first. Working first with Lisa's most effective model allows for the possibility that she will spontaneously self-install her original model and begin playing better immediately. If this occurs, there will be no need to elicit and work with the model she has been employing during her slump because it will have been replaced. NLP values efficiency of effort and timely change.

Elicitation of Lisa's successful performance model begins by asking her to remember a time when she was performing her best. Perhaps Lisa's major tour win is a time she will identify as one of her bests. I will ask Lisa to relax and imagine being back on the course on the first tee during her championship round. I will then ask her to describe her tee shot from each sensory modality. I will ask Lisa for the following information.

- What do you hear happening around you as you walk onto the tee box to hit your drive? (auditory, external)
- What are you saying to yourself? Do you have any internal silent dialogue, music, or sound images? (auditory, internal)
- What do you see around you? What objects are you looking at? Is your visual field narrow or broad? (visual, external)
- Are you experiencing any internal visions? Are you running "movies" through your mind? (visual, internal) What do you look like? (visual, constructed)
- What are you feeling externally? Is the wind blowing on your face? Do you feel the club in your hands? (kinesthetic, external)
- What are you feeling internally? Are you excited or calm? What does your stomach feel like? (kinesthetic, internal)
- What do you smell? Are you aware of any taste sensations? Salivation? (olfactory/gustatory, external)
- Are you remembering any smells or tastes? (olfactory/gustatory, internal) (Dilts et al. 1980, p. 97)

As Lisa describes each sensory state, I will encourage her to describe her experience in as much detail as possible. I will ask her to describe the submodalities of each sensory representation. For instance, I will have her describe the brightness, color, size, and clarity of her visual representations and the loudness and tone of auditory representations. We will go through this sequence with each phase of her preshot, shot, and postshot performance. As Lisa describes her performance on the first tee, I will observe her language and nonverbal indicators for signs of sensory representations. I will note whether her eye movements correspond to her sensory descriptions and look for other indicators of her processing strategy.

Following this procedure, we will examine each of Lisa's shots from tee to green on several holes to make certain we have identified her sensory strategies correctly. If further exploration is necessary to elicit her model, I might ask Lisa to "act out" each shot on a golf course with me as if she were back playing in the tournament. We could also obtain copies of television coverage of her performance and examine the tapes for signs of her sensory strategies. It will be necessary to identify all of Lisa's sensory representations, determine their proper sequence, and investigate how they operate together in her model. As we are exploring each aspect of Lisa's model, I will anchor parts of the model with Lisa by asking her to press her thumb and forefinger together as she re-experiences each aspect of her successful model. This anchoring will allow us to retrigger aspects of her strategies later in our work.

Once Lisa's past successful model has been identified, I will want to test it out on the course by asking her to play using the anchors we have established. As Lisa plays using the model, I will be observing her eye movements and other accessing cues to determine whether she has incorporated her former successful model into her performance or is unconsciously using a different model, perhaps the model she has been using during her slump. If she is using her slump strategies, it might be necessary to compare those strategies with her more successful strategies to identify exactly where they differ. With this knowledge, we can use anchoring and rehearsal techniques to install her more effective model. Repetitively working through each step in the model will help Lisa learn the model and make the transitions from one step in the strategy to the next more automatic. If Lisa encounters a part of the model that is difficult for her, we can work on rehearsing that chunk of the strategy and anchor it to a physical behavior so it is more easily accessed. The chunk can then be inserted into the larger model more easily. Rehearsing accessing cues, such as eye movements and gestures, can also assist the model installation.

After Lisa has mastered the new model and preliminary testing shows it to be effective, we will use future pacing to prepare Lisa to use the model in real competition. *Future pacing* is an exercise in which the athlete mentally practices the model as if she were in a future tournament situation imagining the outcome she desires. I will ask Lisa to put herself into a relaxed state and image herself using the strategies we designed and obtaining the outcomes she desires. Further anchoring of aspects of the model to competition conditions can be done during future pacing exercises.

The real testing of the new model will take place during Lisa's next tournament. If the model is successful and Lisa obtains the outcomes she desires, then our work can be terminated. If the outcome is disappointing, then we will examine Lisa's performance to determine whether

- Lisa used the model in the correct context;
- Lisa unknowingly reverted to another model or altered the model in some way; or
- the model itself was faulty.

Depending on the problem, we would then repeat the procedures to solve that issue and repeat the testing, future pacing, and evaluation in tournament competition.

Termination of our work together is indicated by Lisa's successful employment of her playing strategies. The test of NLP efficacy is its usefulness in producing the outcomes that the athlete desires. Understanding of the interventions and insight into self are not prerequisites for NLP success, but my personal preference is that my clients understand the role of sensory input and the composition of whatever strategies we have worked with in our sessions. I feel that this allows the clients to do some preliminary detective work on their own if their problems recur. For this reason, I offer the clients a strategy guide, or written summary of their strategies, that they can consult if the situation deteriorates. An example of a small portion of Lisa's performance strategy guide might be

- Look at your ball position and the landscape to the pin. (visual, external)
- Look at the precise spot you want to land your shot. (visual, external)
- Make an image of the type of shot that will put your ball on that spot. (visual, internal, constructed)
- Remember an excellent shot from your past that is similar to this shot and visualize making that shot. (visual, internal, remembered)
- Take your stance and feel it is right. (kinesthetic, external)
- Say to yourself, "I'm aimed right at my spot. All I have to do now is relax and swing smoothly to my spot." (auditory, internal)
- Take a deep breath and release it slowly. (kinesthetic, external)
- Say to yourself, "Quiet, please." (auditory, internal signal to quiet the mind)
- Look at the precise spot on the ball where your club will strike. (visual, external)
- Feel the smoothness of your swing. (kinesthetic, external)
- Watch the ball land on your spot. (visual, external)

This is just an outline of the main steps in Lisa's general strategy. There are subroutines or other strategies embedded in these steps that are not written out for Lisa because they make the strategy guide too complicated. In the second step, for example, Lisa must make a series of decisions to select her landing spot. Her decision-making strategy is not included in the guide because it would make it too complex; plus, Lisa's decision-making strategy should be so well anchored into her shot routine that it occurs automatically. In the future, if Lisa experiences another slump and she cannot detect how her strategy is failing her, she would have to consult with me or another NLP practitioner to help her fine-tune her strategy.

I have described in some detail how Lisa's slump could be approached using the NLP model. If Lisa chooses to deal with other issues in her life, a similar approach using NLP techniques can be used. After working her way out of the slump, for example, if Lisa wants to make a decision regarding retirement, I would work with her to access her meta-model of sensory strategies for making decisions and then process her retirement content through her decision-making model.

Additional Case for Discussion

The following case reveals some problems experienced by an elite junior archer who is about to compete in his first international competition. How would an NLP practitioner approach Tony's situation?

Tony Bowen's arrow missed the mark—as did the one before, and the one before that. As he waited for his score, he was definitely dejected and at a loss. He couldn't explain why he was freezing up, unable to release his arrows. He raised his bow and aimed, but then lowered it. He did this repeatedly until time was short. This forced him to rush to get all his arrows off before the time to complete his round ran out. He'd heard about others freezing up—*target panic*, it was called—but this was a new experience for him, a very unpleasant experience.

Sixteen-year-old Tony remembered how excited he was after last year. He surpassed his goals last year by winning not only the junior sectional title but also the junior national archery title. He was a surprise victor—a dark horse—in that tournament, though he had expected to do well. But even Tony didn't dream he would take the national title. It was really a peak experience for him.

The national junior title opened up many opportunities for Tony. He was named to the U.S. international junior squad, and was selected to spend a month at the Olympic training center in Colorado.

It was during his time at the Olympic training center that his hesitation to release the arrows first began. Tony was thoroughly pumped about being named to the international squad and training with the best junior archers and coaches. Secretly, however, he wondered how he would fare at this new level of competition. He questioned whether he could repeat his stellar performance at the national championships against all the champions from other countries.

Compounding his doubt was the fact that he did not feel that he connected very well with the national coach who was to accompany the team to Europe. That coach had a long-term coaching relationship with two of the junior archers that Tony beat in the national championships. Both of the coach's archers were favored over Tony prior to the competition.

"I know he doesn't like me," Tony said. "Nobody thinks I belong here."

"He's messing me up," Tony continued. "He makes me see red with all his talk. I get so angry I feel like a bull who is always having a red cloth waved in his face.

"He's always in my face, telling me to do this and do that. Even when he's not around I hear him in my head—always telling me what to do. I hear his voice and feel his stares in my mind when I'm shooting.

"There is a definite difference between how I shot at nationals and how I'm shooting now. At nationals I was really relaxed. There was pressure to do well, but no one expected me to win, so most of the week I was really loose. I really connected with the target. I saw it so clearly; it was ultra-sharp. I felt I could see every millimeter of the bull's-eye, and I was so clearly focused on the exact center point of the bull's-eye that I knew I had it. It was as if there was a laser beam shooting out of my arrow tip, and all I had to do was put the laser on that center mark. I don't even remember releasing the arrows—just seeing a blur and the arrow strike the target perfectly.

"Time was not an issue. I seemed to have all the time I wanted. I didn't monitor it much because I knew I could just continue at my relaxed pace, putting arrow after arrow in the center of the target, and I felt I had all the time in the world. I even remember taking time to run my eyes down the shaft of each arrow as I placed it on the string.

"There was all the ordinary noise of other competitors, the crowd, and so forth, but it was muffled and distant. In my head I could see my hand, wrist, forearm, elbow, and shoulder, all in perfect position—in their 'slots.' I remember feeling the power in my back muscles as I drew the string. I really felt strong.

"Now I feel I'll never get it back. Worst thing is, I need it more than ever now that I'm going international. I've never been out of the country before, and while it's exciting, it's also scary. I don't know how I'll talk with foreign competitors, as I only speak English. Since I don't know my teammates very well, I wonder if I'll be lonely.

"This will also be the first big competition that my dad has missed. It's too expensive for him to go. We had a difficult time just seeing our way clear to fund my expenses for this trip."

Suggested Readings

Bandler, R. and J. Grinder. 1975. *The structure of magic.* Palo Alto, CA: Science and Behavior Books.

Dilts. R. 1998. *Modeling with NLP.* Capitola, CA: Meta Publications.

Dilts, R., J. Grinder, R. Bandler, J. DeLozier. 1980. *Neuro-linguistic programming: The study of the structure of subjective experience.* Capitola, CA: Meta Publications.

Mackenzie, M. 1984. The metaskills model of sports counseling: Helping athletes achieve excellence. *Quest* 36 (2): 122-133.

Ψ AFTERWORD:
POINTS ABOUT
YOUR PERSPECTIVE

The soul of art is found in the artist's perspective. Likewise, the heart of scholarship is perspective—theoretical perspective—for the theoretical model of the practitioner and researcher is the lens that mediates all observations. For this reason, it is imperative that practitioners and researchers acknowledge the underlying assumptions that shape the lenses they use to observe the world.

Your theoretical style will reflect your experience regarding what "works" and "doesn't work" for you and your clients. It will also reflect your personal training and interests, just as Neuro-Linguistic Programming reflects the experiences of a linguist (John Grinder) and a programmer/mathematician (Richard Bandler).

You must be aware of your own assumptions regarding basic questions such as

- What is the nature of human beings? Are people inherently good, trustworthy, and motivated to fulfill their highest potential? Or are people inherently motivated by drives such as aggression and selfishness? Or are they born as a blank slate and motivated by the experiences they encounter in life? We all make assumptions, usually unknowingly, about the basic condition of human nature, and it is important that the counselor be aware of her assumptions.
- What events and conditions promote change in humans?
- What type of relationship should the client and therapist develop? and
- What determines human behavior?

Your awareness of your basic beliefs allows you to operate with full consciousness of your guiding principles.

Table A.1 summarizes the basic assumptions of five different models used in sport psychology and described in this book. They are not the only models available, and you might want to continue your search for your professional model by studying other models, such as the family systems or Gestalt models. Adopting a model and/or creating your own perspective is a scholarly task, and as such it must be accompanied by an attitude of open-minded skepticism. You will have to consider alternative viewpoints and question everything. It is also a continuous process in that your perspective may change with experience in the field. The process is developmental and should never be considered to be "done." Finding the right balance between change and stability in your model is a major challenge for the growing professional.

Table A.1   Comparison of Psychological Models

Model	Focus	Agents of change	Primary research methods
Psychodynamic	Unconscious inner dynamics	Insight into personal unconscious motives	Case studies
Behavioral	Observable behavior	Learning via conditioning and modeling	Use of empirical methods to examine observable behaviors
Cognitive	Thoughts and thought processes	Change in how one understands and thinks about the world	Empirical measures as well as informal observation and introspection
Humanistic	Subjective experience	Support of individuals' natural motivation to seek full potential	Primarily qualitative and descriptive
NLP	How senses are used to create representations of the world	Enrichment and alteration of representations	Efficacy is determined solely by usefulness to client

Discovering and investing in your own professional model is critical for your practice. Equally critical is your skill at presenting your model of the process to your clients and ensuring that they understand and have confidence in the process model that you use. In the introduction to this book, I asked the question, "How would you explain your model to your client?" In each of the case studies for the various models, explaining the model and process to Lisa was emphasized. It is the client's right to understand the process you will use together before committing to counseling. It is the practitioner's responsibility to be open and forthright with the client regarding the proposed process of treatment. Ultimately, each client must find a model framework that makes sense of, and resonates with, his experiences. The chances of success in the counseling process depend on both the practitioner and the client possessing a clear understanding of the process and a commitment to the procedures inherent in the approach. Success is much more difficult, if not impossible, when either the client or the practitioner lacks synergy with the model employed.

ᴪ BIBLIOGRAPHY

Alder, H. and K. Morris. 1997. *Masterstroke: Use the power of your mind to improve your golf with NLP.* London: London Bridge Trade.

Apitzsch, E. 1995. Psychodynamic theory of personality and sport performance. In *European perspectives on exercise and sport psychology,* edited by S. Biddle. Champaign, IL: Human Kinetics.

Apitzsch, E. and B. Berggren. 1993. *The personality of the elite soccer player.* Lund, Sweden: Studentlitteratur.

Apter, M. 1982. *The experience of motivation: The theory of psychological reversals.* London: Academic Press.

Apter, M. 1989. *Reversal theory: Motivation, emotion and personality.* London: Routledge. Cited in J. Kerr, 1997, *Motivation and emotion in sport: Reversal theory.* East Sussex, UK: Psychology Press.

Bain, L. 1995. Mindfulness and subjective knowledge. *Quest* 47: 238-253.

Bandler, R. 1996. What is Neuro-Linguistic Programming™: The First Institute of Neuro-Linguistic Programming™ and Design Human Engineering™ [Online]. Available: **www.purenlp.com/whatsnlp.htm** [April 13, 1999].

Bandler, R. 1997. Neuro-Linguistic Programming: The Presuppositions of NLP™ [Online]. Available: **www.purenlp.com/nlpresp.htm** [April 16, 1999].

Bandler, R. and J. Grinder. 1975. *The structure of magic.* Palo Alto, CA: Science and Behavior Books, Inc.

Bandler, R. and J. Grinder. 1979. *Frogs into princes.* Moab, UT: Real People Press.

Bandura, A. 1977. Self-efficacy: Toward a unifying theory of behavioral change. *Psychological Review* 84: 191-215.

Bandura, A. 1986. *Social foundations of thought and action: A social cognitive theory.* Englewood Cliffs, NJ: Prentice Hall.

Beck, A. and M. Weishaar. 1995. Cognitive therapy. In *Current psychotherapies,* edited by R. Corsini and D. Wedding. Itasca, IL: R.E. Peacock Publishers.

Begel, D. 1992. An overview of sport psychiatry. *The American Journal of Psychiatry* 149: 606-613.

Benson, H. 1975. *The relaxation response.* New York: Avon Books.

Berger, B. and M. Mackenzie. 1980. A case study of a woman jogger: A psychodynamic analysis. In *Sport psychology: An analysis of athlete behavior,* edited by W. Straub. New York: Mouvement Publications, 360-372.

Biddle, S. 1985. Mental preparation, mental practice and strength tasks: A need for clarification. *Journal of Sports Sciences* 3: 7-74.

Birdsong, L. and J. McCune. 1977. Operant conditioning techniques: A preseason conditioning program for female basketball players. Paper presented at the meeting of the American Alliance of Health, Physical Education and Recreation, Seattle, WA.

Bliemeister, J. 1988. Empirical verification of central theoretical constructs of neurolinguistic programming. *Zeitschrift Fuer Klinische Psychologie. Forschung und Praxis* 17: 21-30.

Buckner, M., N. Meara, E. Reese, and M. Reese. 1987. Eye movement as an indicator of sensory components in thought. *Journal of Counseling Psychology* 34: 283-287.

Bull, S., J. Albinson, and C. Shambrook. 1996. *The mental game plan: Getting psyched for sports.* United Kingdom: Sports Dynamics.

Burton-Nelson, M. 1998. *Embracing victory: Life lessons in competition and compassion.* New York: William Morrow.

Bustamante, L., D. Howe-Tennant, and C. Ramo. 1999. What is humanistic psychology? [Online]. Available: **syncorva.cortland.edu/~ANDERSMD/ HUMAN?WHAT.HTML** [January 25, 1999].

Cameron, J. and W. Pierce. 1994. Reinforcement, reward, and intrinsic motivation: A meta-analysis. *Review of Educational Research* 64 (3): 363-423.

Carroll, R. 1999. Neuro-linguistic programming (NLP) [Online]. Available: **skepdic.com/neurolin.html** [April 15, 1999].

Carver, C. and M. Scheier. 1990. Origins and functions of positive and negative affect: A control-process view. *Psychological Review* 97: 19-35.

Chaplin, J. 1985. *Dictionary of psychology.* New York: Dell Publishing.

Chomsky, N. 1957. *Syntactic structures.* The Hague, Netherlands: Mouton.

Cialdini, R. 1993. *Influence: Science and practice.* New York: HarperCollins College Publishers.

Consumers Union. 1995. Mental health: Does therapy help? *Consumer Reports* 60: 734-736.

Cooper, A. 1998. *Playing in the zone: Exploring the spiritual dimensions of sports.* Boston: Shambhala.

Corey, G. 1996. *Case approach to counseling and psychotherapy.* New York: Brooks/ Cole Publishing Company.

Corsini, R., ed. 1994. *Encyclopedia of psychology.* New York: John Wiley and Sons.

Crocker, P. and T. Graham. 1995. Emotion in sport and physical activity: The importance of perceived individual goals. *International Journal of Sport Psychology* 26: 117-137.

Crossman, J. 1997. Psychological rehabilitation from sports injuries. *Sports Medicine* 5: 333-339. Citing G. Larson, C. Starkey, and L. Zaichkowsky, 1996, Psychological aspects of athletic injury as perceived by athletic trainers. *Sport Psychologist* 10: 37-47.

Dale, G. 1996. Existential phenomenology: Emphasizing the experience of the athlete in sport psychology research. *Sport Psychologist* 10 (4): 307-321.

Dervin, D. 1991. Sports, athletes, and games in a psychoanalytic perspective. In *Mind-body maturity: Psychological approaches to sports, exercise, and fitness,* edited by L. Diamant. New York: Hemisphere Publishing Corporation.

De Witt, D. 1980. Cognitive and biofeedback training for stress reduction with university athletes. *Journal of Sport Psychology* 2: 288-294.

Dilts, R., J. Grinder, R. Bandler, and J. DeLozier. 1980. *Neuro-Linguistic Programming Volume 1: The study of subjective experience.* Capitola, CA: Meta Publications.

Dilts, R. 1996. What is NLP? [Online] Available: **www.nlpu.com/whatnlp.htm** [April 13, 1999].

Dilts, R. 1998. *Modeling with NLP.* Capitola, CA: Meta Publications.

Donahue, J., J. Gillis, and K. King. 1980. Behavior modification in sport and physical education: A review. *Journal of Sport Psychology* 2: 311-328.

Dweck, C. 1975. The role of expectation and attributions in the alleviation of learned helplessness. *Journal of Personality and Social Psychology* 31: 674-685.

Einspruck, E. and B. Forman. 1985. Observations concerning research literature on neuro-linguistic programming. *Journal of Counseling Psychology* 32 (4): 589-596.

Ellis, A. 1993. Fundamentals of rational-emotive therapy for the 1990's. In *Innovations in rational-emotive therapy,* edited by W. Dryden and L. Hill. Newbury Park, CA: Sage Publications.

Ellis, A. 1995. Rational emotive behavior therapy. In *Current Psychotherapies,* edited by R. Corsini and D. Wedding. Itasca, IL: F.E. Peacock Publishers.

Farber, M. October 12, 1998. Stitches in Time. *Sports Illustrated,* pp. 86-96.

Feltz, D., D. Landers, and U. Raeder. 1979. Enhancing self-efficacy in high-avoidance motor tasks: A comparison of modeling techniques. *Journal of Sport Psychology* 1: 112-122.

Feltz, D. and D. Landers. 1983. Effects of mental practice on motor skill learning and performance: A meta-analysis. *Journal of Sport Psychology* 5: 25-57.

Ferris, T. 1997. *The whole shebang: A state of the universe report.* New York: Simon and Schuster.

Festinger, L. 1954. A theory of social comparison processes. *Human Relations* 7: 117-140.

Fitts, W. 1965. *Manual for the Tennessee self-concept scale.* Nashville: Counselor Recordings and Tests.

Fitts, W. 1972. *The self-concept and behavior: Overview and supplement.* Nashville: Counselor Recordings and Tests.

Fletcher, J. 1993. *Patterns of high performance.* San Francisco: Berrett-Koehler Publishers.

Frost, R. 1974. Development of values through sport: The winning edge. *Proceedings of the First National Sports Psychology Conference,* May 18-20, 1973, edited by W. Schwank. Washington, D.C.: AAHPER Publications.

Gallwey, T. 1974. *The inner game of tennis.* New York: Viking.

Gill, D. 1986. *Psychological dynamics of sport.* Champaign, IL: Human Kinetics.

Gould, D., L. Finch, and S. Jackson. 1993. Coping strategies used by national champion figure skaters. *Research Quarterly for Exercise and Sport* 54: 453-468.

Gould, D., S. Jackson, and L. Finch. 1993. Sources of stress in national champion figure skaters. *The Sport Psychologist* 15: 134-159.

Gould, D. and E. Udry. 1994. Psychological skills for enhancing performance: Arousal regulation strategies. *Medicine and Science in Sport and Exercise* 26: 478-485.

Greenspan, M. and D. Feltz. 1989. Psychological interventions with athletes in competitive situations. *Sport Psychologist* 3: 219-236.

Gundersheim, J. 1982. Comparison of male and female athletes and nonathletes on measures of self-actualization. *Journal of Sport Behavior* 5: 186-201.

Hales, D. and R. Hales. 1995. *Caring for the mind.* New York: Bantam Books.

Hall, C. and J. Pongrac. 1983. *Movement imagery questionnaire.* London, Ontario: University of Western Ontario.

Hall, C., W. Rogers, and K. Barr. 1990. Imagery use among athletes. *The Sport Psychologist* 4:1-10.

Hanin, Y. 1994. Individual zones of optimal functioning (IZOF) model: An idiographic approach to performance anxiety. In *Sport psychology: An analysis of athletes' behavior,* edited by K. Henschen. Ithaca, NY: Movement Publications.

Hardy, L. and G. Parfitt. 1990. A catastrophe model of anxiety and performance. *British Journal of Psychology* 82: 81-106.

Harris, J. 1993. Using kinesiology: A comparison of applied veins in the subdisciplines. *Quest* 45: 389-412.

Heward, W. 1978. Operant conditioning of a .300 hitter: The effects of reinforcement on the offensive efficiency of a barnstorming baseball team. *Behavior Modification* 2: 25-40.

Hinshaw, K. 1991. The effects of mental practice on motor skill performance: Critical evaluation and meta-analysis. *Imagination, Cognition and Personality* 11: 3-35.

Howard, W. and J. Reardon. 1986. Changes in the self-concept and athletic performance of weight lifters through a cognitive-hypnotic approach: An empirical study. *American Journal of Clinical Hypnosis* 28: 248-257.

Hunt, J. 1995. Divers accounts of normal risk. *Symbolic Interaction* 18: 439-462.

Hunt, J. 1996. Psychological aspects of scuba diving injuries: Suggestions for short-term treatment from a psychodynamic perspective. *Journal of Clinical Psychology in Medical Settings* 3 (3): 253-270.

Ibrahim, H. and N. Morrison. 1976. Self-actualization and self-concept among athletes. *Research Quarterly* 47: 68-79.

Ingalls, J. 1988. Cognition and athletic behavior: An investigation of the NLP principle of congruence. *Dissertation Abstracts International* 48 (7-B): 2090.

Ivey, A. 1994. *Intentional interviewing and counseling*. Pacific Grove, CA: Brooks/ Cole Publishing.

Jackson, S. 1992. Elite athletes in flow: The psychology of optimal sport experience. PhD diss., University of North Carolina, Greensboro, NC.

Jackson, S. and M. Csikszentimihalyi. 1999. *Flow in sports: The keys to optimal experiences and performances*. Champaign, IL: Human Kinetics.

Jones, G. 1993. The role of performance profiling in cognitive behavioral interventions in sport. *The Sport Psychologist* 7: 160-172.

Jones, L. and G. Stuth. 1997. The uses of mental imagery in athletics: An overview. *Applied and Preventive Psychology* 6: 101-115.

Jones, R. 1977. A modified basketball game: The effects of contingency management on competitive game behavior of girls attending basketball camp. Symposium presented at the Third Annual Convention of the Midwestern Association of Behavior Analysis, Chicago, IL.

Kerr, J. 1997. *Motivation and emotion in sport: Reversal theory*. East Sussex, UK: Psychology Press.

Kirschenbaum, D. 1987. Self-regulation of sport performance. *Medicine and Science in Sport and Exercise* 19 (Suppl.): S106-S113.

Kirschenbaum, D., D. Ordman, A. Tomarken, and R. Holtzbauer. 1982. Effects of differential self-monitoring and level of mastery on sports performance: Brain power bowling. *Cognitive Therapy and Research* 6: 335-342.

Kleiber, D. 1983. Sport and human development: A dialectical interpretation. *Journal of Humanistic Psychology* 23: 76-95.

Kleine, D. 1990. Anxiety and sport performance: A meta-analysis. *Anxiety Research* 2: 113-131.

Knight, S. 1995. *NLP at work*. London: Nicholas Brealey Publishing.

Krane, V., M. Andersen, and W. Strean. 1997. Issues of qualitative research methods and presentation. *Journal of Sport and Exercise Psychology* 19: 213-218.

Kyllo, L. and D. Landers. 1995. Goal setting in sport and exercise: A research synthesis to resolve the controversy. *Journal of Sport and Exercise Psychology* 17: 117-137.

Landers, D. 1988. Improving motor skills. In *Enhancing Human Performance,* edited by D. Druckman and J. Swets. Washington, D.C.: National Academy Press.

Larson, G., C. Starkey, and L. Zaichkowsky. 1996. Psychological aspects of athletic injury as perceived by athletic trainers. *Sport Psychologist* 10: 37-47.

Lee, C. 1988. Behavioural intervention following a sporting injury: A case study. *Behaviour Change* 5: 154-159.

Lee, T., S. Swinnen, and D. Serrien. 1994. Cognitive effort and motor learning. *Quest* 46: 328-344.

Locke, E. and G. Latham. 1990. *A theory of goal setting and task performance*. Englewood Cliffs, NJ: Prentice Hall.

Locke, E., K. Shaw, L. Saari, and G. Latham. 1981. Goal setting and task performance. *Psychological Bulletin* 90: 125-152.

Mackenzie, M. 1984. The metaskills model of sports counseling: Helping athletes achieve excellence. *Quest* 36 (2): 122-133.

Mackenzie, M. and K. Denlinger. 1990. *Golf: The mind game.* New York: Dell Publishing.

Magill, R. 1975. Self-actualization and the college athlete. *Canadian Psychomotor Learning and Sport Psychology Symposium,* 395-398.

Mahoney, M. 1979. Cognitive skills and athletic performance. In *Cognitive behavioral interventions: Theory, research and procedures,* edited by P. Kendall and S. Hollon. New York: Academic Press.

Martens, R. 1975. The paradigmatic crisis in American sports personology. *Sportwissenschaft* 50: 9-24.

Martens, R., R. Vealey, and D. Burton. 1990. *Competitive anxiety in sport.* Champaign, IL: Human Kinetics.

Maslow, A. 1954. *Motivation and personality.* New York: Harper & Row.

McClelland, D., J. Atkinson, and E. Lowell, 1953. *The achievement motive.* New York: Appleton-Century-Crofts.

McInman, A. and J. Grove. 1991. Peak moments in sport: A literature review. *Quest* 43: 333-351.

McKenzie, T. and B. Rushall. 1974. Effects of self-recording on attendance and performance in a competitive swimming training environment. *Journal of Applied Behavior Analysis* 7: 199-206.

Meyers, A., J. Whelan, and S. Murphy. 1996. Cognitive behavioral strategies in athletic performance enhancement. In *Progress in Behavior Modification,* edited by M. Hersen, R. Eisler, and P. Miller. New York: Brooks/Cole Publishing.

Miller, G., M. Galanter, and K. Pribram. 1960. *Plans and the structure of behavior.* New York: Henry Holt.

Mischel, W. 1973. Toward a cognitive social learning reconceptualization of personality. *Psychological Review* 80: 252-253.

Monguio-Vecino, I. and L. Lippman. 1987. Image formation as related to visual fixation point. *Journal of Mental Imagery* 11 (1): 87-96.

Murphy, M. 1972. *Golf in the kingdom.* New York: Viking.

Nelson, L. and M. Furst. 1972. An objective study of the effects of expectation on competitive performance. *Journal of Psychology* 81: 69-72. Cited in Mahoney, M. 1979. Cognitive skills and athletic performance. In *Cognitive behavioral interventions: Theory, research and procedures,* edited by P. Kendall and S. Hollon. New York: Academic Press.

Ness, R. and R. Patton. 1979. The effects of beliefs on maximum weight-lifting performance. *Cognitive Therapy and Research* 3: 205-211.

Nideffer, R. 1976. Test of attentional and interpersonal style. *Journal of Personality and Social Psychology* 34: 394-404.

Nideffer, R. 1989. Psychological aspects of sports injuries: Issues in prevention and treatment. *International Journal of Sport Psychology* 20: 241-255.

Ogilvie, B. 1966. *Problem athletes and how to handle them.* London: Pelham.

Oglesby, C. 1987. *Sport involvement and the potential for psychological growth: Necessary conditions for psychological development.* Association for the Advancement of Applied Sport Psychology, Newport Beach, CA, September 17, 1987.

Olson, J. and W. Heward. 1977. Use of contingent line-bowling to increase rates of bowling practice. Symposium presented at the Third Annual Convention of the Midwestern Association of Behavior Analysis, Chicago, IL.

Onestak, D. 1991. The effects of progressive relaxation, mental practice and hypnosis on athletic performance: A review. *Journal of Sport Behavior* 14: 247-282.

Orlick, T. 1975. The sports environment: A capacity to enhance—a capacity to destroy. In *The status of psychomotor learning and sport research,* edited by B. Rushall.

Pavlov, I. 1927. *Conditioned reflexes.* Oxford, England: Oxford University Press.

Prapavessis, H., J. Grove, P. McNair, and N. Cable. 1992. Self-regulation training, state anxiety, and sport performance: A psychophysiological case study. *Sport Psychologist* 8: 213-229.

Privette, G. 1981. The phenomenology of peak performance in sports. *International Journal of Sport Psychology* 12:51-50.

Privette, G. 1983. Peak experience, peak performance and flow: A comparative analysis of positive human experience. *Journal of Personality and Social Psychology* 45: 1361-1368.

Privette, G. and C. Bundrick. 1987. Measurement of experience: Constructs and content validity of the experience questionnaire. *Perceptual and Motor Skills* 65: 315-332.

Petruzzello, S., D. Landers, and W. Salazar. 1991. Biofeedback and sport/exercise performance: Applications and limitations. *Behavior Therapy* 22: 379-392.

Raskin, N. and C. Rogers. 1995. Person-centered therapy. In *Current Psychotherapies,* edited by R. Corsini and D. Wedding. Itasca, IL: F. E. Peacock Publishers, 128-161.

Ravizza, K. 1984. Qualities of the peak experience in sport. In *Psychological Foundation of Sport,* edited by J. Silva and R. Weinberg. Champaign, IL: Human Kinetics.

Ravizza, K. 1990. SportPsych consultation issues in professional baseball. *The Sport Psychologist* 4: 330-340.

Robin, M. 1993. Overcoming performance anxiety: Using RET with actors, artists, and other "performers." In *Innovations in rational emotive therapy,* edited by W. Dryden and L. Hill. London: Sage, 160-183.

Rogers, C. 1980. *A way of being.* Boston: Houghton Mifflin. Cited in N. Raskin and C. Rogers, 1995, Person-centered therapy. In *Current Psychotherapies,* edited by R. Corsini and D. Wedding. Itasca, IL: F. E. Peacock Publishers, 128-161.

Rogers, W., D. Hall, and E. Buckolz. 1991. The effect of an imagery training program on imagery ability, imagery use and figure skating performance. *Journal of Applied Sport Psychology* 3: 109-125.

Rosa, N. 1998. *Integrating mind and body: NLP for better golf* [audio series]. Philadelphia: Peak Performance Psychology for Golfers.

Rotella, R. and B. Cullen, 1995. *Golf is not a game of perfect.* New York: Simon and Schuster.

Rothschild, B. 1993. RET and chronic pain. In *Innovations in rational emotive therapy,* edited by W. Dryden and L. Hill. London: Sage, 91-114.

Rushall, B. and J. Pettinger. 1969. An evaluation of the effects of various reinforcers used as motivators in swimming. *Research Quarterly* 40: 540-545.

Rushall, B. and D. Siedentop. 1972. *The development and control of behavior in sport and physical education.* Philadelphia: Lea and Febiger.

Sachs, M. 1984. A psychoanalytic perspective on running. In *Running as therapy: An integrated approach,* edited by M. Sachs and G. Buffone. Lincoln, NE: University of Nebraska Press.

Sanderson, F. 1977. The psychology of the injury prone athletes. *British Journal of Sports Medicine* 11: 56-57.

Scanlan, T., G. Stein, and K. Ravizza. 1989a. An in-depth study of former elite figure skaters: I. Introduction to the project. *Journal of Sport and Exercise Psychology* 11: 54-64.

Scanlan, T., G. Stein, and K. Ravizza. 1989b. An in-depth study of former elite figure skaters: II. Sources of enjoyment. *Journal of Sport and Exercise Psychology* 11: 65-83.

Scanlan, T., G. Stein, and K. Ravizza. 1991. An in-depth study of former elite figure skaters: III. Sources of stress. *Journal of Sport and Exercise Psychology* 13: 103-120.

Schindler, T. and M. Waters. 1986. Athletic involvement and aspects of self-actualization. *Journal of Sport Behavior* 9: 59-69.

Schlesinger, H. 1954. Cognitive attitudes in relation to susceptibility to interference. *Journal of Personality* 22: 354-374. Quoted in S. Van Schoyck and A. Grasha, 1981, Attentional style variations and athletic ability: The advantages of a sports-specific test. *Journal of Sport Psychology* 3: 149-165.

Scott D., L. Scott, and B. Goldwater. 1997. A performance improvement program for an international-level track and field athlete. *Journal of Applied Behavior Analysis* 30: 573-575.

Seligman, M. 1998. The gifted and extraordinary. *APA Monitor* 29 (11): 2.

Sharpley, C. 1984. Predicate matching in NLP: A review of research on the preferred representational system. *Journal of Counseling Psychology* 31 (2): 238-248.

Sharpley, C. 1987. Research findings on neurolinguistic programming: Nonsupportive data or an untestable theory? *Journal of Counseling Psychology* 34 (1): 103-107.

Shields, D. and B. Bredemeier. 1995. *Character development and physical activity.* Champaign, IL: Human Kinetics.

Silva, J. 1984. Personality and performance in sport. In *Psychological foundations of sport*, edited by J. Silva and R. Weinberg. Champaign, IL: Human Kinetics.

Simek, T., R. O'Brien, and L. Figlerski. 1994. Contracting and chaining to improve the performance of a college golf team: Improvement and deterioration. *Perceptual and Motor Skills* 78: 1099-1105.

Simon, I. 1983. A humanistic approach to sports. *Humanist* 43: 25-32.

Skinner, B. 1938. *The behavior of organisms: An experimental analysis.* New York: Appleton-Century-Crofts.

Slife, B. and R. Williams. 1997. Toward a theoretical psychology: Should a subdiscipline be formally recognized? *American Psychologist* 52 (2): 117-129.

Smoll, F. and R. Smith. 1984. Leadership research in youth sports. In *Psychological foundations of sport*, edited by J. Silva and R. Weinberg. Champaign, IL: Human Kinetics.

Spence, J. and K. Spence. 1966. The motivational components of manifest anxiety: Drive and drive stimuli. In *Anxiety and behavior*, edited by C. Spielberger. New York: Academic Press.

Stanton, H. 1989. Using rapid change techniques to improve sporting performance. *Australian Journal of Clinical and Experimental Hypnosis* 17 (2): 153-161.

Strean, W. 1998. Possibilities for qualitative research in sport psychology. *The Sport Psychologist* 12: 333-345.

Taylor, J. 1988. Slumpbusting: A systematic analysis of slumps in sports. *The Sport Psychologist* 2: 39-48.

Thorndike, E. 1898. Animal intelligence: An experimental study of the associative processes in animals. *Psychological Review Monograph Supplement* 2 (Whole No. 8).

Thorne, F. 1963. The clinical use of nadir experience reports. *Journal of Clinical Psychology* 19: 248-250

Ursano, R., S. Sonnenberg, and S. Lazar. 1991. Concise guide to pyschodynamic therapy. Washington, D.C.: American Psychiatric Press.

Vallerand, R. 1984. Emotion in sport: Definitional, historical and social psychological perspectives. In *Cognitive sport psychology*, edited by W. Straub and J. Williams. Lansing, NY: Sport Science Associates.

Vallerand, R. 1987. Antecedents of self-rated affects in sport: Preliminary evidence on the intuitive-reflective appraisal model. *Journal of Sport Psychology* 9: 161-182.

Van Schoyck, S. and A. Grasha. 1981. Attentional style variations and athletic ability: The advantages of a sports-specific test. *Journal of Sport Psychology* 3: 149-165.

Vealey, R. 1994. Current status and prominent issues in sport psychology interventions. *Medicine and Science in Sport and Exercise* 26: 495-502.

Weiner, B. 1972. *Theories of motivation: From mechanism to cognition.* Chicago: Rand McNally.

Weiner, B. 1981. The role of affect in sport psychology. In *Psychology of motor behavior and sport*, edited by G. Roberts and D. Landers. Champaign, IL: Human Kinetics.

Weinberg, R. and W. Comar. 1994. The effectiveness of psychological interventions in competitive sport. *Sports Medicine* 18: 406-418.

Weinberg, R., D. Gould, and A. Jackson. 1979. Expectations and performance: An empirical test of Bandura's self-efficacy theory. *Journal of Sport Psychology* 1: 320-331.

Whelan, J., M. Mahoney, and A. Meyers. 1991. Performance enhancement in sport: A cognitive-behavioral domain. *Behavior Therapy* 22: 307-327.

Wilber, K. 1996. *Eye to eye: The quest for the new paradigm.* Boston: Shambhala Publishers.

Wolpe, J. 1958. *Psychotherapy by reciprocal inhibition.* Stanford, CA: Stanford University Press.

Yerkes, R. and J. Dodson. 1908. The relation of strength of stimulus to rapidity of habit formation. *Journal of Comparative Neurology and Psychology* 18: 459-482.

Zaichkowsky, L. and C. Fuchs. 1988. Biofeedback applications in exercise and athletic performance. *Exercise and Sport Sciences Reviews* 16: 381-421.

Ψ INDEX

Ψ ABOUT THE AUTHOR

Karen L. Hill, PhD, is an associate professor in the College of Health and Human Development at Penn State University where she teaches courses in psychology and sport science. In her career, Hill has served as acting director of academic affairs at Penn State University and as a research assistant in pulmonary medicine at the Medical College of Pennsylvania. She earned her PhD in exercise and sport psychology from the department of kinesiology at Temple University.

Hill is widely published in academic journals and texts; has received numerous grants for projects in her field; and has chaired or participated in a full roster of seminars, workshops, and technical and professional meetings. In addition, Hill is a sought-after speaker on subjects such as team cohesion and communication, problem-solving, and electronic collaborative learning with technology.

Her professional affiliations include the Association for the Advancement of Applied Sport Psychology; the International Society of Sport Psychology; the American Alliance of Health, Physical Education, Recreation and Dance of Pennsylvania; the Women's Sport Foundation; and the American Psychological Association.